CONNECTING
THROUGH ENGLISH

ALEXANDRA COUTLÉE ◘ SUZANNE GAGNÉ ◘ LOUIS-PHILIPPE LONGPRÉ ◘ KAREN LYONS ◘ MARTINE PICARD ◘ ELISA SHENKIER

Coordinator: Judith Rohlf

Éditions Grand Duc
Groupe Éducalivres inc.
955, rue Bergar, Laval (Québec) H7L 4Z6
Téléphone: 514 334-8466 ▪ Télécopie: 514 334-8387
InfoService: 1 800 567-3671

ACKNOWLEDGEMENTS

The publisher wishes to thank the following people for their comments and suggestions during the development of this project:

Mr. Taibi Baaja, École St-Henry, Commission scolaire de Montréal
Ms. Marie-France Bastien, École secondaire Hornidas-Gamelin, Commission scolaire au Cœur-des-Vallées
Mr. Jacques Benca, retired teacher
Mr. Alain Bissonnette, École Édouard-Montpetit, Commission scolaire de Montréal
Ms. Julie Boissé, École Jean-Rimbault, Commission scolaire des Chênes
Ms. Julie Bussière, Collège Jésus-Marie de Sillery
Ms. Dominique Cantin, École secondaire Donnaconna, Commission scolaire de Portneuf
Ms. Marie-Guylaine Dallaire, École Père-Marquette, Commission scolaire de Montréal
Ms. Annie Dumay, École Père-Marquette, Commission scolaire de Montréal
Mr. Jean-François Duquette, École Cité des Jeunes, Commission scolaire des Trois-Lacs
Ms. Christiane Emond, École Pamphile-Le-May, Commission scolaire des Navigateurs
Mr. Michel Fontaine, Collège Jésus-Marie de Sillery
Ms. Claire Gaudette, École secondaire Hornidas-Gamelin, Commission scolaire au Cœur-des-Vallées
Ms. Jacqueline Gilbert, Collège Jésus-Marie de Sillery
Ms. Chantale Guimond, Collège Clarétain
Ms. Annick Kerschbaumer, École secondaire de Rivière-du-Loup, Commission scolaire de Kamouraska-Rivière-du-Loup
Ms. Caroline Lavoie, École secondaire Mont St-Sacrement
Ms. Michèle Lavoie, Collège Notre-Dame
Ms. Dominique Le Bot, École Val-Mauricie, Commission scolaire de l'Énergie
Ms. Nadine McElroy-Cadieux, École Liberté-Jeunesse, Commission scolaire de la Seigneurie-des-Mille-Îles.
Mr. André Montmarquette, Polyvalente Hyacinthe-Delorme, Commission scolaire de St-Hyacinthe
Ms. Christiana Pistilli, Polyvalente de St-Jérôme, Commission scolaire de la Rivière-du-Nord
Ms. Caroline Ramsay, Polyvalente de Disraeli, Commission scolaire des Appalaches
Mr. Christofaro Rania, École Félix-Leclerc, Commission scolaire des Affluents
Ms. Johanne Robitaille, École secondaire Donnaconna, Commission scolaire de Portneuf
Mr. Martin Roy, École Augustin-Norbert-Morin, Commission scolaire des Laurentides
Ms. Louise Simard, École Louis-Cyr, Commission scolaire des Grandes-Seigneuries
Mr. Jocelyn St-Pierre, École Vallée-des-Lacs, Commission scolaire du Fleuve-et-des-Lacs
Ms. Laurence Vlach, École secondaire Mont St-Sacrement

Scientific Revision:
Ms. Lilianne Bohémier

© 2008, Éditions Grand Duc, A division of Groupe Éducalivres inc.
955 Bergar Street, Laval (Québec) H7L 4Z6
Telephone: 514 334-8466 ▪ Fax: 514 334-8387 ▪ www.grandduc.com

All rights reserved.

We acknowledge the financial support of the Government of Canada through the Book Publishing Industry Development Program (BPIDP) for our publishing activities.

Government of Québec – Tax credit for book publishing – Administered by SODEC.

PRODUCT CODE 3692
ISBN 978-2-7655-0209-8

Legal deposit
Bibliothèque et Archives nationales du Québec, 2008
Library and Archives Canada, 2008

Printed in Canada

1 2 3 4 5 6 7 8 9 0 S 7 6 5 4 3 2 1 0 9 8

Montreal, September 1

Dear Students,

It's the start of a brand new year and a great adventure in English!

We hope you will find the topics and issues in this book both exciting and challenging. Each unit has been designed to captivate your interest, stimulate your creativity and develop your critical thinking as you continue to learn English. Each unit has been carefully structured to help you develop your ESL competencies and gain confidence in using English.

Our goal is to help you learn English through meaningful tasks. We've given it our best shot. The ball is now in your court. Have a fabulous year learning and... *Connecting Through English*!

Sincerely,
The Team

Alexandra, **Elisa**, *Judith*, *Karen*, *Louis-Philippe*, *Martine* and *Suzanne*

"Learning English opens doors... Connecting Through English opens minds."

Table of Contents

UNIT 1 At All Costs

Is winning really everything?

FOCUS ON... Personal Pronouns, Indefinite Pronouns, Transition Words

HOW TO... Make Ethical Choices, Use the Six-Hats Thinking Strategies, Overcome Stress When Talking

UNIT 2 Tuning In!

What role does music play in our lives and in society?

FOCUS ON... Adverbs of Degree or Intensity, The Future Tense, Future Events, Using the Past Tense

HOW TO... Decode Lyrics, Make Memo Cards

UNIT 3 On the Edge

What do you need in order to cope with adverse conditions?

FOCUS ON... The Conditional Tense, Using Transition Words, Using Quotation Marks, Using Commas, Choosing Between the Simple Past and the Present Perfect

HOW TO... Read a Story, Write a Narrative Essay

UNIT 4 Mirror, Mirror...

How far would you go to change your own image?

FOCUS ON... The Conditional Tense + an "If-Clause", Modal Auxiliaries

HOW TO... Keep a Response Journal

SH00029301

Saint-Henri

The Structure of the Book

This Student Book is organized to help you learn English and make you feel competent as a learner as you carry out various tasks. It contains seven separate units (learning and evaluation situations) and two independent projects. The content of each has been carefully structured to help you develop your competencies in English as you gain knowledge and insights into yourself, others and the world. At the end of the book, there is a Reference Toolkit where you will find lots of helpful information. Have a look!

The Structure of Each Unit

THE OPENING PAGES

Each unit begins with a two-page spread. On these pages, in addition to the title of the unit, you will find a brief summary of what you will be doing in the unit and an illustration or series of illustrations to start off your discussions on what is to come. There are also two guiding questions. These questions will help you make sense of the topic presented in the unit and assist you in focusing on its key issues. Upon finishing the unit, you should be able to answer both questions and explain why they are important.

TASKS AND ACTIVITIES

Each unit is divided into a series of tasks, which are then divided into activities. The tasks are a way of grouping activities together in a meaningful fashion. To introduce each task, there is a brief paragraph that explains what you will be doing. The activities that follow are the steps necessary to accomplish the task.

ICONS

Throughout the book, you will notice three icons:

A ▤ indicates that there is a handout that goes with the activity.

A ⊙ indicates that there is an audio text.

A ▤ indicates that there is an audiovisual text.

THE FINAL TASK

All of the tasks in each unit lead up to a Final Task. The Final Task is something that you will do or make (*a written assignment, a PowerPoint presentation, a storyboard...*) to show what you have learned in the unit. The Final Task is not necessarily long or complicated, but it allows you to use what you have learned in a logical way. Very often, you have a choice of what to do or what media you will use.

EXTRA READING (OPTIONAL)

This section is not really part of the unit per se. That is to say, it is also completely optional. It has been included to provide additional texts to read for students who work faster, who want more or who have more time in English. At the end of each text, there is a question to think about and discuss. Reading the question before reading the text will give you a purpose for reading.

OTHER THINGS TO DO (OPTIONAL)

This section is completely optional. It provides suggestions for fun projects related to the topic of the unit.

WRAP-UP

The Wrap-up is an important page. It allows you to reflect on what you have learned throughout the unit. It will help you make connections with what you have learned and assist you to transfer this knowledge.

The following special features are found throughout the book:

How to...

Step by step procedures and strategies to help you achieve success and develop expertise.

Focus on...

Grammar!

The explanation of a specific grammar point or notion needed to complete the task at hand.

Culture

A wealth of information!

Fun facts, great insights, interesting details about the lives of famous people and the world we live in.

Vocabulary Builder

New words and expressions related to the topic, and activities to do to enrich your vocabulary.

ICT

Suggestions for using computers and other communication technologies in your learning.

Humour

Something to make you laugh, or at least... smile!

Can You Do It?

A challenge. Something more to do, related to the task

 ### Talk About It!

Questions or prompts related to the subject to get you talking and discussing in English.

 ### Think About It!

Thought-provoking questions or statements worth pondering.
Food for thought!

 ### Write About It!

Your chance to express yourself in writing on issues related to the task at hand.

Strategies

Things to do to help you learn or communicate effectively.

Cues

Functional language or prompts to help you discuss.

1 UNIT
At All Costs

In general, when we think of sports, we think about physical skills, discipline, healthy lifestyles and self-esteem. But sport also has a dark side.

IN THIS UNIT...

You will explore how the thirst for victory can lead to cheating. Along the way, you will be confronted with a number of ethical choices. Where do we draw the line when faced with a difficult decision? Is winning everything? Is winning by cheating really winning?

In the **FINAL TASK**, you will be asked to express a point of view on a variety of situations that involve a judgment call.

- Is winning really everything?
- How is cheating in sport equal to cheating in life?

TASK 1 presents an ugly side of sport – cheating. With advances in medicine and biotechnology, the temptation to win at any price is always present. Cheating is big in the field of sports in general, and often leads to sad, sordid endings for those concerned. In this task, you will learn that there is a high price to pay for trying to take shortcuts to victory.

ACTIVITY 1

Cheaters' Hall of Fame

"Something worth having is worth cheating for." We don't know who said this, but it seems that cheating and sports go together like bread and butter or McGwire and creatine. In this activity, you will hear about some of the worst cases of cheating in sports.

① Have a look at the pictures below. Can you recall any of these cases of cheating?

② Try to match the pictures with the athletes.

③ Listen to some of the cases.

④ Complete the handout with information about these athletes.

a) b) c) d) e) f)

Culture

The History of Doping

The ancient Greeks ate hallucinogenic mushrooms, as well as sesame seeds, to improve performance, and gladiators used stimulants to combat fatigue in the arena. In the 19th century, stimulants such as strychnine, cocaine and caffeine were used.

How many of these names can you match with their pictures?

1. Danny Almonte
2. Diego Maradona
3. Michael Waltrip
4. Floyd Landis
5. Mike Tyson
6. Rosie Ruiz
7. Sammy Sosa
8. Ben Johnson
9. Jamie Salé and David Pelletier
10. "Shoeless" Joe Jackson and the Chicago White Sox
11. Tonya Harding and Nancy Kerrigan

g)
h)
j)
k)
i)

Can you find other examples of cheating in sports?

Cues
- I think picture a) is _____.
- Which one do you think is _____?
- I don't know many of these people, but I'm sure _____ is _____.
- It's just a guess, but...
- I think that...
- I don't have a clue who _____ is. Do you?

Culture

And they thought they wouldn't get caught...

Boris Onishchenko was a member of the Soviet Union's modern pentathlon team in the 1976 Summer Olympics. He was disqualified for cheating in the fencing event. He rigged his electric épée with a switch that allowed him to register a hit when there wasn't one. Newspaper reporters dubbed him "Disonishchenko."

Roberto Madrazo may have come in third place in Mexico's 2006 presidential election, but he was first in his category to cross the finish line in the 2007 Berlin marathon. His glory was short-lived, however, when it was revealed that he had cheated by taking a shortcut. An electronic tracking chip showed that, in fact, he had skipped two checkpoints in the race. Stripped of his win, Madrazo said that he had never intended to complete the race, but had gone to the finish line to "collect his belongings."

ACTIVITY 2

Cheating...

The use of drugs in sports doesn't always produce winners.
After all, athletes have a lot to lose, don't they?

1 Watch the video *Artificial Athletes*.

2 Read the article *Cheating Your Health* on the handout.

3 Discuss the *Talk About It!* questions.

4 Compare the information from the video and the article using the graphic organizer on the handout.

5 Share your answers with a partner.

"The most important thing in the Olympic Games is not to win but to take part, just as the most important thing in life is not the triumph but the struggle. The essential thing is not to have conquered but to have fought well."

– Olympic Creed

Artificial Athletes:
The Dangers of Steroids

Talk About It!

a) What's the most surprising information in the video and the text?

b) What does that say about practising an elite sport?

c) Did you realize that steroids are not only used by athletes?

d) Do you think that the use of steroids has spread to high schools? In which sports?

e) Is the damage being done serious enough to stop people using them?

f) What would be the best techniques to use to convince young people never to touch steroids?

 Use the functional language on pp. 232-235 when discussing.

Can You Do It?

While discussing, try to focus on using the correct pronouns.

Think About It!

What if you knew that one of your teammates was using a prohibited substance to enhance his/her performance? What would you do?

a) Would you confront your teammate? Why or why not?

b) Would you report the behaviour? To whom? Why or why not?

c) Would you choose to ignore the situation? Why or why not?

d) How could you tell whether your decision was the best decision or not?

U.S. Anti-Doping Agency (USADA), *The Journey: Struggling with Ethics in Sport*

Personal Pronouns

	Function			
	Subject	**Object**	**Possessive**	
			Adjectives	**Pronouns**
Singular	I	me	my	mine
	you	you	your	yours
	he/she/it	him/her/it	his/her/its	his/hers/its
Plural	we	us	our	ours
	you	you	your	yours
	they	them	their	theirs

	To initiate an action	**To receive an action**	**To show ownership**
Where to look for them:	Just before the verb (except in questions)	• After a transitive verb • After a preposition	Before an object or person (They replace a person's name.)
Examples:	- **She** *wrote an article on cheating.* - **We** *are learning about sports ethics.*	- *They tested* **him** *for illegal drugs.* - *Marianne was running behind* **him**.	- *They used* **her** *cellphone because* **theirs** *was not working.* - *We took* **our** *pledge to be fair very seriously.*

Matt and I or *Matt and me?*
- *Matt and I* *are happy to be here today.* [NOT Matt and me]
  The subject pronoun "I" <u>is doing</u> the action of the verb.
- *They invited* **Matt and me.** [NOT Matt and I]
  The object pronoun "me" <u>is receiving</u> the action of the verb.

ACTIVITY 3

Straight Facts

propensity: a strong tendency to do something.

Why do some athletes cheat? Indeed, why do we as humans have a propensity for cheating in all areas of life? Are bigger rewards, more exposure, more money and beating your competitors the main things on the agenda? Or not?

❶ Listen to what an expert has to say about the reasons why athletes are willing to go to extremes to win.

❷ Discuss the *Talk About It!* questions with a partner.

❸ While discussing, focus on using the right pronoun and *everybody*, *anybody*, *somebody* and *nobody* correctly (see next page).

Strategies

Don't forget to refer to the listening strategies given on pp. 222-223:

- Direct attention
- Pay selective attention
- Activate prior knowledge
- Lower Anxiety
- Infer

💬 Talk About It!

a) Why do some athletes cheat?

b) Who are the cheaters?

c) How do they justify their cheating?

d) Who are the true victims of cheating?

e) Will drug testing ever stop cheating?

"If winning is everything to you, you will do anything to win. Competing without cheating may cost you your chances of winning. Are you willing to make that sacrifice to pursue victory with honour?"

Humour

"I'm not too good at the hurdles."

Unit 1 ■ At All Costs

Indefinite Pronouns

Pronouns	Characteristics	*Examples*
everybody (everyone) nobody (no one) somebody (someone)	• Can be the subject or object of a sentence • Are always singular • Are used only in the affirmative	- ***Everybody*** *I know loves to watch that athlete skate.* - *I saw **everyone** I know there.* - ***Nobody** left early.* - ***Somebody** has a lot of explaining to do.* - *I found **somebody** with a cellphone.*
anybody (anyone)	• Is always singular • Is used with a negative form of the verb or for questions	- *I don't know **anybody** who doesn't like to watch that athlete skate.* - *Does **anybody** have a cellphone I can borrow?*

Practise!

With a partner, write a short paragraph in which you include *everybody*, *anybody*, *somebody* and *nobody*.

Don't forget to use the right ones in your discussions.

**Everybody, Somebody, Anybody, Nobody
That's Not My Job!**

Once there were four people named Everybody, Somebody, Anybody and Nobody.

There was an important job to be done and Everybody was sure that Somebody would do it. Anybody could have done it, but in the end Nobody did it. Somebody got angry about that, because it was Everybody's job. Everybody thought Anybody could do it, but Somebody realized that Nobody would do it. It ended up that Everybody blamed Somebody when Nobody did what Anybody could have done.

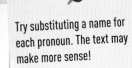

Try substituting a name for each pronoun. The text may make more sense!

Where do we draw the line? What's cheating and what's not? In this task, the intention is not to tell you what is right and wrong. Instead, you will be provided with a few examples of ethical choices from various sports. Decisions are seldom all black or all white, and so you will try and base your judgment on solid grounds: the values of fairness, equality and justice.

ACTIVITY 1

Sports Technology

The story of Oscar Pistorius provides food for thought since it's not a clear case of cheating. You be the judge.

❶ Look at the title and the illustrations on pp. 12-14. Can you guess what the text is about? Read the article to find out if "Cheetahs are cheating."

❷ Be prepared to justify your opinion using the *How to Make Ethical Choices* box on the next page.

❸ Complete the handout.

❹ Share your answers with your partner.

Every day, headlines reveal things that are going wrong in sports. The stories include:

- Athletes driving drunk
- Corrupt officials fixing competitions
- Players shaving points for gambling purposes
- High school athletes selling and taking steroids
- Coaches having inappropriate relationships with athletes
- Parents brawling at youth sporting events
- Fans crossing the lines and assaulting coaches, players and officials
- Athletes breaking records with the help of performance-enhancing substances
- Etc.

These are just a few examples of things that go wrong in sports. Something is missing. Part of the problem is that people ignore ethics when making decisions. ❖

U.S. Anti-Doping Agency (USADA), *The Journey: Struggling with Ethics in Sport*

solid grounds: the foundations for an argument, belief or action; a basis for something.

to shave: to limit the number of points scored by one's own team in an athletic contest deliberately.

to brawl: to fight (in public).

"Sports reveal character."

How to...
Make Ethical Choices

1 | Forget the "me-first" attitude.

2 | Look at how your choice will affect everyone involved: your team, your friends, your parents, your future spouse and children...

3 | Put the decision up against each of the following values:
   • *Trust*   • *Responsibility*   • *Caring*   • *Respect*   • *Fairness*   • *Citizenship*

4 | If something bothers you, it may be because it's not the right choice for you. Take time to think it over and discuss it with people you trust. Use one of the *Quick Tools* below.

Quick Tools for Making an Ethical Choice:

The Sunlight Test

- What would you do if everyone you loved and respected knew what you were doing?
- Would you be proud of your actions?

The Role Model Test

- A role model should be someone you respect and trust to do the right thing.
- When faced with a decision, ask yourself what your role model would do in the same situation.
- As a role model for others, what decision would you want them to follow?

U.S. Anti-Doping Agency (USADA), *The Journey: Struggling with Ethics in Sport*

The idea is not to tell you what is right or wrong. You must make that decision on your own.

Keeping an open mind and using all the tools given here will help you reach a decision that works for you: a decision that may affect the rest of your life.

Culture

What Is Ethics?

The word "ethics" is derived from the Greek word *ethos* (character). It is closely related to the Latin word *mores* (customs). Together, they define how individuals choose to interact with one another. In philosophy, ethics defines what is good for the individual and for society, and it establishes the nature of duties that people owe themselves and one another.

Are Cheetahs Cheating?
Sports Technology Argued

by Ellen Goodman

BOSTON – As someone who lives just a few hundred paces from the Boston Marathon course, I've cheered my share of athletes. This year, it was Masazumi Soejima at the head of the pack, propelling his wheelchair across a rainy 26 miles in 1 hour, 29 minutes and 16 seconds. It took Robert Cheruiyot an extra 44 minutes and 57 seconds to come in first on foot.

I take nothing away from the athleticism and grit of Soejima. But it goes without saying that he didn't "beat" Cheruiyot. Those who compete on foot and those who compete with wheels are categorically different. And succeed in different categories.

The Controversy

I make this point because of the controversy surrounding a 20-year-old South African named Oscar Pistorius. This racing phenomenon recently won the 100 and 200 metre races in an international competition for disabled athletes. He won on a pair of J-shaped carbon fibre blades known as Cheetahs.

Pistorius calls himself "the fastest man on no legs." He was born with defects in his feet, and his lower legs were amputated when he was 11 months old. Nevertheless, he says, "I don't see myself as disabled." He wants to be allowed to race for the Olympic gold on his own two Cheetahs.

This is one of those stories tailor-made for the Olympic coverage: a great athlete overcomes enormous adversity to pursue his dream! But it's also one of the other stories now stalking sports: exactly what kind of technology, training or performance enhancements should we applaud? And what kind should we reject?

This conversation seems to be as common as box scores and doping scandals. On the baseball field, Barry Bonds is creeping up on Hank Aaron's home run record. But there is no joy in Mudville. Bonds' achievement is tainted by the belief that he used steroids to beef up his body and his record.

In cycling, where doping is the bane of the Tour de France, Floyd Landis' inspiring win turned sour

grit: spirit.
to stalk: to haunt; to follow or pursue.
to taint: to corrupt.
to beef up: to make greater or stronger (informal).
bane: a cause of harm or ruin.

with lab reports of testosterone shots. He is still fighting for his crown and his reputation.

Techno-doping

Those who oppose Pistorius compare his Cheetahs to "techno-doping." But it is also true that technology has been used to enhance performance since the first runner put on a shoe and this duffer put Big Bertha in her golf bag.

Training has reached a level of technical sophistication unheard of when Roger Bannister broke the four-minute mile. Athletes train in wind tunnels and travel to high altitudes. But the use of altitude tents to simulate that "high" has been decried as violating the "spirit of the sport."

And what are we to make of the LASIK surgery that gave the nearsighted Tiger Woods his 20/15 vision and four straight championships right afterwards? Is better-than-perfect vision a kind of enhancement, like doping, or a correction, like contact lenses?

Some years ago, I questioned a beauty pageant in which the contestants had been surgically altered and implanted. They didn't owe their beauty to their maker but, rather, to their remaker.

Questions about the remanufacture of athletes, says ethicist Tom Murray, "force us to ask what is the point of sport. Whatever we think is meaningful and beautiful about sports has to do with the ways we admire natural talents and hard work and dedication."

But there are other things we don't admire. "I can climb the mountains of the Tour de France faster than all the other competitors," quips Murray. "All I need is a motor."

Today, we replace hips and knees with titanium. We replace thyroids with pills. NBC is remaking the *Bionic Woman* series for a new run, and ethicists are debating the possibility of real bionic athletes. Michael Sandel, author of *The Case Against Perfection*, warns that "part of what we admire about great athletes is that we are able to see ourselves in their human achievements." Who would applaud the bionic Olympiad?

As for Pistorius and prostheses? So far, the International Association of Athletics Federations has prohibited him from the Olympics. The final decision won't come till August.

duffer: clumsy, maladroit (informal).
Big Bertha: name of a heavy piece of artillery from WWI; here, a kind of golf club whose effect is supposed to be "like a cannon."

The Author's Opinion

But what makes his challenge so compelling is not just his extraordinary courage and talent. His prostheses both enable a disabled man and offer an athlete high-tech equipment. They land somewhere between a sophisticated running shoe and a motor.

I don't think that Cheetahs are cheating. And I am uncomfortable with the talk of cyborgs and transhumans that surrounds this case. These stories will get harder, not easier, over the next years.

But as a fan of Soejima, I don't think that racing on a separate track is an insult. It's still the right place for the "fastest man on no legs."

cyborg: a human who has certain physiological processes aided or controlled by mechanical or electronic devices.

Ellen Goodman, "Are Cheetahs Cheating?" issue from *The Washington Post,* 2007
© 2007, The Washington Post
All rights reserved.

Talk About It!

a) What is the author's position?

b) Is ethics in sports at an all-time low?

c) What do you think should be included in a code of ethics for sport at school?

Write About It!

Should Oscar Pistorius be allowed to compete in the Olympics or should he compete only in the Paralympics? Justify your answer.

The Beam in Your Eye

Here's another case where decisions are not all black or all white. You will listen to a text comparing the use of steroids with eye surgery. In the end, you will have to decide for yourself why, if using steroids is cheating, having laser eye surgery should not be considered in the same light.

① Listen to the text about making ethical choices.

② Complete the handout.

③ Share your answers with a partner.

④ In your group, try to answer the *Talk About It!* question.

"Win with grace. Lose with dignity."

 Talk About It!

What is cheating?

Don't forget to structure your paragraph around a topic sentence. If you need help, refer to p. 249.

Making Ethical Choices

It's now your turn to voice an opinion on what's right and what's not. In the FINAL TASK, you will be asked to carry on a discussion on various issues related to sports and ethics. After that, you will write a short text about one of them.

What to Do

Prepare

1 Read the list of situations on your handout. Choose one to discuss.

2 Read the *How to Use the Six-Hats Thinking Strategies* box on the next page. You will be using them in the discussion.

3 Think about how to explain your situation to your teammates and the reasons why you feel it is or is not acceptable. Try to approach the subject wearing each of the six hats.

4 Use the handout to help you organize your ideas.

Present and Discuss

5 Present your situation and position to your teammates.

6 Listen and react to what they have to say.

7 Share your views on all the situations presented by adding comments, showing appreciation, relating personal experiences, giving examples and/or asking questions. Use the *Conversation Cues* on p. 18 to help you.

8 Feel free to use a six-hats card to indicate your perspective during the discussion.

Reflect

9 Think about how the discussion went. Use the handout to identify both strong and weak points.

Write

10 Choose one of the six hats and write a short text explaining any one of the situations discussed from that perspective. Your readers should be able to identify which colour hat you selected.

11 Use the checklist on the handout.

How to...
Use the Six-Hats Thinking Strategies 📝

When discussing, it can be useful to use The Six-Hats Thinking Strategies. This method was invented by Dr. Edward de Bono in the early 1980s to help people examine a problem or issue from different perspectives without anyone "taking what's being said personally."
By the colour of hat you choose, others will know your intentions for the sake of discussion.

Here's what each colour hat stands for:

> Of course, it's not necessary to put on a real hat.
> You can use coloured cards instead!

Colours (hats or cards)	When you wear this hat, you...
white	• present only the facts. • are objective or neutral.
black	• present the negative points or disadvantages. • can play the devil's advocate without being judged.
yellow	• present the positive points or advantages.
red	• voice your feelings or emotions openly without having to justify them.
green	• express new ideas that may be far-fetched. • take risks to the point of saying something weird.
blue	• reflect on what has been said. • link to other issues.

Using these six hats can:
- *Encourage risk-taking*
- *Improve communication*
- *Expose different perspectives without fear of judgment*
- *Stimulate creative thinking*
- *Help with problem solving*
- *Etc.*

Example:

We all agree that using steroids is bad, but for the sake of discussion, I would like to present why some people think using steroids is OK. I can choose a **black hat** to show that I am playing the devil's advocate and not necessarily giving my personal opinion.

devil's advocate: someone who takes the worst side just for the sake of argument.

"The pursuit of victory with honour is not a destination; it is a journey."

CONVERSATION CUES		
Initiate	• Here's a really interesting (complicated, hot...) issue. • In this situation, ... • In my opinion, ... • I truly believe that... • Would you agree with me that...?	• Some people claim that... • Personally, I feel that... • Here are the facts... • To play the devil's advocate, let me say that...
React and Maintain	• I think that... • I agree. I disagree. • Personally, I... • Do you really believe that...? • I think you're right (wrong)! • Don't take this personally, but... • I know for a fact that...	• On the other hand, • Apparently, • It's a well-known fact; it's common knowledge that... • Everybody knows that... • That reminds me of... • I would rather... • It's better to...
End	• Maybe we should move on to the next issue. • Let's move on to the next question. • Wow! I've learned a lot.	• What an interesting (boring, complicated, difficult) issue that is! • Great discussion, gang!

bind: a difficulty.

How to...
Overcome Stress When Talking

If participating in a more formal discussion makes you nervous, there are a few things you can do to help you lower your anxiety.

1 | Use the models, cues and examples given in class as a starting point.

2 | Add a personal touch or comment.

3 | Take risks. Don't be afraid of making mistakes.

4 | Choose one of the six hats! You won't be judged for your opinion. Everyone will know that it's for the sake of discussion.

5 | Remember, the message doesn't have to be perfect in order to be understood.

6 | Use strategies like stalling for time and gesturing to help you out of a bind.

7 | Say something. Go for it!

Transition Words

Here's a list of common words and expressions to help you link your ideas:

Purpose	Words and Expressions		Examples
To add information	• Additionally, • Also, • Besides,	• Furthermore, • In addition, • And	– *Those drugs are dangerous.* ***Furthermore,*** *they are illegal.*
To give a different point of view or opinion	• However, • In spite of • On the other hand, • Yet, • On the contrary, • Nevertheless, • Unfortunately, • But		– *He was basically an honest person.* ***However,*** *he got caught in the web of fame.* – *Doping is illegal.* ***Unfortunately,*** *it is widespread among athletes.* – ***On the contrary,*** *it is not necessary to cheat in order to win.*
To give an example or to illustrate a point	• For example • For instance,	• Indeed, • In fact,	– ***Indeed,*** *that is one good reason not to cheat.*
To give a conclusion or result	• As a consequence, • As a result, • To sum up, • Consequently, • Therefore, • So, • Thus, • In conclusion,		– *He was caught cheating.* ***Therefore,*** *he was kicked off the team.* – ***In conclusion,*** *cheating never really pays off.*
To put events in sequence	• First, • Second, • Then, • Next, • After that, • Finally,		– ***First,*** *he worked hard.* – ***Then,*** *he made the school team.* – ***After that,*** *he became a professional wrestler.*

Practise! 📝

Read the following paragraph and add transition words to link ideas and events:

What a soccer game! It rained all night. The field was wet and slippery. The game was scheduled for 8 a.m. Half of our team players were missing. Wendy was away on a family trip. Tina had her leg in a cast. Our best player hurt her knee at the beginning of the game. Lucie received a yellow card. Our best defence got a red card for rough behaviour. We were exhausted because we had no replacements. Our coach was really frustrated. The few supporters that were present showed signs of impatience...

Can you think of one of your worst games? Or your best?

Wrap-up

Look Back

- You should be able to:
  - Say what the pictures on the opening pages represent.
  - Explain why this title was chosen for this unit and why it is appropriate.
  - Answer the Guiding Questions.

Think About It

- What are the reasons you participate in an individual or team sport?

- Is winning at all costs important to you?

Now What?

- Consider getting more information about the dangers and consequences of cheating in high school sports and making it available in your school.

- Make your own personal ethical choices about cheating and stick by them.

Select some of your work for your portfolio!

3 Name three things you have learned in this unit.

2 Give two consequences of cheating.

1 Find one argument you could use to convince one of your friends to never use steroids to enhance his/her performance.

OTHER THINGS TO DO

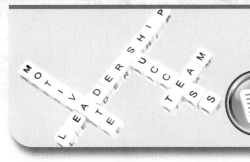

Prepare a word puzzle based on sports issues and cheating.

Search the Internet to find out more about what's happening in baseball and cycling. Explain whether or not you think that the scandals occurring in these two sports might eventually kill them.

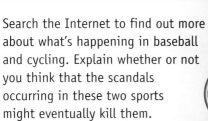

Voice your opinion about the best role models in sport. Justify your choices.

Organize a class debate on one of the issues mentioned in the unit. Refer to *Project 1, It's Debatable*.

Athlete Pledge for Clean Sport & Fair Competition

Preamble

This Pledge for Clean Sport & Fair Competition expresses my hopes, is a commitment of my values, and is my declaration to support doping-free sport. This pledge affirms my commitment for:

Respecting Competition and the True Spirit of Sport

This Athlete Pledge for Clean Sport & Fair Competition expands the current Athlete's Olympic Oath used at the Olympic Games as follows:

"In the name of all the competitors I promise that we shall take part in these Olympic Games, respecting and abiding by the rules that govern them, in the true spirit of sportsmanship, for the glory of sport and the honor of our teams." Olympic Charter Ch.5 Section 1.12

I _____(athlete's name)_____ will specifically honor this Athlete Pledge and promise to:

Respect my sport

I honor the letter and the spirit of the rules of my sport.
I value well-played games and competitions.
I strive for excellence, within the rules of my sport.

Respect competition

I value fair competition where each competitor competes within the rules of the game.
I value competition where each competitor plays at his or her best.
I strive to win – fairly.

Respect my opponents

I recognize that each competitor is striving to do his or her best – within the rules.
I honor my opponent as co-competitor as we strive for excellent sport.

Respect myself

My integrity is found in competing fairly.
Having good health is important to me.
I compete drug-free.

I believe that the only Good Sport is Fair Sport, Sport that is Clean, and I Agree:

To respect the ideals of fair play and the Olympic Movement.
With the values of doping-free sport.
To abide by any and all anti-doping rules that relate to me and to my sport.
To be a role model for other athletes, and people younger than me.

Outside of competition, I am willing to take a stand, and to show my commitment fordoping-free sport by:
- Talking with other athletes, coaches, and my family about doping-free sport.
- Thinking about fairness, and ethical issues with all choices I make.
- To mentor other athletes, who may follow in my footsteps.

U.S. Anti-Doping Agency (USADA)

Question

Do you think participants in school sports should be required to sign this pledge?

Run, Run, As Fast As You Can...

by Judith Rohlf

1 When she was first handed the grey pills, she took them obediently, no questions asked. After all, they came from her coach. And when she received her first injection, she dismissed the funny feeling in the pit of her stomach as nervousness. She was out to win. Besides, she trusted her coach implicitly...

5 And win, Stacey did! She had never been faster or had more endurance. Time after time, she came in first place in both the 200 metres and the 400 metres. The press dubbed her the Gingerbread Girl because of her tanned skin and in reference to the popular fairy tale. She was on the road to becoming a star sprinter! Never mind the fact that her once lanky, deerlike body became thicker and more muscular and

10 masculine, or that severe acne covered her face and arms, leaving deep pit marks in her skin. She was somebody; people noticed her... Her voice changed as well. Deep down, it bothered her that even her mother sometimes had trouble recognizing her now perpetually hoarse voice on the phone, but that too, she passed off. "Don't worry, mom. It's nothing. Just some allergies," she'd say, swallowing her

15 conscience. Stacey hated the way she looked, but she kept on reminding herself that it was a small price to pay for recognition and glory. She shied away from mirrors and old friends and concentrated on running and training and winning. After all, she was the Gingerbread Girl!

Then, when she least expected it, the would-be Olympic gold medallist's world
20 came crashing down. During a major competition, the unthinkable happened. Along with her fellow teammates, Stacey tested positive for doping. Even more quickly than her rise to the top, she fell to the bottom. All her training and hard work slipped down the drain. The cookie crumbled.

As Stacey flipped through the pages of a huge scrapbook bursting with photos and
25 newspaper clippings of days past, her eyes filled with tears. Not for what she no longer could or would be, but for what she had let herself become. In the end, there's one race cheaters never win.

Question

What is meant by the last sentence? What happens to the Gingerbread Man in the classic fairy tale?

---

to dismiss: to reject; to ignore.
lanky: tall and thin.
to shy away from: to stay away from something due to fear or caution.

2 UNIT

TUNING IN!

IN THIS UNIT...

Music is everywhere! In this unit, you will listen to various types of music. You will look at how music is a part of your life and the role it plays in society in general. You will also reflect on what makes a good song. As a **FINAL TASK**, you will work in groups and share a song that you feel will mark your generation.

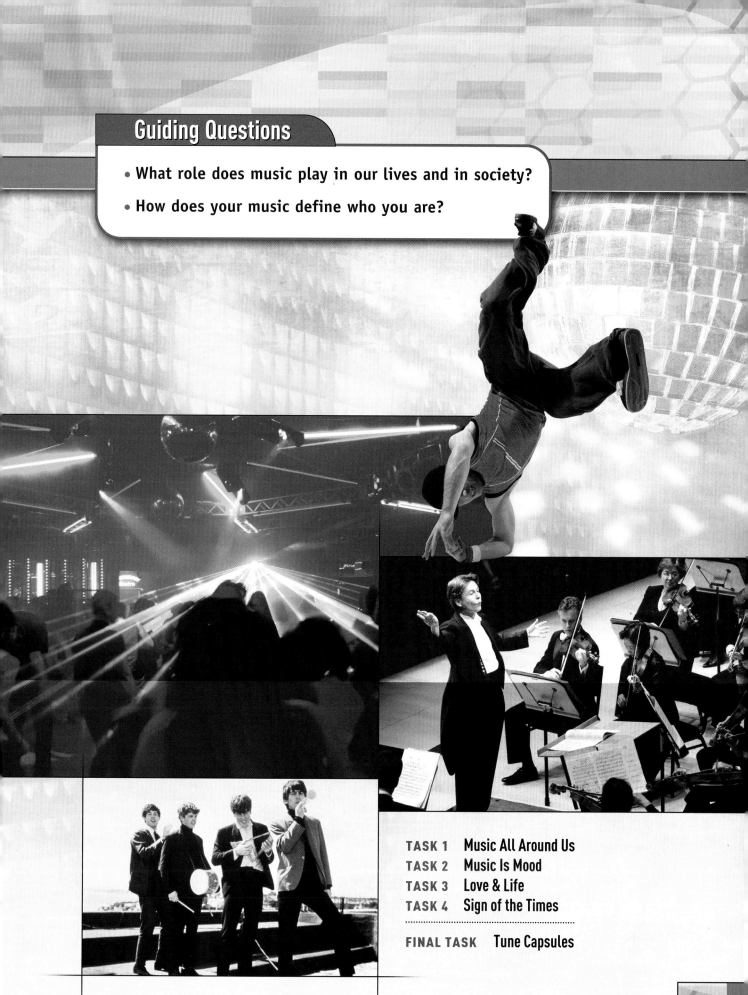

Guiding Questions

- What role does music play in our lives and in society?
- How does your music define who you are?

Music! It's everywhere and we all listen to it. But, have you ever stopped to think about what music is... or isn't? In TASK 1, you will be defining the word <u>music</u> and looking at how music is sometimes used for reasons other than just listening enjoyment.

ACTIVITY 1

Music to My Ears

Several people were asked what *music* means to them. In Activity 1, you will find out what they had to say. After that, you will come up with your own definition of what music is.

1 Look at the illustrations below. Then take a few minutes to think about how you would define the word **music**. Note your ideas on the handout.

2 Listen to the interviews. As you listen, jot down keywords and ideas about music on the graphic organizer.

3 Write your personal definition of music.

4 Compare and share your definition, first with a partner and then in your group.

5 Put your ideas together and write a common definition.

6 Share your definition with the other groups.
- What points did everyone mention?
- Is it possible to come up with a common definition for the class as a whole?

"After silence, that which comes nearest to expressing the inexpressible is music."

– Aldous Huxley

Vocabulary Builder

Did you know that the word **music** comes from the word **muse**?

- Look up the word **muse** in the dictionary and explain how it is related to music.

- Find another common word that also derives from the word **muse**.

- What links can you make between all three words?

It's Everywhere!

Music is everywhere, but not all of the music we hear is by choice. In this activity, you will look at places where music is played for purposes other than our listening enjoyment. In such instances, is it still music?

① Brainstorm about places where music is played.

② Listen to a medley of tunes. As you listen, imagine when and where you might hear each tune.

③ Write your answers on the handout.

④ Based on your definition of music in Activity 1, can everything in the medley really be considered music?

⑤ In your group, discuss the *Talk About It!* questions.

⑥ Finish completing the handout.

 Talk About It!

a) Why do you think music is played everywhere?

b) Do you think that it was the same 50 years ago? Explain why or why not.

c) In what situations do you find that music can be very annoying? When does music become noise?

Can You Do It?

- Make a list of places where music is played. Can you come up with more than 25 places?

- Work in teams and pool your answers. Which group can come up with the most places?

"That's not music, it's just noise. Why don't you play something with a tune?"

to pool: to bring (ideas, resources) together.

Music Is Mood

Whether or not we choose the music we listen to, it's clear that it influences our moods and the way we perceive the world. Background music in elevators and shopping centres, advertising jingles, soundtracks and uptempo tunes to do housework to all contribute to the way we feel and react. In TASK 2, you will explore how music affects you.

ACTIVITY 1

Mood Dispensers

Have you ever thought of speakers as mood dispensers? They fill a room with waves that help shape how we experience reality. In this activity, you will explore how music affects your mood.

1 Does a particular sort of music make you happy? Is there music that affects you so much that you just can't stay still? Take a couple of minutes to think about different types of music and how they make you feel.

2 Read through the *Functional Language for Talking About Music* on the next page.

3 Listen to five short selections.

4 As you listen to them, jot down how each one makes you feel.

5 Share your responses in your group.

6 Discuss the *Talk About It!* questions in your group. Use the *Cues* on the next page to help you.

Culture

- In Montreal, opera music was played in some parts of the Berri-UQAM metro station to dissuade young people from hanging out there.
- Some convenience stores use the same strategy.
- Heavy metal is played in some grain storage rooms to keep rats away.
- Why do these "tricks" work?

Talk About It!

a) Where would you expect to hear each of the selections played?

b) Are there places where playing some types of music would not be appropriate? Explain.

c) What kind of music do you think your principal would select to play in the halls of your school? Would your choice be the same? Explain why or why not.

Functional Language for Talking About Music

This music is...

- boring
- amazing
- relaxing
- inspiring
- nerve-racking
- crazy
- irritating
- awesome
- distracting

- melancholic
- happy
- aggressive
- soothing
- depressing
- invigorating
- catchy
- astounding

It makes me feel...

- happy
- sad
- depressed
- energized
- restless
- relaxed
- sleepy
- moved
- aggressive

- It's too loud!
- Turn it down!
- It's not loud enough!
- Turn it up!
- Pump up the volume!
- Shut it off!
- Change it!
- Play it again!

- It gets on my nerves.
- It makes me feel like... dancing, singing, moving, doing housework, throwing up, tearing out my hair...
- I feel like turning up the volume, buying earplugs, relaxing, dancing...
- This music is good for...

Cues

- I would/would not expect to hear...
- It would/would not be appropriate to hear...
- If I could choose the music played in..., I would choose...

Focus on...

Adverbs of Degree or Intensity

You can combine the following adverbs of degree with adjectives to express how people find music and how it makes them feel.

- absolutely
- altogether
- awfully
- completely

- considerably
- deeply
- drastically
- especially

- extremely
- fairly
- immensely
- intensely

- nearly
- practically
- profoundly
- quite

- rather
- somewhat
- terribly
- totally

- tremendously
- truly
- unbelievably
- uncontrollably

Examples:

– I found this music **considerably** <u>refreshing</u> – This song is **completely** <u>annoying</u>! – It makes me feel **totally** <u>energized</u>!
                   adjective   adjective   adjective

Practise!

Make up at least five different sentences using adjectives and adverbs of degree to express how different types of music make you feel or how you feel about them. Classify the adverbs by degree.

 ### Write About It!

Choose a public place and explain how the music played there influences your mood.

astounding: surprising and impressive.
altogether: completely, totally.

ACTIVITY 2

Mood on the Screen

Music is essential to films because it catalyzes intense emotions and manipulates the way we perceive various scenes. In Activity 2, you will listen to two separate pieces, both composed by Ennio Morricone for Sergio Leones' 1968 film *Once Upon a Time in the West*. You will see how the music played during a scene influences our perceptions.

1 Look at the picture below. What is going on? What do you think will happen next?

2 Listen to the two selections.

3 As you listen to the first one, write what you think will happen next. The music will last two minutes; write as much as you can while it is playing.

4 Listen to the second selection. Now what do you think will happen? This extract will also last two minutes. Write your answer while the music plays.

5 Compare your answers. Did your perceptions change with the music? How did the music influence your mood?

6 Share in your group.

Culture

Once Upon a Time in the West tells a story of revenge and lust for money, centred around the development of the railway in the Wild West of the United States.

A mysterious man (Harmonica) helps a beautiful widow kill the desperados who slaughtered her family. But he is also out to avenge the killing of his own brother...

to catalyze: to cause or increase a reaction.
lust: a passionate desire for something.

What will happen next?

Focus on...

The Future Tense

- Use:

  | will + the verb to express a future action |

  Examples:
  - *He **will play** guitar at the concert but he **won't sing (will not sing)**.*
  - *We **will be** there, but we **won't stay** too late.*
  - *After that TV appearance, the Bobbins **will be** famous all over the country.*

- You can also use:

  | To be going to + the verb |

  Examples:
  - *He's **going to play** guitar, but he **isn't going to sing**.*
  - *We **aren't going to stay** there late.*
  - *After that TV appearance, the Bobbins **are going to be** famous all over the country.*

Focus on...

Future Events

To string together events happening in the future, use linking words and expressions like:

- *soon*
- *in a little while*
- *after that*
- *from now on*

- *any second now*
- *next*
- *from then on*
- *starting today*

- *shortly*
- *then*
- *from this moment on*
- *in the future*

Practise!

Write four sentences about an event in the future. Use linking words to string them together into a logical paragraph.

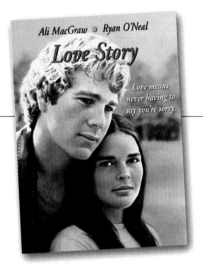

Do you listen to the music or do you listen to the words? Just as the music often influences our moods, the lyrics can also stir up emotions. They portray our lives, dreams and tribulations. In TASK 3, you will look at lyrics as an integral part of music.

ACTIVITY 1

My Endless Love!

The recurrent theme of **love** in song lyrics is unsurpassed. This is probably because songwriters are by nature romantic people! Or perhaps it is because love, like music, is a universal language...

All generations have their favourite love songs. Musical styles change, but the message remains the same, an echo of the timeless myth of love.

❶ Listen to the song *Down by the Old Mill Stream*, a love song from 1910!

❷ As you listen, make a list of keywords that express the myths of love.

❸ Write two sentences that express what you think this song means.

❹ Compare your answers with a partner.

❺ Read *How to Decode Lyrics* on the next page.

❻ Divide the tips up among your group. Each of you will be responsible for applying some of them to the song.

❼ Complete the first part of the handout individually.

❽ In your group, take turns presenting what you have learned about the song from your tips.

❾ Together, answer the *Talk About It!* questions and finish completing the handout.

Can You Do It?

- Work with a partner to make a list of at least 10 love songs you know.
- Not all songs speak of love. Find at least five other recurrent themes and give an example of a well-known song for each.

Culture

Myths are universal stories rooted in human nature and history. They convey emotions and perceptions.

Myths are things that never happened but always are.
– Sallustius, 4th century A.D.

Two examples of myths are the images of the ideal lover and that of a perfect life without any problems.

tribulation: a difficulty.
recurrent: occurring again and again.
A.D.: *anno Domini*; used for dates that come after the supposed year Christ was born.

How to...
Decode Lyrics

Trying to figure out what a song means is not always easy. Like poems, lyrics express the author's state of mind, often in artistic ways. Like abstract paintings, lyrics may lead to different interpretations, depending on the interpreter.

Use these tips to help you understand the lyrics of a song:

1 **Use a dictionary.**
- Look up recurrent words and expressions.

2 **Make links with the title.**
- A serious author makes sure the title reveals part of his message.

3 **Uncover the three words or expressions repeated most often.**
- They should point to the meaning of the song!

4 **Find the theme of the song.**
- Is it a song about war, friendship, love...?

5 **Make a list of the action verbs.**
- Verbs are the motors of sentences and carry a lot of meaning.

6 **Make a separate list of stative verbs.**
- These are verbs that don't really show action, yet they provide descriptions. Some common stative verbs are: *to be, to have, to appear, to become, to grow, to look, to seem, to feel* and *to taste.*

7 **List the subject of the verbs.**
- Who is the song about?

8 **Determine the prominent verb tense.**
- Is the song in the past, present or future?

9 **Make links with the period in which the song was written.**
- Was the song written during a war or some other event? Are there references to specific events in the song?

10 **Find out about the author's life.**
- Did he/she travel a lot? Did he/she lose a child or go to prison? Look for links between the author's life and the song.

11 **Locate the metaphors.**
- A metaphor uses an image to express an idea: *Example: He fell into the trap of love.*

12 **Reveal any myths that the lyrics are hiding.**
- Songwriters also tell old stories in their songs. They speak of heroes, perfect love, broken wings...

Talk About It!

a) Does taking the time to decode the lyrics of a song help you appreciate it more? Explain your answer.

b) In what ways is this old classic like a modern love song?

ACTIVITY 2

In Tune with the World

From nursery rhymes to romantic melodies, the songs we sing and listen to play a capital role in our existence. The songwriters who compose them allow us to explore various aspects of life that are at times universal and at times very personal.

1 Listen to Rufus Wainwright's song "Going to a Town."

2 As you listen, fill in the missing words on the handout.

3 Listen to the song again and circle the words that you think contain the essence of the message.

4 Using the tips on the previous page, find the general meaning of the song. Why exactly is Wainwright tired of America? Why does he refer to religion?

5 In your group, discuss the political message of the song.

6 Finish completing the handout.

Culture

Traces of song lyrics go back to Ancient Greece in 1100 B.C. Some of the first songs ever written were for the Greek god **Apollo**, who was associated with many aspects of life, including music and poetry.

Apollo was the leader of the Muses.

nursery rhyme: a simple song or poem for children.

Culture

Rufus Wainwright is a singer and songwriter. He was born in 1973 in Rhinebeck, New York, but he grew up in Montreal in a family of folksingers.

Wainwright began playing piano at age 6 and started touring at 13 with *The McGarrigle Sisters and Family* because his mom was in the band.

By the way, *The McGarrigle Sisters and Family* are a folk music ensemble from Saint-Sauveur-des-Monts, Quebec.

Sign of the Times

If songs can carry important messages, what happens when millions of people listen to the same tunes? The radio and record industries have made this possible. As a result, music has helped shape zeitgeists that, in turn, have had an impact on lifestyles, values, attitudes and fashion.
In TASK 4, you will look at music as a sign of the times.

ACTIVITY 1

Music and Fashion Stereotypes

Throughout the generations, songwriters and musicians have *strived* to find new and different ways to sell their music. Over time, various stereotypes have been produced.

> *to strive: to try very hard.*

1 Look at the four illustrations below. They illustrate the following music styles: R&B, rap, rock and punk.

2 Listen to the four selections. Each of them is linked to one of the four characters.

3 As you listen, think about your perceptions of the **values** and **lifestyles** associated with each of the four music and fashion trends.

4 Compare your perceptions in your group. How are they alike? How are they different?

5 Discuss the *Talk About It!* questions.

6 Complete the handout.

Culture

A **zeitgeist** (pronounced |tsïtgïst|) is the defining spirit or mood of a particular period of history, shown by the ideas and beliefs of the time. Each generation has its own zeitgeist.

The word comes from the German words for time (Zeit) and spirit (Geist).

💬 Talk About It!

a) What are some other stereotypes related to music and fashion? Which musicians or groups made these styles popular? Do any of these styles have roots in other generations?

b) In Unit 4, you will be discussing body image. Do you think that fashion stereotypes are related to body image? Why or why not?

ACTIVITY 2

Would-be Classics

Of the hundreds of songs recorded each year, some tunes manage to remain more popular than others and end up marking an entire generation. Songs like "Hotel California" by The Eagles and "Let It Be" by The Beatles are good examples. In this activity, you will take a look at songs from today to see if they might pass the test of time for generations to come.

❶ Read the *Making a Classic* box on the next page.

❷ In your group, think about a recent song that you think might still be popular 30 years down the road.

❸ Rate your would-be classic on a scale of 100 using the 10 criteria on the list. What score do you think it would take to make the grade?

❹ Exchange song titles with two other groups and evaluate each other's songs. Does your song pass their test? Does their song pass yours?

Culture

A **classic song** has nothing to do with classical music, as in that of Beethoven or Mozart. Rather, the term classic describes a song that has remained popular and appealing for several generations. It is a song that has passed the test of time.

"I never expected to be anybody important."

– Elvis Presley

down the road: in the future.
to make the grade: to measure up to a certain standard.
appealing: attractive.

 Think About It!

At school, a passing grade is usually 60%. Do you think this would be a high enough score for a song to become a classic?

Making a Classic

We could argue forever about what makes "a truly classic song," but no matter what your opinion is, there are certain aspects of songs that are recurrent when it comes to describing one that is a true classic.

1 **Theme:** Is the theme of the song (what it is about) able to touch a vast audience or is it restricted to a specific group? /10

2 **Lyrics:** Are the lyrics easy to understand and remember? /10

3 **Message:** Does the song tell a story or convey a message? /10

4 **Melody:** Do you end up whistling it in the shower? /10

5 **Beat:** Does it make you want to tap your feet, bob your head or get up and dance? /10

6 **Mood:** Does it put you in the mood for love, make you smile or soothe your soul? /10

7 **Lasting Impression:** Does it move you deeply or stay in your head? /10

8 **Symbols:** Does it use images that are universal? /10

9 **Success:** Did it enjoy instant success on the hit parade? /10

10 **Popularity:** Do your parents know it as well? /10

/100

Culture

The Doors was the name of a popular rock band formed in 1965. Lead singer Jim Morrison was responsible for much of its fame.

Although the group was dissolved in the early 70s, interest in The Doors has remained high all over the world and the group continues to sell 1 million albums a year.

One of their great classics is "Light My Fire."

Talk About It!

a) Which criteria on this list do you think are the most relevant?

b) What other elements would you add to this list?

c) Do you think that it is harder for a song to become a classic these days? Explain why or why not.

> **to whistle:** to blow air through the lips to make music.
> **to soothe:** to calm.

ACTIVITY 3

Sounds of the Times

Each generation has its classic songs and listening to them becomes a fine way of reminiscing about the *good old days*. Is it possible for someone from one generation to make links with the times and music of another generation?

❶ Read the texts about the 1920s, 40s, 60s and the 80s on pp. 40-43.

❷ Using the handout, organize the information from each text into categories.

❸ Compare answers with a partner.

❹ Add any other knowledge you may have about these decades.

❺ Exchange handouts with students in another group and look for new information to add.

❻ Retrieve your handout and pool any new ideas in your group.

❼ Listen to the songs from the 1920s, 40s, 60s and 80s. As you listen, make links between the sounds, lyrics, fashion and history in order to add even more information to your handouts.

❽ Choose ONE of these decades and write a short paragraph in which you make links between music and time. Explain how the music of that time reflected that generation.

❾ Refer to the *Focus on Using the Past Tense* box on the next page to help you use the past tense correctly.

to retrieve: to get (something) back; to regain possession of.

 Talk About It!

Which of these decades do you find most intriguing or exciting? Explain why.

"Yesterday's just a memory, tomorrow is never what it's supposed to be."

– Bob Dylan

Culture

The Roots of Radio
(even before the 1920s!)

In 1886, German physicist, Heinrich Rudolph Hertz demonstrated that rapid variations of electric current could be projected into space in the form of radio waves similar to those of light and heat.

Using the Past Tense

Here are three ways to use the past tense:

	Simple Past	The Past Perfect	The Past Continuous
Use this tense to express:	a **completed action** that took place at a specific or non-specific moment in the past	• an **action completed before** some other action in the past • an **"if" clause** that is followed by the past condidional • an action that people wanted to do, but for some reason didn't	• an **incomplete** action in the past • an action that **was going on in the past** when something interrupted it • **two actions** happening at **the same time** in the past
Examples:	• He **wrote** the lyrics to the song. • He **didn't record** them.	• He **had** already **written** the music to the song. • If he **had recorded** the song, it would have been a big hit. • He **had planned** to record the song, but in the end he didn't.	• He **was writing** the lyrics to the song. • He **was writing** the lyrics to the song when the telephone rang. • He **was writing** the lyrics to the song and **working on** a new video.
Common markers:	• Last night, yesterday, in the past...	• Already, just, until...	• While, at the same time that...

Practise!

1. Write a sentence about music for each of the uses of the past tense listed in the table.

2. Exchange papers with a partner and check the work.

3. Read the sentences below. State which tense is used in each example and explain why.
   a) He lived the life of a rock star.
   b) Imagine you had been as famous as the Beatles.
   c) If rock had existed before, people would have evolved much faster.
   d) They were playing the Thriller video twice every hour in those days.
   e) She had thought about writing an article on heavy metal and its influence on young people.

   f) Hippies had planned to change the world, but their influence didn't last long enough.
   g) While she was practising her solo, he was getting his trumpet ready.
   h) Elvis had a huge influence on the Beatles.

4. Circle the verbs in the paragraph you wrote about one of the decades. What verb tenses did you use? Were you able to integrate all three tenses?

THE 1920S AT A GLANCE

The "Roaring Twenties" is a term used to describe this decade's social, artistic and cultural dynamism. After the Great War (WWI), jazz music blossomed, the Charleston dance was hot, art deco was in, and finally the Wall Street Crash of 1929 came to punctuate the end of the era as The Great Depression set in.

The period was also distinguished by numerous inventions, unprecedented industrial growth, accelerated consumer demand and important changes in lifestyle.

The spirit of the Roaring Twenties was marked by a general feeling of renewal associated with modernity and a break with tradition. Everything seemed to be feasible through modern technology. New technologies, especially those associated with automobiles, movies and radio, brought "modernity" to a large part of the population. At the same time, entertainment, crazy fashions and light-hearted fun and games were being promoted in dance halls and jazz clubs, in defiance of the horrors of World War I, which remained present in people's minds. The period is also often called "The Jazz Age," although strangely enough, it coincided with the Prohibition period in the USA. ❖

The first talking movie, *The Jazz Singer*, was produced in New York in 1927. It is the story of a young Jewish man from a long line of cantors who decides to break with family tradition and become a jazz singer.

Flappers were young women who challenged women's place in society. They smoked, drank and frequented jazz clubs.

Culture

■ In the USA, between 1920 and 1933, it was illegal to manufacture, sell or transport alcohol. This period is referred to as **Prohibition**.

Prohibition made millionaires out of bootleggers and the owners of underground saloons, called "speakeasies."

■ The **Golden Age of Radio** began in the 1920s and lasted until it was replaced by television in the late 50s and early 60s.

The first commercial radio station in the world was XWA in Montreal. It began broadcasting on the AM frequency in May 1920.

cantor: an official who sings and leads prayer in a synagogue.
unprecedented: never seen before.
feasible: possible.

 Talk About It!

Do you think a new period of Prohibition could ever occur?

The 1940s at a Glance

To sum up the Fabulous Forties in a few paragraphs is nearly impossible. The events and changes that the Second World War (1939–1945) brought about are literally countless. Moreover, WWII split the decade into two parts.

There were virtually no attacks or warfare on North American soil, yet all eyes and ears were glued to newspapers and radios for news from the fronts in Europe and the Pacific, and all economic efforts went to support the troops abroad. Industries were booming and women were called to work in factories to replace the men who had gone to war.

In the United States, music and movies began to take on new roles as creators of an imaginary world of romance, glitter and dreams. Big bands played happy, swinging music that had couples dancing and romancing. The film industry entertained the masses with glitzy musicals depicting beautiful people living in ideal worlds of glamour and romance.

Meanwhile, on the other side of the globe, in order to put an end to the war with Japan, the Americans launched the first ever nuclear attack.

After the war, America went through a strong period of economic growth. Women were encouraged to stay at home and enjoy a new modern way of life brought about by new machines and products. The ordinary citizen's life was regimented by broad stereotypes that defined the perfect family, husband, wife and children.

On the political side, the post-WWII period was characterized by a fear of communism and the development of the Cold War between the United States and the Soviet Union and their respective allies.

All in all, it's hard to say that the 40s was really such a fabulous period. Life was great, at least on the big screen, and the 40s paved the way to today's fast American lifestyle, but those years also involved the most destructive war ever to strike humanity... ❖

Clarinetist **Benny Goodman** (1909–1986) was one of the first bandleaders to achieve widespread fame. He influenced almost every jazz musician who played clarinet after him and was responsible for making significant steps in racial integration in the United States.

ICT

Go on the Internet and find out more information about the music of the 40s.

Rock and roll developed in the United States in the late 1940s and early 50s and quickly spread to the rest of the world. Its immense popularity had an unprecedented impact on lifestyles, fashion, attitudes and language.

Culture

■ Post-war Masculine Fashion

The end of the war brought about a dramatic change in men's fashion. Long coats, full-cut trousers and colourful clothing became trendy and were taken as a sign of opulence and luxury. Hand-painted ties also became popular. This change was partly a reaction to wartime shortages and rationing.

■ Glenn Miller (1904–1944) was an American jazz musician and leader of one of the best-known big bands of the Swing era. His music still remains alive, decades after his death.

glitzy: flashy; showy; ostentatious.
meanwhile: at the same time.
trousers: pants.
trendy: fashionable; popular.

The 1960s at a Glance

> "Elvis is the greatest cultural force in the twentieth century. He introduced the beat to everything, music, language, clothes, it's a whole new social revolution... the 60s comes from it."
>
> – Leonard Bernstein, composer and conductor

The 60s is mostly remembered for the complex cultural and political trends that occurred between 1958 and 1974 in many Western countries. The 60s saw the rise of a counterculture movement, which moved away from traditional values toward more open and socially-oriented ones.

The decade was also called the Swinging Sixties because of the libertine attitudes that emerged during this time. The 60s slogan was "Make love, not war!" Widespread drug use also became a symbol of the 60s counterculture.

The 60s was a time of immense change in all aspects of public and private life and is often referred to as a period of worldwide social revolution. In the United States, huge changes were brought about by the civil rights movement, the rise of feminism and the fight for gay rights. This exciting period also saw the invention of the microchip! Quebec didn't miss out on the wave either; it had its own "Quiet Revolution."

The 60s saw the development of a host of new, exciting, radical and subversive events and trends, which continued to develop into the 70s and 80s and beyond. The spirit of the 60s still glows in the hearts of all hippies, old and young alike! ❖

Elvis Presley (1935–1977) was an American singer, musician and actor. He is an icon of popular music and is known as "The King." Presley started becoming popular in 1956.

The Ed Sullivan Show was a popular American variety program that ran on TV from 1948 to 1971. Sullivan hosted all the "greats," including The Beatles, Elvis, The Doors and the Rolling Stones.

The Beatles was a group from Liverpool composed of John Lennon, Paul McCartney, George Harrison and Ringo Starr. It is one of the most widely acclaimed and influential bands in the history of popular music. The Beatles is the best-selling musical group of all time. It is estimated that the band has sold over 1 billion discs and tapes worldwide.

subversive: against established order.
catchphrase: a phrase that serves as a slogan for a group or movement.

Culture

"Flower power" was a catchphrase used by hippies during the late 60s and early 70s. It was a symbol of non-violence rooted in opposition to the Vietnam War.

Hippies were also known as flower children because of their bright flowery clothes and the flowers often worn in their hair.

The 1980s at a Glance

This decade is sometimes referred to as "the Me decade" or "the Greed decade," reflecting the economic prosperity and social climate of the period. During this time the word "yuppie" (young urban professionals) became fashionable. The decade also witnessed a religious revival and the rise of conservatism, which began with a backlash against disco music late in the 70s.

Disco music, which had started in 1972 and peaked in 1979, began to lose ground on the charts in 1981. The 80s is also known for its own particular pop culture, which featured things like exaggerated fashions, big hairstyles and the commercialization of music via video clips.

In the world of politics, the 80s saw the fall of the Berlin Wall. It had been built to separate the west side of Berlin from the east, which had been controlled by communist Russia ever since the defeat of Germany in WWII.

The Cold War between the United States and the Soviet Union also came to an end. After some 30 years of an ongoing nuclear arms race, capitalist USA and communist Russia, both stocked with enough nuclear warheads to destroy the entire planet many times over, signed a treaty putting an end to this period.

This transitional period also saw massive democratic revolutions and demonstrations, such as the Tiananmen Square protests of 1989 in China and the breaking up of the Soviet Union with events such as the Czechoslovak Velvet Revolution, and the end of the dictatorial regime in Romania and other communist states in Central and Eastern Europe.

The 80s was also characterized by an increase in telecommunications and the rise of liberal (free trade) market economies. ❖

The **CD** was first launched on the market late in 1982. It became the standard playback medium for commercial audio recordings for over 20 years.

In Quebec, **MusiquePlus** began playing commercial music videos in 1986.

ICT

Go on the Internet and find out more information about the different kinds of music of the 70s and 80s, like disco, bubblegum, alternative, techno, New Wave and punk.

Culture

The golden age of the Broadway musical is generally considered to have begun with *Oklahoma* in 1943 and ended with *Hair* in 1968. In the 80s and 90s, pop operas like *The Phantom of the Opera* and various Disney productions became popular.

greed: an intense desire to keep or have for yourself.
to peak: to reach a high point.

Tune Capsules

In your group, you will choose and present a song that you feel marks your generation. Based on what you have learned throughout the unit, you will explain what this song is all about and why you feel it could become a classic.

What to Do

❶ Your presentation may take on many different forms. For example, it may be a:

- formal presentation
- skit
- panel discussion
- PowerPoint presentation
- game show
- etc.

❷ The choice is yours! But, there are steps to follow in order to make it a hit!

Step 1: In your group, **choose** a song to present using the *Checklist for Choosing a Song* box on the next page.

Step 2: **Plan** and **organize** your presentation.

Step 3: **Present** your song to the class, **evaluate** your work and reflect on how you did both individually and as a team.

Choosing a Song

Finding the right song is crucial to the success of your presentation, so you will want to give it some thought.

You probably understand that in a school context, your flavour of the month might not be your best card to play... You will have to submit the lyrics of your song to your teacher for approval, so you may have to dig a little deeper in your MP3 files to find something appropriate. The checklist below will help you.

CHECKLIST
for Choosing a Song

1 Does your song promote violence, sex or racism? If so, forget it!

2 Can we hear and understand the lyrics as we listen to it?

3 Does the song repeat the same verse 75 times? If so, maybe you won't have much to say about it...

4 Are you able to explain the lyrics, or are they too complicated?

5 Is the song a long one? If so, will you have enough time to present it?

6 Do the lyrics really represent your generation? Remember, you're looking for a future classic.

7 Can you find information about the group or singer and describe their roots and philosophy?

8 Can you make links between the song and society?

9 Does your song pass your *Making a Classic* test, using the tips on p. 37?

10 Does your song meet with your teacher's approval?

"My version of Georgia *became the state song of Georgia. That was a big thing for me, man. It really touched me. Here is a state that used to lynch people like me suddenly declaring my version of a song as its state song. That is touching."*

– Ray Charles

to lynch: to kill without legal sanction, usually by hanging.

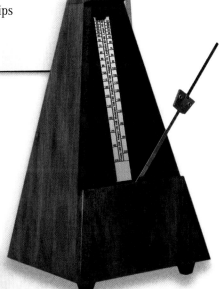

STEP 2

Planning and Organizing Your Presentation

Throughout the unit, you have had occasions to look at music and songs from the angles of mood, lyrics and society. You probably have some ideas about what you would like to say about your song. Now it's time to plan how you will do this. Dare to be creative!

1 Decide when and how you will play your song. (You don't necessarily have to play it; you could read, sing or simply show the lyrics instead. It's up to you.)

2 Use the handout to plan and organize your presentation. Follow the checklist carefully to make sure you don't forget anything.

3 Decide who does what, making sure each person has equal time in the limelight.

4 Individually, organize your part of the presentation and validate your ideas with the other members of your group.

Presenting and Evaluating

Once your planning is done, you will get ready for your presentation. Depending on the form you have chosen, you may find it useful to make memo cards. They will help you stay focused and organized without having to read a text. It will make your presentation more interesting.

❶ Read *How to Make Memo Cards* on the next page.

❷ Make memo cards for your part of the presentation. Get ready to present a future classic!

❸ Use the *Tips* on p. 49 to help you during your presentation.

❹ Be an active listener and participant during your classmates' presentations.

❺ Use the handout to evaluate your participation and reflect on your performance.

❻ Answer the *Talk About It!* questions.

 ## Talk About It!

a) Of the songs presented, besides your own, which ones do you think have a good chance of becoming classics? Explain why?

b) Which one would you rate at the very top of the list? Why is that?

 ## Write About It!

Choose one of the songs presented (but not your own!) and write a paragraph explaining why you think it could become a classic (or why it wouldn't).

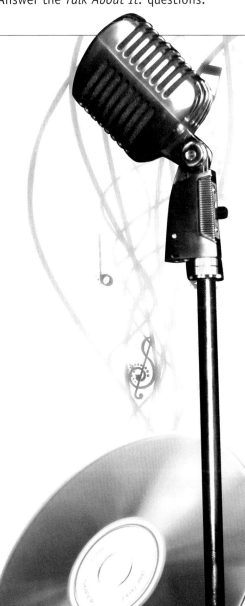

How to...
Make Memo Cards

1 | Write only one main idea per card.

2 | Write only a few keywords.

3 | Avoid sentences, except for the transition sentence.

4 | Use large letters and colours to help you see the words more clearly.

A typical memo card looks like this:

Memo Card Title or Number: **4**

Main idea: The Beatles on *The Ed Sullivan Show*

Important details and keywords:
- Sunday, Feb. 9, 1964
- most important event in history of rock music
- over 73 million viewers

Transition: From that moment on, "Beatlemania"
hit America.

Using a short transition sentence can help you if you get nervous.

COMMUNICATION ALLEY

TIPS ON DEALING WITH NERVOUSNESS

- Prepare all your material beforehand; last-minute problems make stress levels go through the roof!
- Make sure all equipment is working.
- Know your first two sentences very well.
- Wait for complete silence before you start.
- Take time to breathe.
- If you feel nervous at the beginning, remind yourself that the stress will go down once you start.
- Look at students that are listening attentively.

to go through the roof:
to intensify enormously;
to explode (metaphorically).

Wrap-up

Look Back

- Look back at the pictures on the opening pages and explain why they were chosen to introduce the unit.

- Answer the Guiding Questions.

Think About It...

- What do you think music will be like 20 years from now?

- Do you think your generation has a lot in common with the one that preceded it, even though you listen to different sounds?

Now What?

- You might want to print the lyrics of the songs you like and analyze their meaning.

- Perhaps you would like to write your own lyrics to express how you feel or to communicate the messages of your generation.

- You could even organize a slam competition or other music event at your school!

Select some of your work for your portfolio!

3 Name three things you've learned about the role music plays in our society.

2 List two new vocabulary words or expressions you remember.

1 Imagine the theme of your generation's number one classic song.

OTHER THINGS TO DO

Find out more about a favourite songwriter, musician or group. Make links with mood, lyrics and society. Present your findings in a creative way.

Choose a favourite film and listen to the soundtrack. Write about how the music defines the mood.

Compose or perform a song or dance and explain what it expresses to your peers.

Choose a song from the past and illustrate the lyrics, perhaps in the form of a comic strip or as a photo book.

Canadian Singers and Songwriters

Besides Céline Dion, Shania Twain, Leonard Cohen and Bryan Adams, numerous other Canadian singers and songwriters have left their mark on the music world and helped shape Canada's culture and identity.

Acknowledging Canadian musicians of the past and present is a way of paying tribute to some of the world's greatest talents. Here are but a few of them.

A Few English Canadian Greats

Paul Anka was born in Ottawa in 1941, but became a naturalized citizen of the United States in 1990. He is a singer, songwriter and actor of Lebanese origin who became a teen idol in the late 1950s and 60s. His hit "Diana" is one of the best selling 45s in music history. Anka is also known for writing many hits sung by various artists. These include the theme for *The Tonight Show Starring Johnny Carson*, the English lyrics to Frank Sinatra's signature song "My Way", and Tom Jones' hit "She's A Lady." Anka was elected to the Canadian Music Hall of Fame in 1980. He has a star on both the Hollywood Walk of Fame and Canada's Walk of Fame. In 1991, the Government of France honoured him with the title of Chevalier in the Ordre des Arts et des Lettres and he was appointed an officer of the Order of Canada in 2005.

Paul Anka

Oscar Peterson

Oscar Peterson (1925–2007) was a Canadian jazz pianist, vocalist and composer. He made more than 200 recordings, won seven Grammys and numerous other awards and acclaims, and received honorary doctorates from a number of Canadian universities. He was famous for being able to play in every known jazz style and was considered to be one of the greatest jazz pianists of all time. Peterson grew up in Little Burgundy, Montreal, where, at age 5, he began playing the trumpet and piano. After a bout of tuberculosis at age 7, he turned all his attention to the piano, which he practised for four to six hours a day. When he was 14, he dropped out of school and became a professional pianist. During his brilliant career, Peterson made many duet and trio performances and recordings. In 1993, he suffered a severe stroke that left him with limited control of his left hand. He continued to perform however, relying principally on his right hand. He died in his home in Mississauga, Ontario, on December 23, 2007.

The Guess Who is a Canadian rock band from Winnipeg, Manitoba, which began in 1962 as Chad Allen and the Reflections. The group's first gold single was "These Eyes," which hit number 6 on the US charts in 1969. In 1970, they had the honour of being the first Canadian rock group to have a number 1 hit in the United States. This hit, "American Woman," dethroned The Beatles for three consecutive weeks. The band broke up in 1975, with some of the members going on to perform solo. Then, in 1983, members Randy Bachman, Burton Cummings, Jim Kale and Garry Peterson reunited as The Guess Who to perform a series of concerts in Canada. In 2001, The Guess Who was inducted into Canada's Walk of Fame.

The Guess Who

Joni Mitchell

Canada's own folk singer **Joni Mitchell** was born in Alberta in 1943. Her 1974 album *Court and Spark* is now a classic example of Canadian folk/rock. Mitchell explores and combines pop and jazz, and has developed a unique guitar technique. She has influenced many musicians and composers, including Madonna, Prince and Björk. Besides being a musician, Mitchell is an accomplished visual artist who created the artwork for her albums. Mitchell has received numerous awards both in the United States and Canada. Her achievements include being inducted into the Rock and Roll Hall of Fame in 1997 and Canada's Walk of Fame in 2001. In 2007, she was featured on a Canadian postage stamp.

Glenn Hebert Gould (1932–1982) was born in Toronto. He was one of the most well-known and celebrated pianists of the 20th century. He is especially recognized for his recordings of the music of Johann Sebastian Bach. Gould greatly preferred the control and intimacy of the recording studio to the atmosphere of the concert hall, which he compared to a competitive sporting arena. His final public performance was in 1964. Gould was known for his eccentric personality and incredible technique at the piano. He received many honours before and after his death. He won four Grammy Awards and in 1983, was inducted into the Canadian Music Hall of Fame.

Glenn Hebert Gould

K.D. Lang was born Kathryn Dawn Lang in Edmonton, Alberta, in 1961. While in college, she was drawn to country music and became determined to pursue a career as a professional singer. Although Lang started out singing country, she has since often turned to mainstream pop and sometimes, dance rock or jazz. Her album *Hymns of the 49th Parallel* includes only songs by Canadians, including Joni Mitchell, Leonard Cohen and Neil Young. In 2008, Lang released *Watershed* (her first collection of original material since 2000), which she says is a culmination of everything she has ever done. Lang, a lesbian, is an advocate for gay rights. She has also supported many other causes including HIV/AIDS care and research. In 2007, she collaborated with Annie Lennox in the production of the charity record "Sing" to raise awareness of the transmission of HIV to unborn children in Africa. Lang has had numerous hits and won many awards, including four Grammys and eight Junos. In 1996, she was made an Officer of the Order of Canada. ❖

K. D. Lang

Question

Which of the musicians mentioned do you feel is the greatest?

MP3 Players and Your Ears at 30

1 You have probably been warned not to use your MP3 player for long periods of time, especially at high volume; but were you told why?

First, most MP3 players come with stock ear buds, which fit snugly in the ear canal and do not allow any sound to escape. When those trapped sound waves
5 enter your ears, they vibrate tiny hair-like cells, sending nerve impulses to your brain that tell you to hear. Loud noise damages those hair cells, usually temporarily at first. This causes ringing in the ears or temporary deafness.

Extremely loud noises, such as a close gunshot, can immediately destroy hearing cells. But they can also be killed by repeated waves of loud sound,
10 such as those coming in from digital music headphones or speakers at a concert. The longer the exposure, the greater the chance of permanent damage.

Musicians, whose ears are their foremost working tool, now use earplugs onstage to avoid the kind of hearing damage faced by first-generation rockers. It's sad that kids who attend their concerts don't know enough to bring their
15 own sets of earplugs.

It is recommended not to use your player at a level louder than 6. At level 7, you can listen for four hours a day or so; after that there's a potential for hearing loss. At level 8, no more than an hour and a half can be tolerated.

20 Hearing experts advise MP3 users not to turn the volume up higher than 80 per cent and to limit their listening time to 90 minutes. They call it the "80 for 90 guideline." Alas, experts know that despite their warnings, many an MP3-addicted youth will continue to fuse with their player, mostly because there doesn't *seem* to be any impairment. However, as with
25 the consequences of too much sunburn on exposed skin, the damage doesn't appear right away. By the time ears hurt or start ringing 24 hours a day, they will already have been permanently damaged. The aftermath of such trauma in the ears will only show up at age 20 or 30, a time that seems very far away at age 16... ❖

Adapted from Experts worry about harm to hearing from MP3 players
by Marla Jo Fisher, January 4, 2007 smh [online]

Question

Can listening to your MP3 player really damage your hearing?

---

snugly: tightly.
foremost: most important.
alas: unfortunately.
to fuse: to cause to become one.

The Power of Music

Music has great power. It can move us to tears, take us back in time to a special event, make us want to get up and dance, or help us relax after a long day.

But did you know that...?

- Some hospitals play background music in the intensive care units for premature babies. It is found that doing this helps them develop.

- Music also helps calm Alzheimer patients, and in nursing homes, playing the right type of music reduces tension at the dinner table.

- Athletes often use music to pump them up before a big game or a special race.

- On the other hand, certain types of music can help lower heart rates.

- Harp music has been found to have soothing effects, not only on humans, but also on both domestic and wild animals.

- Studies show that high school students who study music get better grades.

- At age four months, babies react both positively and negatively to music. Harsh notes cause them to squirm and turn away, and tunes they like often make them coo.

No culture is known that did not have music.

Question

What other examples can you find of the power of music?

"THAT'S THE BEST HOLD MUSIC I'VE HEARD. I'D LIKE TO SIGN YOU UP AT ONCE!"

"And if he starts telling you that it was his generation that invented Rock 'N' Roll, just humour him."

---

to squirm: to twist about.
to coo: to make soft sounds.

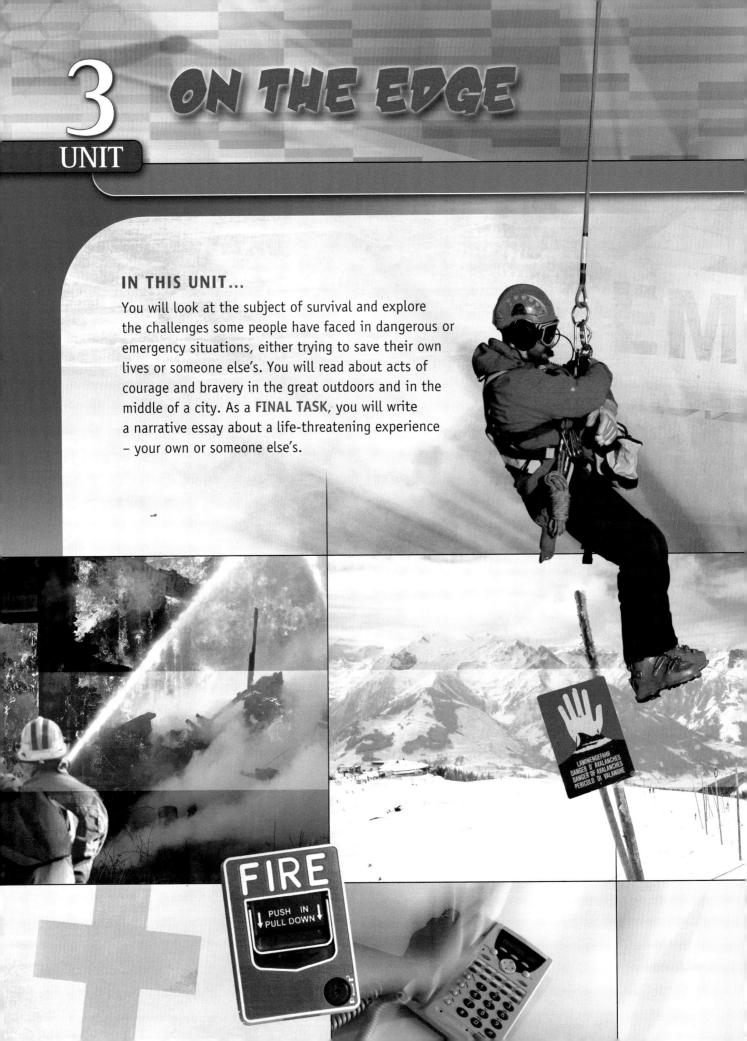

3 ON THE EDGE

UNIT

IN THIS UNIT...

You will look at the subject of survival and explore the challenges some people have faced in dangerous or emergency situations, either trying to save their own lives or someone else's. You will read about acts of courage and bravery in the great outdoors and in the middle of a city. As a **FINAL TASK**, you will write a narrative essay about a life-threatening experience – your own or someone else's.

LAWINENGEFAHR
DANGER D' AVALANCHES
DANGER OF AVALANCHES
PERICOLO DI VALANGHE

FIRE

↓ PUSH IN ↓
PULL DOWN

- What is meant by the word "stamina"?

- What do you need in order to cope with adverse conditions?

TASK 1 presents a survival story. You will learn that there are a number of things to take into account when placed in a potentially life-threatening situation.

ACTIVITY 1

A Snowboarder's Amazing Tale of Survival

In this activity, you will read the amazing survival story of Eric LeMarque, who managed to survive a life-threatening situation thanks to some smart thinking.

❶ Read *How to Read a Story* on the next page. Try to use these strategies as you read the text about Eric LeMarque.

❷ It has been divided into three parts. Read <u>Part One</u>.

❸ As you read, focus on what the snowboarder did to stay alive.

❹ Validate your understanding of <u>Part One</u> with a partner.

❺ Continue with <u>Part Two</u> and <u>Part Three</u>.

❻ After each part, validate your understanding by answering the questions at the end.

❼ Once you have finished the story, discuss the *Talk About It!* questions on p. 62 in your group.

❽ Complete the handout.

How to...
Read a Story

Before reading

1 Look at the **title** and **illustrations**.
- What information do they give you about the story?
- Can you make any predictions?
  - *I think this story is about...*

While reading

2 Read for the **general idea**.
- Don't try to understand every word. Pick out words you know.

3 If there is a word you don't know, **keep on reading**. You may get the meaning from the context, or you may be able to understand the text anyway.

4 **Visualize** what's going on, like a film in your mind.
- Let yourself become part of the action. Imagine you are there.

5 Don't try to read the whole thing at once. **Read a section and stop**.
- Just say what you think it means. Do you have any questions?

6 Then, try to **predict** what might happen next.
- *I think that...*

After reading

7 Try to make sense of the story. Identify:
- The characters
- The setting (where and when)
- The problem or conflict
- The climax (turning point)
- The **resolution** or the **ending**

8 Think about why the author wrote this story:
- *The message the author wished to convey is...*
- *I think the author wanted to show that...*

9 **Share** your opinions:
- *I think this story is... because...*

A Snowboarder's Amazing Tale of Survival

By Andrew Murr | Newsweek Web Exclusive, March 5, 2004

Rescuers are still stunned that Eric LeMarque's smart thinking got him through frostbite and seven below-freezing nights in the High Sierras.

HOW THE SNOWBOARDER KEPT HIMSELF ALIVE

Part One

to duck out: to move swiftly, especially so as to escape being seen.
kindling: small, dry sticks used to start a fire.
soggy: wet.
to dog: to track or to follow persistently.
to trudge: to walk heavily and firmly; to plod.
numb: deprived of the power to feel or move normally.

March 5 – The sun was dropping quickly through the frozen air when Eric LeMarque realized he was lost. An hour earlier, the 34-year-old snowboarder had ducked out of bounds on 11,000-foot Mammoth Mountain in California's Sierra Nevada, looking for a "fresh line" – virgin powder. But a wrong turn sent him into the wilderness on the back of the mountain, and now he was cold and wet and stuck. His cellphone battery was dead. He had no food beyond four pieces of gum and no protection beyond the clothing he wore. He built a fire pit and gathered kindling in hopes the ski patrol would see the smoke, but his soggy matches wouldn't light. "I thought, God, I've got to get out of here," he recalls. LeMarque strapped on his board again and plunged downhill in the darkness, unknowingly speeding further from

safety and rescue every minute. He would spend seven nights in the High Sierras last month before he was found alive by a stunned Army National Guard helicopter crew. He was on the point of exhaustion and death on what became for him a very lucky Friday the 13th. LeMarque endured nights of single-digit temperatures and days that often failed to crack freezing. The snow lay 12 feet deep. Frostbite dogged him early on, and he trudged on feet that were increasingly numb until, finally, he could no longer walk or even stand up. What food he ate consisted of tree bark and pine seeds – he lost 35 pounds. By the end, he was hallucinating and dreamed that his struggle was just a videogame that he was losing. "I was thinking, the game is over," LeMarque told NEWSWEEK. "Let's reset it. I give up."

Part Two

LeMarque was well suited for survival. Born in Paris but raised in Los Angeles, he grew up to be a solid college hockey player – good enough to be drafted by the NHL's Boston Bruins. When he didn't make the pros, he played in Europe for five years, including a tour with the French national team during the 1994 Winter Olympics. In recent years, he's taught hockey and kept in shape with sports and frequent snowboarding. A risk-taker and an optimist, he had no doubt he wouldn't mind boarding by himself, even after friends returned to Los Angeles the morning he became lost. Even after dark that first night, he was sanguine. "I figured it was an adventure," he recounts. "I'll wake up in the morning, and I'll be saved."

He should have worried more. LeMarque continued downhill for another day, putting miles between him and safety and getter ever colder. He found a riverbed and found hopping on the rocks easier going than navigating the deep snow – until he fell in and got soaked. Fast-moving water pushing against his snowboard threatened to drag him over an 80-foot waterfall.

He was soaked. The next day in the cold sunshine, he peeled off his frozen socks and tore the soles off his feet. "They were already black and purple and red," he recalls. "I tried to forget them."

The will to live and some clever thinking kept him alive. He avoided eating snow, which lowers the body temperature dangerously. At night, he used the edge of his board to shave pine boughs and branches for a bed to keep off the snow. Recalling a movie, he jury-rigged a compass by floating a metal needle on a bit of wood floating in water. He turned the radio on his MP3 player into a direction finder after he noticed that reception on a station broadcast from Mammoth grew stronger when pointed north. So he turned course and headed in that direction, pushing step by slow step up the side of a mountain called Pumice Butte where he might be seen. His endurance helped, but by day five, he ran out of energy. He stayed in his snow shelter for two nights, barely able to move. "I was too tired." By Friday morning, Feb. 13, "I knew today was the day." He would either be saved that day or die.

For your own information
1 kg = 2.2 lb.
1 lb. = 454 gr

sanguine: cheerfully confident; optimistic.
bough: a tree branch, especially a large or main branch.

Questions

1. *Besides snowboarding, what did LeMarque do to stay in shape?*

2. *What was his personality like?*

3. *What happened to his feet?*

4. *Why did LeMarque decide to change direction?*

5. *Why was February 13th an important date for LeMarque?*

Part Three

Luckily, rescue efforts had finally geared up. For days, no one knew LeMarque was on the mountain. Friends he'd stayed with in Mammoth had returned to L.A. the morning he was lost. It wasn't unusual for him not to check in with his parents. "We didn't worry at first," says his mother, Susan LeMarque. "He's 34." By mid-week, they were panicked, and his father and stepmother drove to the resort and pushed a search. The only things missing from his condo, police found, were his board, keys and season pass. That meant he was on the mountain. But where?

Search and rescue patrols swung into action on Thursday, Feb. 12. The next day, patrollers found the abortive fire pit, then the tracks. By 3:30, a helicopter crew spotted him using infrared imaging. Semiconscious, LeMarque rose to his knees, waving frantically in the air. Stunned rescue workers were shocked to find him alive.

"It amazed everybody," says Bill Greene of Mono County Sheriff Search and Rescue. "I don't think anybody was not surprised to find him alive." Rescue workers radioed the chopper crew to double-check his name, figuring that maybe this guy was a second lost skier. Eric LeMarque couldn't have survived.

He was alive, not well. His feet and ankles were suffering from stage IV frostbite – water in the cells had frozen causing muscle, blood and tissue cells literally to burst, explains Dr. Peter H. Grossman of the Grossman Burn Center at Sherman Oaks Hospital in Los Angeles, where LeMarque has been treated since he was stabilized at a Mammoth hospital. Doctors had amputated both feet, and this week they took off six more inches of shin bone to close the wounds. He'll be fitted with prosthetic limbs this spring and begin the long task of learning to walk again. He says he'll face life with a new humility. He even vows to hit the slopes again. "I'll be snowboarding next season," he promises. But next time, he'll be much, much better prepared. ❖

to gear up: to get ready for a coming action or event.
to swing into action: to get going.

Questions

1. Why did it take so long for rescue workers to start looking for LeMarque?
2. How was he when they found him?
3. What consequences did he suffer?

Talk About It!

a) Would you be able to find the courage to cheat death against the odds?
b) Do you think it's all right for people to expose themselves to danger by acting irresponsibly? Explain your thinking.
c) LeMarque claims he'll be back on the slopes. Do you believe him? Would you go back?

Had He Known...

In this activity, you will look at LeMarque's story from a very different point of view. You will approach it with hindsight.

1 Read the definition of **hindsight** in the *Vocabulary Builder* box.

2 In your group, make a list of at least eight things LeMarque would surely have done using hindsight. Use the conditional tense in your answers.

3 Share your answers as a class. Be prepared to explain your choices.

4 Discuss the *Talk About It!* questions below in your group or as a class.

Vocabulary Builder

Hindsight

The word *hindsight* is a compound word formed with <u>hind</u>, meaning "back" and <u>sight</u>, meaning "vision."

Hindsight is the perception or understanding of events after they have occurred. It is usually used with the word <u>in</u>:

Situation: Eric LeMarque's cellphone was dead. He could not call for help.

In hindsight, he would make sure the battery in his cellphone was charged before going snowboarding.

The antonym of *hindsight* is *foresight*. Foresight means seeing things in advance:

If I use foresight, I will do something "just in case."

Think of the words <u>behind</u> and <u>before</u>.

"Hindsight has always been better than foresight."

– (popular saying)

 ## Talk About It!

a) What does the popular saying about hindsight mean?

b) What example can you give from your personal experience where hindsight would have been very useful and kept you out of trouble?

In TASK 2, you will see that it takes much more than knowledge, skills and equipment to survive. The right mental attitude and the will to stay alive constitute the winning combination.

ACTIVITY 1

What If...

When an emergency situation occurs, there's no relying on hindsight! You're stuck with trying to make the best decision under the existing circumstances. Sometimes what you decide may have dire consequences. And there may not be much time to think. How would you cope? What would you do?

Part One

1 Look at the illustrations on this page and the next one.

2 Brainstorm about the emergency situations they evoke.

3 Your group will receive a set of cards. Each one describes an emergency situation related to one of the illustrations. Read the first card.

4 Together, discuss what you would do. Practise using transition words in your discussions.

5 Continue in the same manner with the other cards.

Part Two

6 Think up a new emergency situation in the great outdoors.

7 Write it down.

8 Exchange your situations with another group.

9 Discuss and write down what you would do using the conditional tense.

10 Return the situation and your answer to its owners.

11 Complete the handout.

to rely on: to depend on.
dire: horrible, awful.
to cope: to try to overcome difficulties.
to evoke: to bring to mind, to suggest.

"Climbing is not a battle with the elements, nor against the law of gravity. It's a battle against oneself."

– Walter Bonatti

Focus on...

The Conditional Tense

How to form the conditional tense

would + the verb   **wouldn't** + the verb

*Examples: – We **would take** a first-aid kit.   – I **wouldn't go** alone.*

When to use the conditional tense

- To talk about hypothetical choices (choices that may or may not be possible)
- For actions that could be done only under certain conditions

Example: I would call the ski patrol if I had my cellphone with me. (But unfortunately, I forgot it at home.)

Note

After **if**, use the **past tense** (not the conditional):

*Examples: – **If** they **went** camping, they would take a first-aid kit.*
*– **If** I **had** a dog, I would take him with me for safety.*
*– I wouldn't go hiking **if** I **were** not fit.*

Using Transition Words

In your writing and speaking, make sure you use transition words to go from one event to the next.

Examples:
– At first   – Next
– After that   – Before
– Then   – Subsequently
– Initially   – Finally...
– Later

In an "if" clause, the verb *to be* takes the form *were*.

*Example: If I **were** a better skier, I'd go skiing in the Rockies.*

 ## Talk About It!

a) Have you ever had to act rapidly in an emergency or in a critical situation? Explain.

b) How do you think you would react in a moment of crisis? Could you cope?

c) What do you think your greatest strength would be in a moment of crisis?

Cues
- *I would panic if...*
- *I'd be too nervous, (scared, uptight, panicky, out of it...) to...*
- *I would break down.*
- *I (don't) think I could cope with...*
- *I'd stay calm because...*
- *I'd try to focus on...*

ACTIVITY 2

The Scare of a Lifetime

In the short story, "A Pail of Berries," a teenage girl was out picking blueberries with her younger brother Corey when they met face to face with a black bear. Would they manage to escape?

❶ Read the description of the short story above and the introduction below and look at the illustrations. What do they tell you about the story? Write that information on your handout.

❷ Listen to Part One of the story.

❸ Answer the questions on your handout.

❹ Read Part Two on the next page.

❺ Answer the Think About It! questions.

❻ Listen to Part Three of the story.

❼ Complete the handout, then share your answers with a partner.

Culture

Bear Facts

- Black bears are abundant in most of Canada.

- Adult female black bears weigh on average 68 kg and adult male bears, 125 kg.

- Standing up on its hind feet, a black bear can be up to 2.13 metres tall. And, although black bears can stand and walk on their hind legs, it is more normal for them to walk on all fours.

- Black bears don't usually attack unless they are wounded or feel cornered or threatened.

- Playing dead is ineffective with black bears. So is running because black bears can easily outrun humans. They also climb trees.

> **to outrun:** to run faster than someone or something.
> **hustle and bustle:** energy and excitement.

Introduction

Every summer for as long as she could remember, Cassie went to visit her grandparents for a week. They lived on a small ranch just outside of town, where the air was fresh and pure. She'd spend her days horseback riding, picking blueberries and lying in the hay reading romance novels and dreaming of true love. In the evening, they played cards and watched old movies. Cassie wouldn't give up her life in the city for anything, but for a few days in August, it was great to leave all the hustle and bustle and noise behind and enjoy the simple life...

A Pail of Berries

by Judith Rohlf

PART TWO

Everything began to unfold quickly, much too quickly...

Without warning, the bear dropped back down on all fours and was wandering over to Corey, who suddenly became aware of the danger. Terrified, he jumped to his feet and began swinging his arms wildly and screaming and crying and yelling, all at the same time.

As if mesmerized by the boy's actions, the bear stopped moving and stood there eyeing him.

Numb with fear, Cassie just sat there staring at both her brother and the bear.

"Cassie, help! Help me... Cassie!" Fearing an attack, Corey had dropped to the ground in a ball, using his arms to protect his face. This sudden, unexpected movement seemed to anger the bear. It let out a long, loud growl.

Cassie saw the look of hunger in its eyes. She felt the supplication and panic in her brother's voice. Still she sat there, unable to move a muscle.

In the seconds that followed, Cassie's whole life flashed before her eyes. She thought of her parents and her friends back home... She remembered when Corey was born and what a cute baby he had been and how he was always getting on her nerves by following her around and spying on her and her friends... Then, in her mind, she saw the bear mangle her young brother as she just sat there, horror-stricken... That's what fear does. It sharpens the memory at the same time as it deprives you of your senses and defences...

The bear let out another growl as it slowly and deliberately moved in on Corey and gave him a quick tap on the head with its front paw. She saw Corey try to jerk away. He was at the mercy of the bear. So was she.

At once, Cassie snapped out of her trance. Everything was up to her. She knew she had to act, but how?

In desperation, she picked up her metal water bottle, which was still over half full, and flung it at the bear. But, her aim was off and it sailed to the ground, not even touching the animal. The bear snarled and showed its teeth. Cassie's heart skipped a beat...

 Think About It!

a) What happened when Corey stopped waving his arms and dropped to the ground?

b) What do you think will happen next?

Can You Do It?

- Make a list of all the verbs in the text.

- Identify the verb tense of each verb and explain your choice.

- Refer to pp. 274-275 of the Toolkit if you need help.

mesmerized: hypnotized.
to mangle: to mutilate.
to fling: to throw with violence.

The Urban Jungle

When speaking of survival, we often think about adventures in the snow or the wilderness, while mountain climbing or doing extreme sports. But emergency situations can occur anywhere. In this TASK 3, you will explore some survival stories from the "urban jungle" and meet people who did what it took to save themselves or others.

ACTIVITY 1

9-1-1

In this activity, you will hear about how a young boy saved his mother's life by dialling 9-1-1.

❶ Listen to the script about a medical emergency.

❷ As you listen, focus on the emotions in the 9-1-1 call.

❸ Answer the questions on your handout.

❹ Validate them with a partner.

❺ In your group, discuss the *Talk About It!* questions.

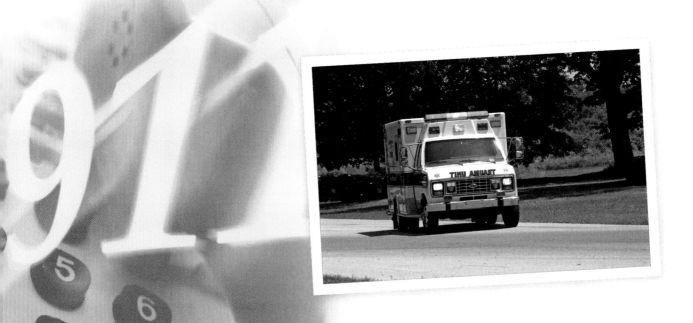

Culture

Did You Know That...?

When the 9-1-1 system was originally introduced, it was advertised as the "nine-eleven" service. This was changed when some panicked individuals failed to find the "eleven key" on their telephones.

 Think About It!

a) What image comes to mind when you hear the expression "urban jungle"?

b) Do you think you would make a good 9-1-1 operator? Why or why not?

Talk About It!

a) What qualities does it take to survive an emergency like the one in the 9-1-1 call?

b) What did the 9-1-1 operator do to help the child?

c) What other emergency situations can you think of that might happen in the "urban jungle"? Refer to the illustrations on these two pages to help you.

d) What are the differences between urban stories of courage and survival and those that happen in the great outdoors?

Focus on...

Using Quotation Marks

Quotation marks are used as punctuation in order to quote a person's exact words when they are incorporated into a text.

Using Other Punctuation with Quotation Marks

Punctuation	Examples
Use a **comma** to introduce the quotation.	- *The pilot said, "That looks like a smoke signal."*
Put **commas** and **periods** <u>inside</u> quotation marks.	- *"We were stuck in the elevator for 12 hours before help came."* - *"We found them," was all he said.*
Put **question marks** and **exclamation marks**: • <u>inside</u> quotation marks when they are part of the quotation • <u>outside</u> when they are not	- *"Wow! That's incredible!" he exclaimed. "Where did you hear that?"* - *Is it about the "urban jungle"?*

Practise!

a) Compose a short dialogue about one of the emergency situations illustrated. Make sure you use quotation marks and other punctuation correctly.

b) Exchange texts with a partner and check your work.

ACTIVITY 2

Decorations of Courage

All over Canada, people risk their lives to save fellow citizens. Some of these good Samaritans even die. Every year, decorations of courage are awarded to some of these individuals by the Governor General of Canada during a special ceremony.

1 Read the introduction to the activity and the *Culture* box.

2 Look at the illustrations below.

3 Listen to the report about how a few of the recipients earned a decoration of courage.

4 Complete the handout.

Culture

Canada awards three different decorations for bravery. These are the **Cross of Valour**, the **Star of Courage** and the **Medal of Bravery**. They were created by Her Majesty Queen Elizabeth II in 1972.

Talk About It!

a) Which of the stories impresses you the most? Why?

b) Do you know anyone who has received one of these prestigious decorations or some other recognition for bravery?

c) Do you know anyone who deserves to receive one? If so, explain.

d) Do think there are as many good Samaritans around today as there were in the past? Explain.

good Samaritan: a compassionate person willing to help others.

To the Rescue

Sometimes people act to save a loved one; sometimes, as with medical personnel, firefighters and police officers, they do so in the line of duty. At still other times, a rescue operation involves ordinary people doing extraordinary things for complete strangers. Whatever the circumstances, it takes a special blend of courage, strength and unselfishness.

In this activity, you will read about one example of people pulling together in a time of catastrophe to save others. It is Karen Nelson's story of how she survived Hurricane Katrina.

❶ Read the story on the next pages.

❷ Try to imagine the action and feel the emotion.

❸ Complete the storyboard of the major events on the handout.

❹ Share your work with a partner.

Vocabulary Builder

Nouns

- An **emergency** is a sudden or unexpected situation or event that demands immediate action or attention.

- An **accident** is an unpleasant, unforeseen, unintended event that results in loss, damage or injury. Negligence may or may not be involved. By accident means something that was not intentional or done on purpose.
  Examples: – The fire was not an accident. It was lit intentionally.
  – I was there by accident. The bridge I usually take was closed for repairs.

- A **crisis** is a time of great danger or trouble. It is not necessarily urgent, but threatens to result in unpleasant circumstances. It is a turning point or a crucial time or event. (*Example: economic crisis*)

- A **red alert** is a warning of imminent danger.
  Example: – Officials issued a red alert for the approaching storm.

Adjectives

- **Urgent** is used to describe something that requires immediate attention or action.

- **Life-threatening** is used for something extremely dangerous that may result in death. (*Example: a life-threatening experience*)

- **Critical** means "requiring immediate attention." (*Example: a critical situation*)

- **Imminent** means "likely to happen without delay."
  Synonyms include: **impending**, **approaching** and **threatening**.
  Example: – In spite of adverse weather conditions, they were in no imminent danger.

In life-threatening danger, people find the courage to face amazing challenges. They use their understanding of how the world works, their ability to consider possible solutions, and their natural creativity to survive on their own or until help arrives. Sometimes, the saving edge comes from tools or special materials. But above all, it's people's indomitable spirit that helps those at risk stay alive. This spirit gives hard-working heroes a chance to accomplish amazing rescues.

unselfishness: generosity; altruism; concern for the welfare of others.
indomitable: invincible; incapable of being defeated.

SURVIVING KATRINA

At 6:10 a.m. local time on Monday, August 29, 2005, Hurricane Katrina slammed ashore near Buras, Louisiana, just 48 kilometres south of New Orleans, along the Gulf of Mexico.

With 233 kilometre-per-hour winds and sheets of rain, Katrina roared into New Orleans. The winds overturned dumpsters and pushed cars along streets. Chunks of roofs, loose boards, road signs and other debris were hurled into buildings. Giant trees fell, crashing through roofs and smashing cars. Power lines snapped and transmission towers toppled, cutting off electricity throughout much of the city.

At the city's Tulane University Hospital, the lights blinked, signalling the backup generators had just switched on. Karen Nelson, a nurse in the Pediatric Intensive Care Unit, hurried to check on fifteen-year-old William. Until a new heart was found, his life depended on the 226-kilogram artificial heart-assist machine attached to his chest. Karen was relieved

to see the machine hadn't missed a beat when the generator switched on. Then she heard reports that the storm had passed through the city. The hospital apparently had withstood nature's worse punch with little more that a few broken windows and some roof damage. But that was about to change.

Water began to pour into the city. Tulane University Hospital quickly became an island surrounded by water. Then water started pouring into the first floor of the hospital.

Evacuate!

By Tuesday morning, people who had survived the storm were fleeing the flooding city. The Tulane Hospital management decided that patients, visiting parents and staff – more than one thousand people altogether – would have to be evacuated. Government agencies did not respond to calls for help. So the hospital managers hired private helicopters to rescue the most critically ill patients.

Karen said, "It was absolutely chaos. Seeing all of this, William was afraid. He knew that if anything happened to his machine, he would die. I told him I'd tell him when to worry, but that for now he was safe."

Tulane Hospital had never before needed to land a helicopter on the roof and didn't have a helipad. The hospital

dumpster: a large container for garbage.
to withstand: to resist successfully.
to flee: to run away from danger or trouble.

directors decided the roof of the parking garage connected to the hospital would work as a landing site. Teams of workers carried the young patients from the fourth-floor <u>pediatric</u> unit to the second-floor sky bridge. The team then took the children across the bridge to the hospital's parking garage and up to the roof. The helicopter rescues were going smoothly. But, that night the generators <u>ran out of</u> fuel, so the hospital was without power. Fortunately, the hospital had a small generator, and it was plugged in to keep William's artificial heart-assist device working.

Team Effort

On Wednesday William's rescue became everyone's focus. A battery pack with a one-hour charge was hooked up to keep the heart-assist machine operating during the trip to the garage roof. Since the elevators were no longer working, a team of men carried William, the heavy heart-assist machine and the battery pack all the way to the garage roof. Karen went along in case the battery pack failed. If that happened, she would have to use hand pumps to take over the machine's job until power could be restored. But everything went well. Once the helicopter's door closed, its power supply took over operating the heart-assist machine, and William was his way to safety.

On Thursday, helicopters continued to carry away the critical-care patients. Boats also arrived and ferried less critical patients, parents and some hospital staff to safety.

By dark, Karen was one of the few remaining staff members still to be rescued. She and the others went to the parking garage to be ready for the helicopter they were told was coming in the morning.

Daylight came, and hours dragged by with no helicopter. Finally, an army helicopter arrived. It had been five long, difficult days since Hurricane Katrina had struck. Karen had helped see that her patients, including William, were rescued. Now, she too was safe.

Afterward

William was moved to another pediatric intensive care hospital well outside the hurricane-damaged area. Karen said, "It wasn't until later when I saw the city on TV that I realized how fortunate we were to get out. Through it all, the nurses on my team stuck together, determined to go out together – and we did." ❖

Markle, Sandra. *Rescues!* Millbrook Press, Minneapolis, 2006, pp. 4-11.

Markle, Sandra. *Rescues!* Millbrook Press, Minneapolis, 2006, pp. 4-11.

to be hooked up: to be connected.
to stick together: to be loyal, especially in times of trouble or danger.

My Story

Throughout this unit, you have been reading about courage, survival and rescue. Now it's your turn to share your story. In the FINAL TASK, you will write a narrative essay about your survival story. It may be real or fictitious, but you must follow the structure of a narrative text and address the physical and mental strengths it took to survive.

What to Do

"To have a great adventure, and survive, requires good judgment. Good judgment comes from experience. Experience, of course, is the result of poor judgment."

– Geoff Tabin

Step 1: Choose Your Subject

1 Look through the unit for ideas for your narrative.

2 Jot down your ideas.

Step 2: Plan Your Narrative

3 Read *How to Write a Narrative Essay* on the next page.

4 Use the graphic organizer on the handout to structure your ideas and help you organize your text.

5 Use the tools presented in this unit to help you compose your text.

Step 3: Write a Draft Copy and Proofread Your Text

6 Read your draft for coherency. See p. 76.

7 Use the grammar explanations in this unit to help you edit your text.

8 Work with a partner. Proofread your texts together before writing your final copy.

9 Refer to the checklist on the handout to make sure you have complied with all the requirements of the task.

Step 4: Make a Final Copy

10 Make a polished copy of your text on the computer. You may add illustrations.

Step 5: Share Your Narrative

11 As a class, decide on how to share your narratives. For example, you could choose to put together a class book, organize a reading, publish your texts in the school newspaper or on a website...

How to...
Write a Narrative Essay

The Parts

In a narrative essay, you are basically telling a story. Therefore, you will use the conventions found in any story:

- The **setting** and **characters**
- A **climax**
- An **ending** (how the incident resolved itself)

The Characteristics

A narrative:

- Is based on a **personal experience** (your own or someone else's)
- Communicates a main idea or a **lesson learned**
- Is written in the first person "**I**" or the third person "**he**" or "**she**"

The Structure

- The **INTRODUCTION** states the **importance of the experience**.
- The **MAIN PARAGRAPHS** use **concrete, specific details** to describe persons, scenes and events. You may include dialogue as long as you use proper punctuation.
- The **CONCLUSION** makes a point or **illustrates once again the importance of the story**.

The Steps

1. **Choose an experience** you want to write about.
2. **Think about why it is significant.**
3. **Follow the Writing and Production Processes** to write your essay.

Language

Narrative essays use **descriptive language** to make the reader feel the action and the emotion.

Choose **vivid verbs** and add **adjectives** and **adverbs**.

Examples:

- *We listened to the speaker.* → *We gave the incredible guest speaker our undivided attention.*
- *The man was walking down the road.* → *The elderly fellow was hobbling painfully down the narrow, unpaved country road.*

Use a thesaurus to find synonyms and enrich your vocabulary!

Revising and Editing

Use the guidelines below to help you with these two important steps of the **Writing Process**. Your text will surely be more coherent, interesting and grammatically correct.

REVISING YOUR NARRATIVE

1 **Reread your opening sentence.**
- Will it capture your **reader's attention**? What does your partner think?
- Is it too long?

2 Did you explain the intention or **purpose** of writing the narrative?
- In your opening paragraph, you must say why this experience is important.

3 **Is the storyline easy to follow?** You don't want to lose your reader!
- Is your narrative **logical**?
- Does what happens **make sense**?
- Did you use **transition words**?

4 Did you **describe the setting** in a way that makes the reader feel like he/she is there?

5 **Can the reader identify with the characters?**
- Are they realistic?
- Do they have personality?

6 **Did you get the reader emotionally involved?** Can the reader share the emotions (fear, discouragement, despair, hope, anger...) of the main character?

7 Does your narrative have **conflict** that rises to an intense breaking point?

8 Did you bring your story to a **conclusion**?

EDITING YOUR NARRATIVE

1 **Read your text aloud.** Your ears may catch what your eyes didn't see.
- If a sentence is too long, it can be confusing. Shorten it!

2 **Vary your vocabulary.**
- Find synonyms for words that are overused.
- Use lots of adjectives and adverbs.
- Use action verbs.

3 **Check for spelling** mistakes.
- Watch out for homophones. (See the *Vocabulary Builder* box.)

4 **Check punctuation.**
- Remember all sentences need at least one punctuation mark!
- Make sure you use quotation marks for dialogue.

5 **Watch the verb tense you use.**
- Underline every single verb in your text; look for consistency.
- You should be able to explain why you chose the tense in each sentence. Use the tools on pp. 274-275 to help you.

Vocabulary Builder

Homonyms are words that sound the same, but have different meanings and spellings.

Examples:
- *your/you're*
- *there/their*
- *its/it's*

Make sure you choose the right one according to the context.

Using Commas

Use a comma	Examples
• To separate items in a list	– I had duct tape, flares, matches and a first-aid kit.
• To separate two phrases	– When the fire broke out, I was sleeping. – If the weather is bad, we promise not to leave camp.
• To separate adjectives	– The mountain climber wore thick, woollen socks. – It was a scary, squeaky, old elevator.
• After an introductory word or phrase	– In the mountains, be prepared for a quick change in the weather. – In case of an emergency, dial 9-1-1.
• Before coordinating conjunctions: and, but, for, or, so, yet	– I knew the terrain was a challenge, so I took my GPS. – We climbed all day, but we didn't reach the summit.
• To set off interjections and the words yes and no	– Well, I think we must help him. – Yes, Marianne was there.
• To address someone	– That was very kind of you, Robert. – Sir, could you tell me where I can find a phone?
• For appositions	– The girl, a former athlete, was able to survive because of her stamina.

Choosing Between the Simple Past and the Present Perfect

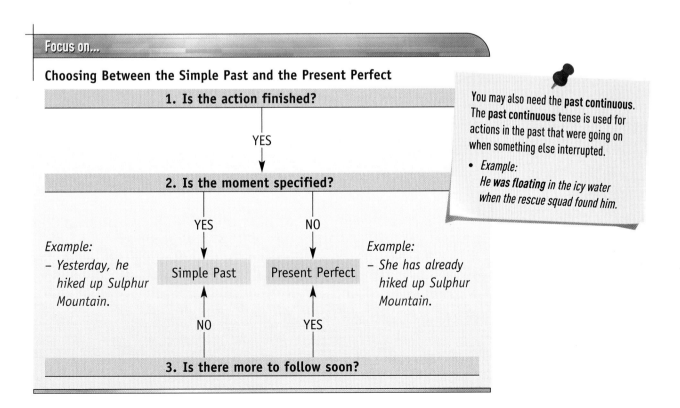

1. Is the action finished?

YES

2. Is the moment specified?

YES   NO

Example:
– Yesterday, he hiked up Sulphur Mountain.

Simple Past   Present Perfect

NO   YES

3. Is there more to follow soon?

Example:
– She has already hiked up Sulphur Mountain.

You may also need the **past continuous**. The **past continuous** tense is used for actions in the past that were going on when something else interrupted.

• *Example:*
He **was floating** in the icy water when the rescue squad found him.

Wrap-up

Look Back

- You should be able to tell what the pictures on the opening pages represent.

- You should be able to explain the title and say why it is an appropriate choice for this unit.

Think About It

- The importance of knowing survival techniques

- The power of inner strength

Now What?

- Can you answer the Guiding Questions?

- Can you trust your instincts when it comes to dealing with difficult situations?

Select some of your work for your portfolio!

3 Name three things you have learned in this unit.

2 List two qualities that could get you out of difficult situations.

1 Find one action that you will put into practice.

OTHER THINGS TO DO

Watch a movie on survival or about a rescue. Use a graphic organizer to the show the storyline.

Make a board game or a trivia game based on survival.

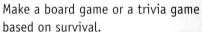

Do some research to learn about possible expeditions and present your findings on the risks involved, as well as the precautions that have to be considered before embarking on such an adventure.

Create a Survival Guide for the adventure of your choice (hiking, mountain climbing, camping in the forest, canoeing, sea-kayaking, snowboarding, skiing...).

Being Prepared for the Unexpected

You never know when an emergency situation will arise, but knowing how to deal with one may help save someone's life. Here are the basic guidelines to follow:

- Stay calm and assess the situation quickly.
- Call 9-1-1.
- Be prepared to give the 9-1-1 operator as much information as possible about the victim's condition and the nature of the emergency. He or she will walk you through what to do while help is on the way.
- Follow the person's instructions.
- Stay on the line!
- Expect to have some sort of delayed reaction afterwards. It's normal!
- CPR, the Heimlich manoeuvre and other first-aid procedures are not difficult to learn. The Red Cross and St. John Ambulance are leaders in teaching first aid and offer a variety of courses. They are worth looking into.

CPR

Cardiopulmonary resuscitation (CPR) is an emergency procedure that involves chest compressions (pressing down on the chest) and artificial respiration (rescue breathing). Although it doesn't restart the heart, CPR can keep the victim alive until an ambulance arrives. It should be followed by defibrillation as soon as possible.

When a person stops breathing and the heart stops beating, the condition is called **cardiac arrest**. Causes of cardiac arrest include heart attack, electrocution, suffocation, motor vehicle accident or other injury, etc. Almost 80% of cardiac arrests occur in or near the home.

CPR increases a cardiac-arrest victim's chance of survival by almost four times. On the other hand, the chances of survival drop nearly 10% for every minute that passes without CPR.

The Heimlich Manoeuvre

The Heimlich manoeuvre is a technique used to dislodge a foreign body that is blocking the airway. It involves a series of thrusts to make the diaphragm move air out of the victim's lungs. It acts like a kind of artificial cough that should cause the choking victim to dispel the object. Learning the Heimlich manoeuvre is not difficult.

Question

What can you do to be prepared in an emergency situation?

---

defibrillation: to restore normal contractions of the heart by means of drugs or an electric shock.

thrust: a sharp blow with force.

to dispel: to drive out.

A Hero on Skates

As told by Simon Lauzon to Alexandra Coutlée

1 In January 2005, a young boy fell through the ice. He was saved by a teenage hockey player's courage and quick wits.

Every year, Simon's family rented a cottage in Sainte-Beatrix, in the Lanaudière region. The area around the cottage and lake is very beautiful. Surrounded by cottages, some rented for the weekend, some used
5 by owners, the lake attracts many visitors. People come and take long walks and lots of beautiful photos.

Each winter, part of the lake is cleared to create a skating rink. This particular year, in January, when the ice was just thick and solid enough, Simon, his brother Vincent and some of their cousins started playing a friendly game of hockey.

While the game was still going on, another family was out taking a walk and enjoying the view. While
10 the parents took pictures, the kids were running and playing, simply enjoying the beautiful winter day.

Part of the lake was restricted and yellow banners surrounded an area where the ice was not thick enough and therefore not safe. Unfortunately, that's where the family's little boy tried to walk and within seconds, he went through the ice into the freezing water.

Simon was skating around, waiting for the puck when he heard a commotion in the distance. He looked
15 up and saw the little boy's head bobbing in and out of the water. His instincts kicked in. Being a good skater and having played hockey for years probably helped, because he was there in seconds. Everybody around him seemed frozen in place, not knowing what to do and very afraid for the little boy.

Simon jumped into the frigid water and took hold of the boy. He then hoisted himself out of the water, still holding the small child. Sliding like a snake on the ice, he waited until he felt the ice was thick
20 enough to stand, stood up and handed the youngster back to his family.

Until then, Simon had not noticed how cold the water was. The cold air quickly reminded him, and he and his brother hurried to their cottage where Simon warmed up in a hot bath.

The family later came by to thank him and since that day, they send him a Christmas card every year. Simon has also received a medal from the Governor General, Adrienne Clarkson, as well as other
25 awards from the RCMP and his hockey league. When asked why he reacted so quickly and bravely, Simon says he doesn't know. He says he just acted on instinct.

Question

How do you think that Simon's hockey training helped him react in this emergency situation?

---

to hoist: to lift; to raise.

4 UNIT

MIRROR, MIRROR...

IN THIS UNIT...

You will learn about the concept of body image.
You will explore the different things people do to change
their physical appearance and why they do it.

Throughout the unit, you will keep a *Response Journal*,
which you will use for the **FINAL TASK**, in which you,
yourself, will take a peek into the looking glass.

Mirror, Mirror on the wall,
Who's the fairest one of all?

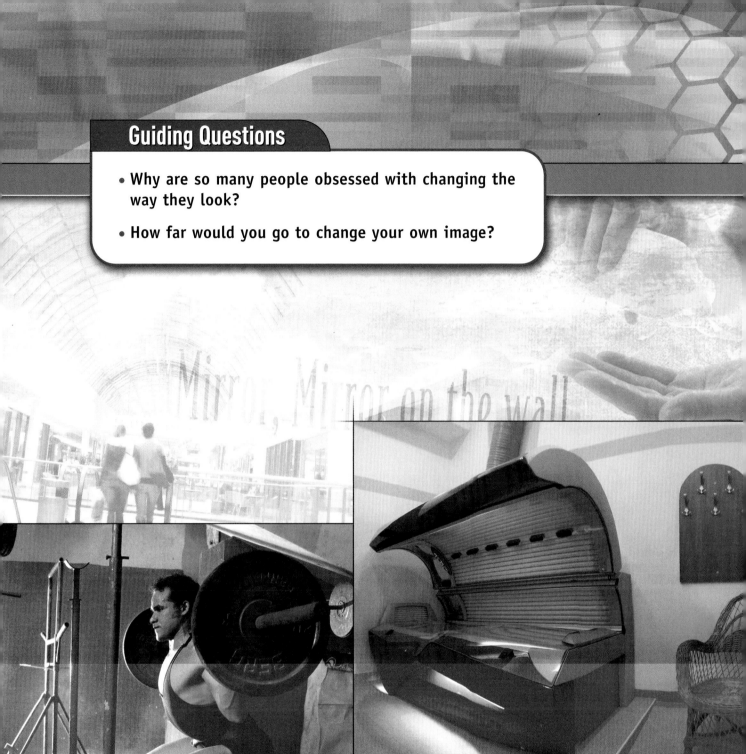

Guiding Questions

- Why are so many people obsessed with changing the way they look?

- How far would you go to change your own image?

Mirror, Mirror on the wall

TASK 1

Metamorphosis

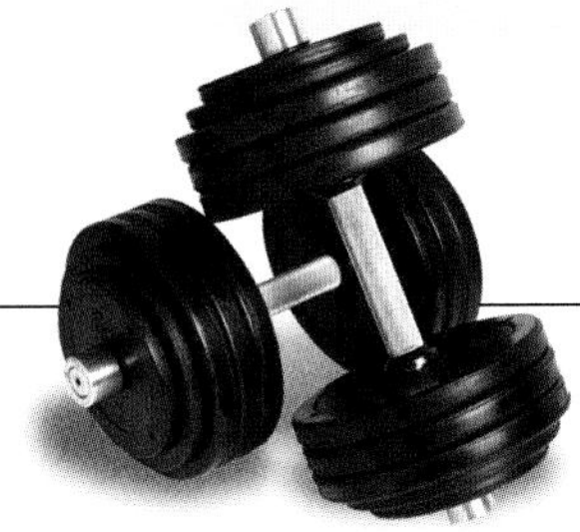

In TASK 1, you will learn about different things people do to change their body image.

ACTIVITY 1

On the Street

There are many ways to change one's body image. While some people are more conservative in their choices, others are more drastic. Listen to these live interviews on the street to find out more.

1. Look at the pictures below. Can you tell what each one represents?
2. Write your answers on the handout.
3. Listen to the interviews and match each picture on this page, with the correct person.
4. Listen again. This time match the picture with the short texts describing the side effects.
5. Answer the questions on your handout.
6. Read *How to Keep a Response Journal* on the next page.
7. Answer the *Write About It!* questions in your *Response Journal.*

Strategies

Here are some strategies to help you understand the text:

- Lower Anxiety
- Infer

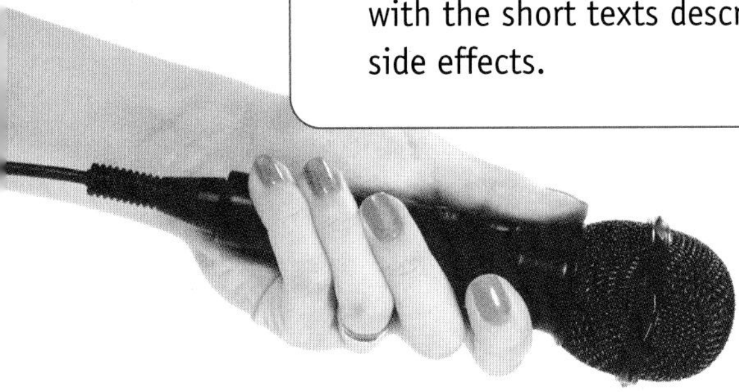

People Interviewed
Westley, Jessica, Stacey, Brian, Neal, Julia

a) There is always a risk of damage, but if the proper equipment is used to do the transplant, problems should be minimized.

b) Known side effect is headaches (because of all the tugging and pulling of the hair).

c) Overexposure can cause eye injury, premature wrinkling of the skin and skin rashes. It can also increase your chance of developing skin cancer.

d) It can last up to six months. The known side effects are usually temporary, but it is important to get the right person to do this procedure and not to receive misplaced injections or doses that are too large.

e) They must be prescribed by a specialist. Corneal ulcers can result from prolonged use.

f) As with every procedure, there are risks involved. Although rare, there could be fatal damage to internal organs, permanent numbness in the treated area and breathing problems.

1
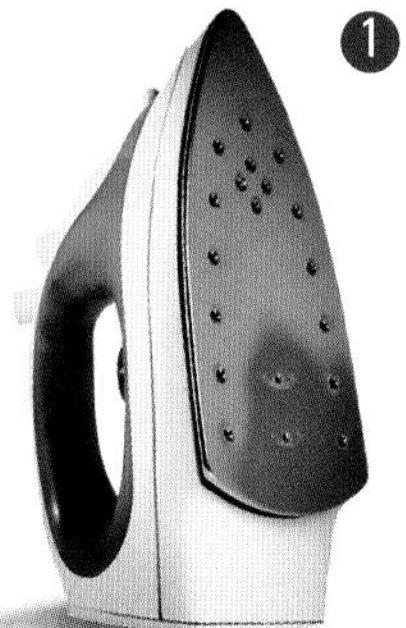

2
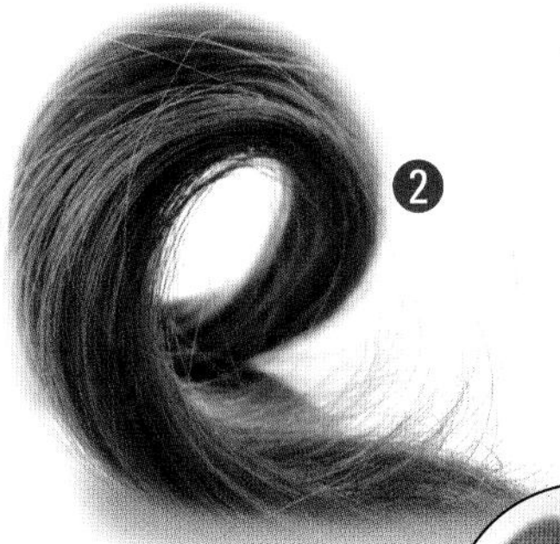

3
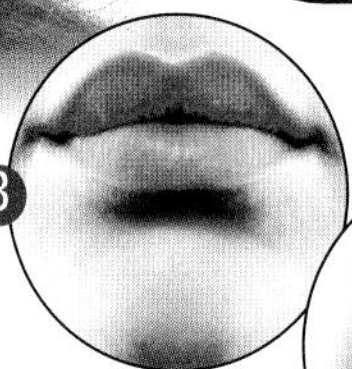

4
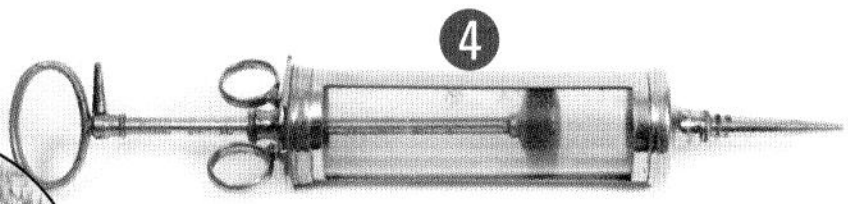

5
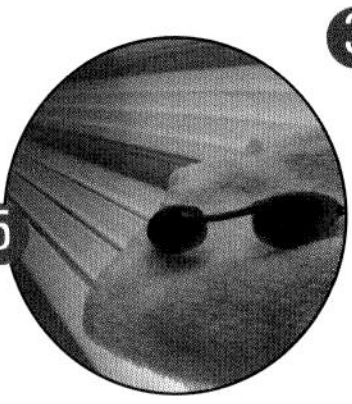

6
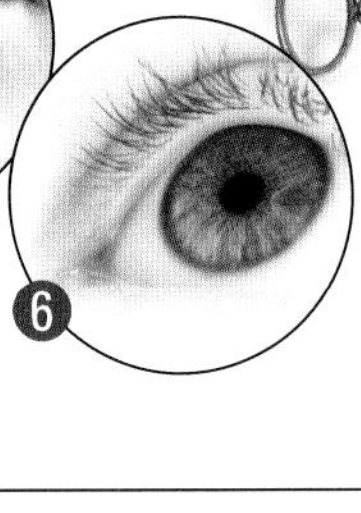

How to...
Keep a Response Journal

Your *Response Journal* is much like a diary or other personal journal. There are no truly right or wrong ways to keep it, but here are some guidelines to follow:

1 | Start each entry on a new page.

2 | Copy the *Write About It!* questions, then answer them.

3 | Date each entry.

Important!

Throughout this unit, you will be asked to keep a *Response Journal* with your personal opinions about the topics presented.

Your *Journal* will be useful in carrying out the FINAL TASK. Feel free to write what you really think. Be honest. Don't censor yourself.

Other Suggestions

- You should try to be neat, but remember, your *Journal* is personal. It's okay to **write in the margins**, include **drawings** and even **cut things out** of magazines and newspapers.
- Your *Journal* will be easier to read if you find a way to make the questions stand out. For example, you could **highlight** them or write them in a **different colour**.
- The length of your texts may vary. Once you have finished an entry, draw a line to indicate the fact, or move on to a new page.

Write About It!

a) Which of the procedures discussed in the interviews would you get done yourself? Explain your reasons.

b) Are there any other body-altering procedures you might consider?

c) What is something you would never do to enhance your image?

ACTIVITY 2

Tattoos Anyone?

Do you know why people get tattoos? Have you ever thought about getting one yourself? Read an interview with Éric Gougeon, a tattoo artist in Montreal, and find out what all the tattoo hype is about.

1 Before you read the text, think of some questions you would ask a tattoo artist. Write at least three on your handout.

2 Read the interview. Did you find the answers to your questions?

3 Complete the handout to check your understanding.

4 Discuss the *Talk About It!* questions with a partner.

Éric Gougeon was born in Montreal in 1969. He has been tattooing since 1992. His first love is painting and his artwork is displayed throughout his studio in Montreal.

According to his estimates, he has tattooed over 3,000 people. He was interviewed in his studio in August 2007.

to flinch: to draw back or tense the body in pain.

An Interview with
A TATTOO ARTIST

Éric Gougeon, better known as Ouzill, has been in the tattooing business for 15 years. As I enter his studio, two big dogs welcome me: a pit bull and a husky. I'm a bit intimidated by strange dogs, so my entrance into the world of tattoos is not too reassuring. But as the artist comes to greet me, I am made to feel right at home and I begin to relax...

by Karen Lyons

While I was in the shop, Gary, a return customer, was getting his leg done. Ouzill took the picture Gary had brought in and made a decal of it. He had Gary shave his leg and transferred the picture onto it. Then he began his artwork, talking away, answering my questions as his customer, visibly in pain, got the lettering filled in.

"Is it really as agonizing as it seems?"

"That depends on the person's tolerance to pain, but it's generally not a pleasant experience. Contrary to popular belief though, the pain is not necessarily worse in places with bone. And it's not always more tolerable where there's more fat. I have seen people with big beer bellies squirm in pain, while others barely flinch while being tattooed on the ankle. For me personally, elbows are the worst place and mine are still tattoo free."

So, how much does a tattoo cost? As in most tattoo shops nowadays, prices are by the hour and can range anywhere between $20 and $1,000. Some people start off with just a small tattoo. Then later on, they have color and background added and it takes on a life of its own.

Ouzil goes on to explain: "A few years ago, tattoos were mostly associated with rockers and criminals. Today, they're pretty much mainstream. I have tattooed both men and women from ages 16 to 65, from all walks of life. I won't tattoo anyone under 16 though, and if you're

under 18, you've got to be accompanied by a parent. Teenagers under 16 are more impulsive and might regret it later on."

So, why do people get tattoos? Some say it's for the art. For others, it's a way to show their colours. For some, it's seen as a rite of passage; for others, it seems to be a way to recapture their fleeting youth. Whatever the reason, Ouzill says most people are return customers. Apparently it's like an addiction. Once you start, it's hard to stop.

"What happens if you end up regretting a tattoo?" I ask.

"Well, tattoos can be removed with a laser, but the results aren't all that great and often leave scars. Or, you can get your old tattoo covered by a new one. Other than that, they're permanent, so it's really important to weigh all the pros and cons beforehand."

I also learn that some tattoo shops dilute their ink to make more money, so it's a good idea to ask questions and take a good look around when you're shopping for body art. "Clean instruments are essential, so look for a sterilization oven in the shop. And the needle must be a disposable one from a sealed package," Ouzill warns.

As Gary breathes a sigh of relief that the first part of the job is over with, I start wondering if I dared... Ouzill explains to me that for men, arms are the most tattooed place, while the lower back is very popular for women. He goes on to say that although tattoos are now widespread, they're still not accepted everywhere and many employers won't hire you if you have a tattoo in plain view. "That is why most people choose to put their tattoo in a place that can be hidden by clothing or hair. It's another thing to think about before getting body art," he reminds me.

I thank Ouzill for his time, gingerly say goodbye to the dogs and promise to be back soon. Maybe even for a tattoo... ❖

Culture

Tattoos

The word **tattoo** comes from the Tahitian word *tatau* or from the Polynesian word *ta* which mean, respectively, to mark or to strike something.

It is hard to put a date on when tattoos first began, although in Japan, tattooing is thought to go back at least 10,000 years.

In many civilizations, tattoos have a religious connotation, but in some religions, they are forbidden.

Tattoos can help identify burned or mutilated bodies. The pigment goes deep enough into the skin so that even severe burns often fail to destroy tattoos.

Use the functional language on pp. 232 to 236 when discussing.

Talk About It!

a) Would you get a tattoo? Why or why not?

b) If so, what would your tattoo look like? Where would you put it?

c) Do you agree with Ouzill about teenagers making choices they might regret later on?

d) Do you think some people go too far? How much is art, and how much is just plain obsession?

As you learned in the interview, tattoos can become an addiction for some people. This is also true of other ways of modifying one's body image. In TASK 2, you'll take a look at a few of them. Then you can decide how much is too much.

ACTIVITY 1

How Much Is Too Much?

In this activity, you will explore three extreme ways people modify their body image. For you, how much is too much?

❶ Look at the pictures.

❷ Do you think these people have gone too far?

❸ Read the three short texts.

❹ Complete the handout about what you see and read.

❺ Discuss the *Talk About It!* questions in your groups.

Extreme Body MODIFICATION

A practice known as extreme body modification has started to appear in underground circles and may slowly be making its way into the mainstream. There are many different modifications, such as eye jewellery implants, which are inserted under the membrane in your eye, and transdermal modifications, where an object is lodged in the skin on one end and the other end sticks out.

Another modification, called beading, consists of having foreign objects, such as jewellery or metal objects, implanted under the skin. This practice originated among African, South American and New Zealand tribes and traditionally had spiritual overtones. It was used to show status within the group or as a rite of passage, from childhood to manhood, for example.

Unfortunately, some people's bodies reject implants, causing various degrees of infection. If left untreated, the resulting damage could be serious. Also, if an implant is made of low-quality material or if the procedure is not performed by a trained professional, the risk of complications is even greater. ❖

✏️ Write About It!

There is an expression that says "Beauty is in the eye of the beholder." What does it mean? Is it true?

STEROIDS

A steroid is a chemical drug that produces testosterone synthetically. Steroids are widely used by male and female bodybuilders to augment their body mass and physical strength. They permit the user to train harder and increase endurance.

Steroids are available in tablet, liquid, gel and cream forms. They are either rubbed on the skin, taken orally or injected intramuscularly. People who abuse steroids may take doses that are 10 to 100 times higher than those taken for medical reasons.

There can be temporary side effects associated with the use of steroids, such as high blood pressure and jaundice, but also more long-term side effects, such as shrinking of the testicles and development of breasts in men, and growth of facial hair and a deepening voice for women. For teenagers who are still growing, steroid abuse can halt their growth prematurely and cause extreme acne. ❖

Dieting

Karen Carpenter at the Billboard Music Awards

Lots of people, teens included, would like to lose a few pounds and many try various diets. Most of these are relatively safe, at least when followed for a short period of time. However, for some people, dieting becomes an obsession that leads to anorexia or bulimia. Although these two conditions are usually associated with females, males may also suffer from them. Untreated anorexia or bulimia can be life-threatening.

Many TV stars and top models suffer from anorexia or bulimia. One of the most well-known cases is that of Karen Carpenter, a famous musician. In 1983, her death from this fatal eating disorder brought anorexia out into the open and spurred public awareness. Unfortunately, more than 8 million people still suffer from severe eating disorders today. ❖

💬 Talk About It!

a) Why do you think that people undertake extreme body modifications?

b) Do you think that athletes should be allowed to use steroids and other similar drugs?

c) Do you know of any other famous people who have struggled with an eating disorder?

d) How about people close to you?

jaundice: a yellow discoloration of the skin.

anorexia: an eating disorder characterized by markedly reduced appetite or total aversion to food.

bulimia: binge eating, followed by self-induced vomiting, use of laxatives and fasting.

ACTIVITY 2

Plastic Surgery

Plastic surgery can be done for purely aesthetic reasons (cosmetic surgery) or for physical reasons (reconstructive surgery). Either way, plastic surgery involves medical procedures that may have serious side effects or complications.

In addition, for some individuals, plastic surgery can get out of hand and become an addiction. How much plastic surgery is too much?

For this activity, you will be working in groups of four. Each member of your group will read a different text about plastic surgery.

❶ Read the text assigned to you.

❷ Get together with others who have read the same text in order to validate your understanding.

❸ Go back to your original groups and explain your text to your team members.

❹ Together, complete the handout about the four texts on plastic surgery; then discuss the *Talk About It!* question.

❺ Read the narrative essay on pp. 92-93 and complete the handout.

❻ Answer the *Write About It!* question in your *Response Journal*.

Culture

Plastic Surgery

In this context, the word **plastic** derives from the Greek, *plastikos,* meaning to mould or shape. It has nothing to do with the synthetic material known as plastic.

Talk About It!

Would you ever encourage a friend your age to have plastic surgery? If so, under what circumstances?

Write About It!

Would you consider having plastic surgery yourself? Explain your reasons.

The Conditional Tense + an "If-Clause"

- The conditional tense + an if-clause is used to express a hypothetical or unreal situation. We say it is hypothetical because it tells us how things would be if the situation were different.

   Examples: – *I **would get** breast implants **if I had** enough money.* (But I don't have enough money.)
   – *She **would move** to Japan **if she spoke** Japanese.* (But she doesn't speak Japanese.)
   – ***If I didn't have** a bicycle, **I would walk** to school.* (But I do have a bicycle.)

- This structure has two parts:

   – the **main clause** with **the conditional tense** (would + the base form of the verb)

   *Example: **I would train** at least twice a week **if I had** a subscription to the gym.*

   AND

   – the **if-clause** + **the simple past tense**

   *Example: **If we wanted** to get a tattoo, **we would go** to see Ouzill.*

Exception:
In the if-clause, the verb <u>to be</u> takes **were** for all persons:
***If she were** any thinner, she would need medical attention.*

Practise!

Answer the following questions:

1. What would happen if...
   a) Your boyfriend got your name tattooed on his arm?
   b) Your girlfriend got her tongue pierced?
   c) Your friends wanted you to take steroids?
   d) Your mother came home with pamphlets about breast implants?

2. When would you consider the following:
   a) Having plastic surgery?
   b) Going to a tanning salon?
   c) Joining a gym?

Narcissus

A nymph by the name of Echo was in love with Narcissus, a handsome teenager. He rejected her advances, and as punishment, the gods made him fall in love with his own reflection in a pool of water. Narcissus eventually died of sorrow at not being able to consummate his relationship and turned into the flower that bears his name.

The word *narcissistic* is mostly used pejoratively. We say of someone who is self-centred and vain that he is a *narcissist* or that he is *narcissistic*.

sorrow: the expression of sadness.
to consummate: to be intimate physically.
vain: excessively proud of one's appearance.

Read about one young teacher's life story and the operation she underwent.

The Decision That Changed My Life

by Marie-Guylaine Dallaire

My Childhood

As far back as I can remember, I was always overweight. At nine years of age, I weighed 135 pounds, which at the time was only five pounds less than my mother. I was put on numerous diets, but I didn't lose weight. Instead, I would end up gaining five or 10 pounds more than when I started each diet. I say that I was "put on" diets because the only motivation I can remember was trying to please my parents. They had my best interests at heart, but every time I asked for sweets, they would remind me that I was on a diet. I could see that my being fat disappointed them so much, especially my mother. Obviously, she didn't intend to hurt my self-esteem. She wanted to motivate me. She wanted to "save" me from her own nightmare. As a youngster, she had been teased a lot about being a little plump and she wanted a better life for me. At the time though, all I could understand was that in the "beauty" department, I left something to be desired. I was not a pretty "little" girl.

As I grew older, I had such poor self-esteem that I would not eat in public and I absolutely hated shopping. Whenever I felt sad, inadequate or repulsive, I would comfort myself with food. Food didn't judge me. Needless to say, I had very few romantic relationships up until the age of 22. I also thought that I was so ugly and fat that I had to be extremely nice to everybody in order to be accepted. I prioritized other people's wants and needs before my own. Those were my "Dark Ages."

The Surgery

I decided to have surgery when I turned 18. My mother, who is a hairdresser, had a client who had undergone a then-new procedure called a "gastric bypass." I met with her. I could not believe my eyes when I saw how thin and happy she was! She explained what the surgery entailed and gave me the surgeon's phone number. I was put on a waiting list. It took four years to receive the call that I was no longer waiting for. I was to be operated on two weeks later. I was overwhelmed with anticipation.

Before I went in for the operation, I was told that 4% of patients die during the procedure. I didn't care. Weighing in at 327 pounds and still gaining, I didn't have that many years ahead of me anyway. The procedure took about eight hours to complete. They removed $\frac{3}{4}$ of my stomach, my gall bladder, about six metres of my small intestine and, while in the neighbourhood, my appendix. Believe me, it was no picnic. The physical pain was excruciating, but during my eight days in hospital, I kept saying I was fine, that I couldn't be better and that the pain was nothing. I said all of that with the biggest, broadest smile, and I meant it too... The psychological relief was so great that I cried with joy instead of pain. I could not wait to be able to walk out of the hospital and go home.

GASTRIC BYPASS: BEFORE

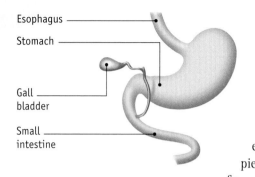

Esophagus

Stomach

Gall bladder

Small intestine

When they finally pulled the tubes out of me and told me to eat, however, it was a different story. I couldn't eat or drink normally. I remember not being able to take a regular sip of water for several weeks. It was drop by drop. With food, it was even worse. It took two months before I could eat meat and even then, I couldn't finish my one-inch piece of chicken. In addition, I would vomit frequently, five or six times a day. It felt like my stitches were going to burst open. That is a "normal" side effect that still ails me today.

The Results

This new life comes with a price. The induced malabsorbtion of food brings with it many problems and side effects. Some people have to have the surgery undone. The body can't completely digest food and absorb the nutrients you need to survive. You lose weight, but also the resistance needed to fight infections and disease. To compensate, you must take megadoses of vitamins every day and sometimes, as in my case, get iron shots regularly. For some people, additional plastic surgery is needed to remove the excess skin left after the weight loss. I was lucky; I didn't have to go through this. My weight stabilized after three years or so, and all I have left now are some unpleasant but bearable side effects. I am often sick and I still have to watch what I eat closely. Some foods are too hard to digest and cause a lot of pain if consumed.

My weight loss was quite phenomenal. I went from 327 pounds down to 153 pounds in 14 months. I didn't believe my clothes and when I looked in the mirror, I still saw a fat girl. The physical change that occurs after an operation like this is only 20% of the entire change. The remaining 80% has to do with body image, personality changes and self-acceptance. THAT IS THE HARDEST PART: to see yourself as you really are and love the stranger in the mirror.

GASTRIC BYPASS: AFTER

At the risk of sounding clichéd, when you can manage to see yourself for who you really are, you realize that **inner** beauty is more important... REALLY! I didn't go through what I did to look like a top model. I now see myself as a normal person who has learned the hard way that your image is sometimes limiting, both physically and socially. I have decided that I will never limit myself again because of how I look. Ironically, I had to go through the operation in order to realize that. ❖

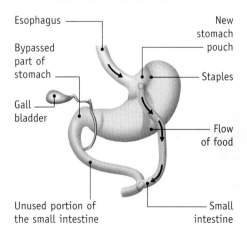

Esophagus

Bypassed part of stomach

Gall bladder

Unused portion of the small intestine

New stomach pouch

Staples

Flow of food

Small intestine

In *TASK 3*, you will take a closer look at who and what influences the choices we make regarding our physical appearance and how we perceive body image. You will continue to write in your *Response Journal*.

ACTIVITY 1

The Media

Have you ever stopped to think about how much the media really influences us? How much say does it actually have on the choices we make? Let's find out.

1. Look at the titles of the following two texts. What information do they give you about the texts?

2. Read both texts.

3. With a partner, discuss the *Talk About It!* questions.

4. Answer the *Write About It!* question in your *Response Journal*.

The Scam

Does looking at fashion models make you want to run out and get an extreme makeover? You might want to read this first.

Did you know that the models you see on the cover pages of magazines or on billboards at the side of the road have had major reconstructive surgery? **Digital surgery,** that is.

The Cover Up

In fact, the changes can be major. Scars, imperfections and wrinkles are taken away. Even pores are digitally removed, so it seems to us that the model has perfect skin. Graphic artists add breasts, make the waistline smaller and add highlights to the model's hair. They whiten the teeth and the eyes; they give the person a nose job. Even the men are getting it these days: bigger pecs, squarer jaw lines, darker or lighter hair. Anything and everything can be done. In fact, some pictures are completely computer-generated.

Revealing the Truth

A popular soap manufacturer created a virtual video to show the evolution of a regular looking girl to a super model. They filmed each step, so that we could actually watch the transformation take place. They then took pictures of the final product and digitally altered the pictures. They made her neck longer, lifted her hairline and made many other adjustments. The results are stunning! They did this to show how beauty in mass media is fabricated, not real. ❖

reconstructive: serving to correct the appearance of certain body structures.
wrinkle: a line or crease in the skin, caused by age.
pecs: pectoral muscles.
to alter: to modify.

Buy, Buy, Buy

by Karen Lyons

Eye cream, day cream, night cream, too
Body lotion, peelings, all this goo?
Curlers, relaxers, sprays and gel
I need all these to be a Southern Belle?

Ab Roller, Cruncher, Buns of Steel,
Do I really need these? What's the deal?
Pilates, kickboxing, I can't keep up
All I want is a decent butt!

Four-blade razors, moisturizers, aftershave,
Loofa sponge and scrubber I need to bathe?
A crewcut, a suit, the perfect tan
Do I really need well-manicured hands?

Bodybuilding, boxing, yoga's cool
Will I really be happier, or am I just a fool?

> **goo:** a sticky, wet substance.
> **loofa sponge:** a washing sponge, often with coarse texture.

Can You Do It?

Make a list of all the "beauty" products you have at home. Compare lists with a partner.

What are all these products supposed to do?

 ## Talk About It!

a) What role do you think advertising plays in getting people to buy beauty products?

b) Should retouching photos be permitted? Explain your thinking.

 ## Write About It!

Most people have something they would change about themselves. What about you? Refer to p. 91 if you need help with the Conditional.

Humour

ACTIVITY 2

Fashion   Fashion Fashion

Another major influence on the way we see ourselves is the fashion industry. In this activity, you'll learn more about the role fashion plays in moulding body image.

❶ Look at the pictures.

❷ Can you put them in order and say from which era they're from?

❸ Complete the handout.

❹ Answer the *Talk About It!* questions in your group.

Culture

Men's Wigs: A Short History

- **Ancient Egyptians** wore wigs to protect their bald heads from the sun.

- **In the 16th century,** wigs were worn to improve one's appearance, or to compensate for hair loss. Also, because of poor hygiene, people were getting head lice. Shaving your head and wearing a wig was a great alternative.

- **In the 17th century,** wigs became very elaborate and were seen as status symbols.

- **In the 18th century,** wigs were powdered white.

- **In the 19th century,** wigs became smaller and were adopted by many professions as part of their official costumes.

- **Today,** wigs are mostly used by people who have severe hair loss due to age, heredity or a medical condition.

Can You Do It?

Imagine what the fashion might be 10 years from now. Use modals to express your predictions for future trends.

For help on using modals, see p. 271.

Culture

Corsets

Corsets were worn by women of all ages from the 16th century up to the 1920s.

They were used mostly to accentuate a women's waistline, which was considered to be her best asset. Women were even known to stuff their clothing at the hips, to make their waist seem more petite.

In the 18th and 19th centuries, men also wore corsets to help their posture when doing activities like horseback riding and hunting.

Corsets also gave men a slimmer waist and made their shoulders seem wider, which was very popular back then.

Although the corset is still around today, it's mostly worn by women as a fashion statement.

Talk About It!

a) What are the similarities and differences between the eras? What did you notice about the body types?

b) Today, fashion is greatly influenced by the media. How do you think fashion evolved before the age of communications?

c) Do you think it's important to follow fashion trends?

ACTIVITY 3

Others and <u>Your</u> Body Image

Have you ever done anything against your better judgment or something you didn't feel comfortable doing because you let yourself be influenced by someone else? The truth is that many of us often do what we think others expect us to do.

❶ Look at the illustration, the title and the subtitles. What predictions can you make from them about the text?

❷ Read the text. What does the author mean by "Not all that liberating, wouldn't you say?"

❸ In your group, discuss the *Talk About It!* questions on the next page.

❹ Write an entry in your *Response Journal* based on the *Write About It!* question.

Who Sets the Standards?

Traditional Standards

For centuries, women of Mauritania in Northwest Africa have vied to conform to men's beauty standards. Does that sound familiar? Read on; it may not be what you think.

Mauritanian men prefer their female counterparts to be pleasantly plump. This has traditionally led to outrageous behaviour. *Gavage,* for example, was practised for centuries. Young girls, mainly between the ages of 5 and 10, were grossly overfed to make them fatten up and be ready for marriage as soon as possible by making them look more mature physically. They were given great amounts of food and milk until they could no longer take it. Some young girls were forced by their mothers to eat their vomit when they purposely regurgitated the food.

The men of Mauritania, who, ironically, are very slim, frown upon thin women, saying they look ghastly and sick.

Breaking from Traditions

In certain parts of Northwest Africa, women have begun to break from tradition. Tired of making themselves do crazy things to attract a man's attention, and influenced by the trends of North America pouring in from the media, the women of the current generation have started exercising and watching what they eat.

They say they are liberating themselves from unhealthy beauty standards set by men. They want to look like the stars they see on television, feel better about themselves and do what they want with their bodies.

What they might not realize is that jumping on the North American bandwagon may not be the ideal thing either. Instead of liberating themselves from men's stranglehold on their body, they are only conforming to another society's not-so-healthy prevailing ideal. Not all that liberating, wouldn't you say? ❖

to vie: to compete, to struggle for victory.
pleasantly plump: overweight.
purposely: intentionally, deliberately, on purpose.
to frown: to show disapproval.
ghastly: pale, resembling a ghost.
to jump on the bandwagon: to follow a current trend.
stranglehold: dominating force.
prevailing: predominant, generally current.

Talk About It!

a) How are the people in the text different from us, and in what ways are they the same?

b) Do you think we have anything to learn from the old traditions of Mauritanian society?

c) Are teens too easily influenced by their peers and the media?

d) What is peer pressure?

 Write About It!

Can you think of a situation in which you made a decision based on the influence of your peers instead of your own intuition? Did you regret it later on? Why didn't you listen to your gut feeling?

Focus on...

Modal Auxiliaries

Modal auxiliaries are used with a main verb to change the meaning or tone of a sentence.

They are used to show **capability** and **obligation**, **make requests**, **give advice** and **grant permission**.

Modal	Function	Example
Can	Capability Possibility	– She **can** run very fast. – She **can** go if she wants to.
Could, would	Offer Polite request	– **Would** you like some juice? – **Could** you help me please?
Should	Advice, suggestion	– You **should** eat more veggies and fewer sweets.
Must, have to	Obligation	– You **must** eat and exercise to stay healthy. – You **have to** see a doctor to get a prescription.
May, might	Possibility	– **I may** go to the gym to work out, or **I may** stay home and be a couch potato. – She **might** consider breast implants. – He **might** grow a moustache.
May, can	Permission	– **May** I go to the gym? – **Can** I go too?
Would	Result of a condition	– If I had more money, I **would** go to Europe.
Could	Possibility Suggestion	– He **could** be sick. – You **could** consider getting contacts.

Note: *Would* is also used to express the conditional.
Would you like to have a new hairdo?

Practise!

1. What advice would you give?
   a) Your friend wants to get a nose job. It's true his nose is a bit big, but...
   b) Your friend has become obsessed with body-building. He spends all his time in the gym lifting weights.
   c) Your best friend seems to try one diet after another without success.

2. Make a list of seven things people around you say in order to try to influence teens your age about their image.

3. Get together with a partner and compare lists. Did you come up with similar items? How do you feel about this "advice"?

In TASK 4, you will focus on the links between body image and self-esteem and learn the true definition of beauty.

ACTIVITY 1

Body Image and Self-esteem

In this activity, you will watch a video in which teens like yourself give their opinions about body image and self-esteem.

❶ Before watching the video, think of strategies you can use to help you understand what you will see and hear.

❷ Choose at least two to use while watching the video. Note them on the handout.

❸ Watch the video.

❹ Complete the handout about the video and then share your answers with your partner.

❺ In your group, discuss answers to the *Talk About It!* questions.

❻ Individually, answer the *Write About It!* questions in your *Response Journal*.

"Nobody can make you feel inferior without your consent."

– Eleanor Roosevelt

"The way you treat yourself sets the standard for others."

– Sonya Friedman

 Talk About It!

a) Do you think looks really matter?

b) Do you think role models are important as far as self-esteem is concerned? Do you have a role model?

c) How can someone learn to accept his/her body as it is?

 Write About It!

a) How have the people around you helped or hindered your self-esteem?

b) Can you think of another factor that has influenced the way you perceive yourself?

What It All Boils Down To

Throughout the unit, we have been talking a lot about body image, but we've never really stopped to define the term. In this activity, you will do just that!

1 Take a couple of minutes to write down what you think the term **body image** means.

2 Compare notes in your group and together come up with a common definition.

3 Read the text and the quotation. In light of these, do you want to change or add anything to your definition?

4 Make a final entry in your *Response Journal* by answering the *Write About It!* questions.

Beauty

Have you ever heard the expression "Beauty is only skin deep"? It refers to the beauty of your appearance. Skin-deep beauty has nothing to do with who you are inside, your feelings, your personality or your character. It has nothing to do with whether you are a good person or a bad one, how much fun you are or how charming. It has everything to do with a preconceived notion of physical beauty for a particular time period. This is especially important to remember today, when the definition of beauty is standardized by the media – in order to get consumers to spend money.

For sure, physical appearance is important, but your real image is defined not by your looks, but how you come across to people. There will always be bad-hair days and people more stunning, thinner, taller, more muscular, cuter, sexier than you. So what. Given the choice, would you really choose to be the "dumb blonde" or the "incredible hunk"?

Dare to be yourself! There is no one who can do that better than you! Sit up a little straighter, stand a little taller, reach a little higher and smile! Be yourself and do it with confidence. Show some real beauty, beauty that's not just skin deep. ❖

Write About It!

a) Do you know anyone, famous or not, who is exceptionally beautiful because of his/her charisma or winning personality?

b) What's your definition of beauty?

"Always act like you're wearing an invisible crown."

A Peek into the Looking Glass

Throughout the unit, we have been exploring body image from many different angles. You have learned about different things people do to modify their image and some of the reasons for doing so. You have been keeping a Response Journal. *Now, it's time to look into the mirror and voice openly what you see.*

What to Do

1 Think about body image in light of everything we've explored in the unit. Think about your own body image and how it defines how you feel and who you are. Read through what you've written in your *Response Journal*. Then prepare to write **one** of the following:
- An opinion letter
- A personal reflection
- An essay
- A poem or song

2 Choose one of the following two options:

Option A: You may write about your own body image.

OR

Option B: You may voice your personal opinion on one or more of the issues discussed in the unit.

3 The choice is yours, but you must write your text in the first person and your text must include the following expression: **"when I look into the mirror…"**. This prompt may be anywhere in your text.

4 In either case, make sure that your text is about body image and that you voice a personal opinion. Also be sure that you have written:
- An **introduction**
- At least **three arguments**, **reasons or ideas** properly supported with information from the unit
- A **conclusion**

5 Use the **Writing Process** on the next page and the handouts to help you plan and structure your text.

6 Use the checklist on the handout to make sure you've followed all the requirements of the task.

7 Reflect on your work.

The Writing Process

PREPARE TO WRITE

- Flip through your *Response Journal.*
- Decide on the form your text will take.
- Select and organize your ideas.
- Do any additional research that is necessary.

WRITE A DRAFT

- Write a first version of your text.
- Don't worry about errors yet.

REVISE

- Read your text to see if the ideas are complete, coherent and well-organized.
- Make sure your text respects the features of the text type you have chosen.
- Vary your vocabulary and sentence structure.
- Ask someone for feedback on the above points.
- Make changes to your text.

EDIT

- Use a dictionary, the Toolkit and other resources to help you correct any grammatical or spelling errors.

PUBLISH

- Add a title page.
- Consider adding illustrations.
- Make a polished copy.

"Beauty is but skin deep, ugly lies the bone; beauty dies and fades away, but ugly holds its own."

Look Back

- You should be able to explain what the pictures on pp. 82-83 represent and why they are there.

- You should be able to answer the Guiding Questions.

- You should be able to explain why the title was chosen for the unit.

Think About It

- Think about the important things in your life. What role does your physical appearance play?

- Think about the different factors that influence the decisions you make about your image. Are you easily manipulated?

Now What?

- Is there something you would like to get more information about?

Select some of your work for your portfolio!

3 Name three things you have learned about body image.

2 List two new words or expressions you have learned.

1 Name one good reason to spend less time worrying about your image.

OTHER THINGS TO DO

Write an opinion letter to a fashion or fitness magazine.
Explain your point of view about the impact (positive or negative) the magazine has on teenagers' self-esteem. Send your letter to the magazine editor.

Have a *Love Your Body Day*.
As a class, make posters and flyers inviting people to accept and like themselves the way they are. Find a date to celebrate.

Read the book *Nobody's Perfect* by Kimberly Kirber.
In this book, teenagers share their stories about body image, self-acceptance and the search for identity.

Watch the movie *Mask*.
This classic is about a boy with a facial deformity and his efforts to live a normal life.

Successful People

1 **Stephen Hawking** was born in 1942 in Oxford, England. As an adult, he developed motor neuron disease, or MND, which put him in a wheelchair and makes it impossible for him to feed himself. After a tracheotomy, he could no longer speak, so a computer program was designed especially for him, which allowed
5 him to be heard. It is activated by a hand or by eye or head movement. In spite of his handicap and appearance, Stephen Hawking has a beautiful family with three children, and is one of the leading physicists in his field.

Stephen Hawking

Steven Paul Jobs was born on February 24, 1955. With Steve Wozniak, he co-founded Apple computers. This duo popularized the personal computer
10 in the 1970s, making it accessible to the general public. Wozniak was the genius behind creating the product and Jobs, the genius at marketing it. Jobs left Apple in 1985, but later returned as CEO. Although he is one of the richest people in the world, Jobs always wears jeans, a black turtleneck and sneakers. He's been quoted as saying that he dresses like
15 this because it's one less thing to worry about in his day. Whatever the reason, it's obvious that image plays a secondary role in his life and he's happy the way he is.

Steve Jobs

Janis Lyn Joplin was born on January 19, 1943, and died on October 4, 1970, from an accidental drug overdose. She was a rock-and-roll singer with
20 a rebellious look. She wore no makeup, loose clothes and had long, unkempt hair. She wanted to prove that women could succeed as something other than pin-ups. She is rumoured to have once won an "ugliest person on campus" contest.

Melissa Emme Aronson was born in New York City but raised in Saudi Arabia. She returned to the U.S. for her studies and had great success on her university's
25 rowing team. She has always been in great physical shape and is an advocate for adopting a healthy lifestyle. Emme was one of the first plus-size women to attain supermodel status and the first model in her field to sign a cosmetics contract with Revlon. She is 1.80 m tall and a size 16. She was named one of the 50 most beautiful people by *People* magazine in 1994 and 1999. Today,
30 she travels around the world to give lectures about body image and self-esteem.

Janis Joplin

Renée Kline and Ty Ziegel were high school sweethearts. While serving in Iraq, Ty was injured when a suicide bomber attacked his unit. He was stuck in a burning truck and the heat melted his face. Renée stood by her man and they got married in 2006.

Question

What role does beauty play in success?

Renée Kline and Ty Ziegel

---

motor neuron disease: Motor neuron diseases (MNDs) are a group of progressive neurological disorders that destroy motor neurons, the cells that control essential voluntary muscle activity such as speaking, walking, breathing and swallowing.
tracheotomy: a surgical procedure that makes an incision through the neck to make an artificial opening for breathing.

CEO: Chief Executive Officer. The chief executive is responsible for a company's operations and is usually the President or Chairman of the Board of Directors or both.
advocate: a public supporter of a cause.

Does Beauty Make a Difference?

Remarkably, some studies have proven that looks do make a difference. Better-looking students tend to get higher grades and more attention from their teachers; good-looking people get better jobs. Some studies have even shown that people are more willing to help out gorgeous people than average-looking ones. They'll go out of their way to give them directions, help them pick up the contents of a dropped purse or stop to help them fix their car. It seems that good-looking people will even get more time in with the doctor and that good-looking criminals may get off scot-free if they're defended by an attractive lawyer.

Certain studies even suggest that this is innate; babies are prone to look at better-looking faces. Good-looking babies also get more attention right from the start.

Question

Have you ever witnessed such discrimination?

"Honey, you need to put away those fashion magazines and put on some weight!"

"How did the facelift go?"

Foul Ball ⊙

by Judith Rohlf

1 He wasn't the best player around. Nor was he the tallest or the fastest. But Benny worked hard, and he certainly had the willpower. All summer he spent working out, lifting weights and practising his free throws. The effort finally paid off. He made the basketball team.

5 Benny, or Beany, as he was called, wasn't part of the "in" crowd. He wasn't invited to hang out. He didn't party. He wasn't cool. He was just this scrawny, way-too-skinny kid who was all feet. He was also very nearsighted. Not exactly every basketball coach's dream. Rumour had it that the only reason he had made the team in the first place was because he worked so hard and everyone

10 felt sorry for him.

At first, any real chances of him actually playing were quite slim. But, he was on the team and he had a uniform. No matter that it was a little too baggy and that the top sometimes slipped off his bony shoulder... he had a uniform. Then one day in January, his break came. Eric was kicked off the team for using

15 drugs, Jack and Curt had been suspended for drinking and Scott was grounded for flunking math. Talk about getting your big break because of your teammates' ill fate. Anyway, there he was, suited up for the game, ready to give it his best shot.

Practice had gone badly for Benny that afternoon. First, he got hit in the head

20 with the basketball and stumbled onto the floor, nearly knocked out cold. Then his shoelace came untied (again) and he tripped and skinned his elbow. Coach Baker looked at him and shook his head.

The Ravens were losing 53-54, with only 11 seconds remaining in the game. The Huskies had the ball and called time. Coach Baker explained

25 his plan, THE plan... "Okay, Benny, you're in. Just head down the centre and stop in front of their basket. That's it. Don't move. Just stand there. You can manage that, can't you?"

"Bbbu... bbb..." Benny started to protest. That was another thing. He stuttered when he got nervous. "B bbbu but..."

30 Benny wanted to tell the coach that he didn't really like THE plan, that it didn't feel good being run into and knocked over... that his body couldn't take too many more floor burns... but it was no use. That's what the coach wanted. It was THE plan.

35 The ref blew the whistle, signalling the end of the time out. Benny scrambled onto the court. The ref tossed the ball to the Huskies and the game resumed. Benny headed down the centre as he had been told. He stopped at

40 the designated spot. He gritted his teeth and closed his eyes, bracing himself for the hit...

Nothing!

Then, all of a sudden, he heard the crowd chanting, "4... 3... 2... 1..." The whistle sounded. The crowd roared.

45 Benny opened his eyes and looked up at the scoreboard. 55-54. They had done it! The Ravens had won! And, he had missed seeing the winning basket...

Down at the other end of the court, he watched his teammates congratulate each other and high-five it.

It was then that it hit him. He would never really be a real part of the team.

50 But, for once, that was okay with him. He bent over and tied his loose shoelace. Then, he wiped his glasses off on his shirt and slipped out the side door of the gymnasium, unnoticed. Tomorrow, he'd go back and get his stuff. Right now, he needed some time just to be himself. Funny how self-esteem hits you when you least expect it.

Question

How did Benny change at the end of the story?

5 UNIT

Nothing but the Truth

IN THIS UNIT...

You will set a critical eye on the media. You will learn how different interests can play a role in journalism, and how words and images are used to convey messages. Throughout the unit, you will develop a personal media literacy portfolio. In the **FINAL TASK**, you will create a checklist to help you in your quest for truth.

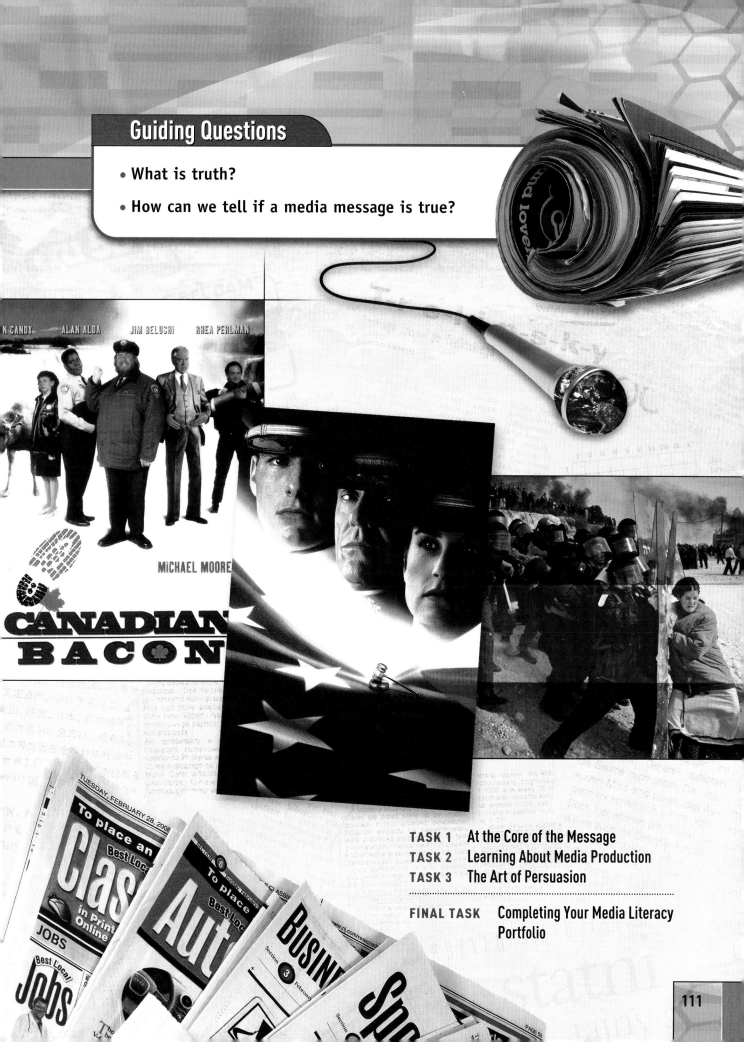

- What is truth?
- How can we tell if a media message is true?

In TASK 1, you will explore how an event can be viewed from different angles. You will realize that different points of view can lead to different interpretations of the truth. You will also begin your Media Literacy Portfolio.

ACTIVITY 1

A FAN-atic!

Imagine the sports section of any newspaper. If the journalist is biased and doesn't stick to the facts, the article will be filled with agreeable terms, positive superlatives and comments in favour of a particular team. On the other hand, negative terms will be used when referring to the opponent. You will begin this unit by reading such a sports story.

❶ Read the title of this activity. What do you think it means? What is a fanatic? Why is FAN written in capital letters?

❷ Look at the picture below. What do you think the article will be about?

❸ Read the article.

❹ Discuss the *Talk About It!* questions.

❺ Complete the handout.

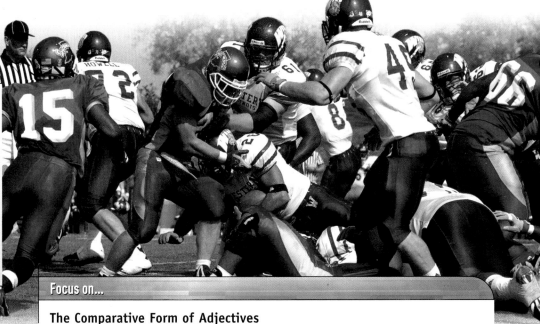

Culture

Media is the plural form of <u>medium</u>. It includes all means of communication, not only newspapers, television, radio and the Internet, but also billboards, comic books, T-shirts, instant messaging and so many other things!

biased: favouring one side or person over another, partial.

Focus on...

The Comparative Form of Adjectives

Choose a sport and make a list of five positive and five negative adjectives that could be used to compare two competitors.

Refer to p. 265 in the Toolkit for help on forming the comparative of adjectives.

Vikings Cheated of Victory

By Patricia Tally

Our mighty Vikings were robbed of a much-deserved victory in last night's game against the Carlton Cheetahs. The cheating Cheetahs sneaked by the Vikes in the last minute of the fourth quarter and won the game 23 to 20. What a disappointing way for our vibrant Vikes to end such a brilliant season! What a rip-off!

Luck was just not on the side of the mighty Vikes. They had to do without their star player for most of the game when Edward "Pit-Bull" Philips was badly injured early in the second quarter. He had been heading toward breaking the all-time record for field goals when he took a hard block from the aggressive Cheets. It was a terrible blow for the glorious Vikings and certainly contributed to the bitter defeat. To top that off, with only a minute remaining, the Cheetahs lucked out when the blind, dillydallying referee called a first down on a play that was, in fact, offside. This led to a fluke field goal and an unfair victory for the Cheets.

The most exciting moment of the night occurred when Cedric Rock and Johnny Garnett shattered the Cheetah's defences and tied the score 20 to 20 late in the third quarter. It showed that, despite their bad luck, the Vikings are definitely in much better shape than the second-rate Cheetahs.

Regional playoffs begin next Saturday when the Vikings welcome the St. Louis Tigers. It should be an easy, hands-down win. Game time is set for 2 p.m. with a mega pep rally beginning at one o'clock on Pierson Field. Come lead the Vikes to victory! See you there! ❖

> **rip-off:** a cheat.
> **dillydallying:** hesitant, showing uncertainty.
> **fluke:** caused by luck or accident.
> **to shatter:** to crush; to damage completely; to destroy.

 Talk About It!

a) In your opinion, which team is better?

b) What words or expressions indicate that the journalist is biased?

c) Who might the author of the article be? Justify your answer.

 Think About It!

a) What do you think of Orwell's quote?

b) How could it relate to the article in the student newspaper?

Culture

In 1945, **George Orwell**, a famous writer and the author of *1984*, wrote an article called "The Sporting Spirit" in the London *Tribune*.

In this article, he questioned the attitudes of spectators at sports events and the passions that sports provoke that lead to animosity between people and countries.

He wrote: *"At the international level, sport is frankly mimic warfare... in other words, it is war minus the shooting."*

ACTIVITY 2

Zeroing in on Witnesses

to zero in on: to focus on.

The press is always looking for the scoop that will make front-page headlines. News is news and truth is truth, or so you might think. But, is it possible that different people might interpret the truth differently? Listen to a funny story about a reporter and his answering machine and see what you think.

1. Read the title and look at the illustrations.

2. Predict what the text will be about.

3. Listen to the text.

4. Identify the different points of view and draw a timeline of the events.

5. Compare notes with a partner.

6. Read the *Think About It!* questions. Take notes on how you would answer them.

7. Share your answers in your group.

Culture

A person who is **media literate** doesn't take anything for granted. Like a detective, the media literate person is always asking around, questioning and wondering about truth and objectivity.

 Think About It!

a) Is anyone lying in this story?

b) What is the truth?

c) How is it possible to have different truths?

Looking for the Truth

As you've seen, truth can appear to vary quite a bit. Is it the same in the media? What is truth anyway?

1. Read the text *Truthfulness* on the next page.

2. In your group, discuss the *Talk About It!* questions on the next page.

3. Complete the handout.

"How many legs does a dog have if you call the tail a leg? Four; calling a tail a leg doesn't make it a leg."

– Abraham Lincoln

"If you don't read the newspaper you are uninformed; if you do read the newspaper you are misinformed."

– Mark Twain

 Think About It!

What do these two quotations mean?

Truthfulness

The media plays an essential role in today's society. We depend on the information we hear and read to stay informed, but by nature, we're more likely to believe what agrees with us most.

In other words, we have a tendency to believe what we want to believe. For example, if you read or hear that your bottled water, a leading brand, contains harmful bacteria, you'll probably switch brands. But if you really prefer the taste of that water, you may pass the news off as "hogwash." After all, you can't believe everything you hear or read in the media...

Journalists take an oath "to publish the truth." They follow a code of ethics. But are they always as objective as they seem? What if you learned that the publisher of the article about the water was also selling another leading brand of bottled water? Wouldn't you wonder about the article's credibility? Is there, in fact, a hidden agenda somewhere? Is the real purpose of the article to sell

more of that second brand of bottled water perhaps? Does the first brand of water really contain harmful bacteria or have you been manipulated by the press? What's the whole truth?

Don't forget that journalists and editors are real people. They have different origins, backgrounds and beliefs. And they have their own sets of values. They see the world through their own lenses. For example, it's pretty obvious that the European, Middle Eastern and American press will all have different views on the same event. Each might be attempting to tell the truth and nothing but the truth quite honestly, but their perspectives and interpretations may be completely opposed to one another. Truth can thus take on many forms. ❖

> **hogwash:** nonsense.
> **to take an oath:** to make an official promise with regard to behaviour.
> **ethics:** a set of rules.
> **hidden agenda:** an unstated ulterior motive or goal.

The Quest for the Truth

You should always question how a text fits in with your personal beliefs.

It's through your own lenses, your own set of values and by exerting critical thinking that you'll be able to form your own opinion and develop your personal vision of the truth.

💬 Talk About It!

a) What is the main idea of each paragraph?

b) Why is truth not always what it seems?

c) In Unit 1, you discussed sports ethics. What links can you make?

Left Wing, Right Wing

Religions and political ideologies are lenses through which we view the world.

In politics, being left wing or right wing isn't a question of being wrong or right. It's a question of values. All over the world, these tendencies exist and attempt to counterbalance each another. They take on different names (liberal, socialist, republican, communist, democratic, conservative, etc.) and can be more or less extreme.

Generally speaking, right-wing people put more importance on justice, religion, military power, capitalism and globalization. They believe in people rising through their own efforts and want less government involvement in social programs. On the other hand, left-wing people sponsor social programs and value democracy, civil rights, consumer rights, environment, feminism and education. Some people and political parties are also said to be in the centre, which means they have mixed feelings and opinions, depending on the issues involved.

In order to be objective, you must be able to examine an issue from different perspectives. Knowing where a newspaper or TV network stands can help you understand the news they showcase. It's one step in your quest for truth. ❖

Humour

" DO YOU WANT TO BE MANIPULATED BY THE LEFT WING MEDIA OR THE RIGHT WING MEDIA ? "

Write About It!

a) Read the cartoon.

b) Imagine the conversation.

c) Write a short dialogue between the man and the woman. Make links with the two previous texts. Remember to use quotation marks!

Culture

The term **left wing** is often a synonym for "liberal" while **right wing** is used for "conservative." This goes back to the seating arrangements of the French National Assembly in 1789.

At this time, just before the French Revolution, nobles who were more "conservative" were seated on the right side of the assembly, while the left side was occupied by more liberal individuals, who eventually led the revolution.

Since blue was the colour associated with the king of France, it remains associated with the conservative right wing. Red is still generally linked to the left wing.

Left wing = red = liberal

Right wing = blue = conservative

ACTIVITY 4

Your Media Literacy Portfolio, Take 1

In this activity, you'll get your first taste of real hands-on media literacy by beginning your *Media Literacy Portfolio*.

1 Read the explanation of a media literacy portfolio below.

2 Take the article given to you by your teacher or choose an article from an English newspaper or magazine, or the Internet.

3 It will be the first document in your *Media Literacy Portfolio*.

4 Read your article and answer the following questions:
  - Whose point of view is expressed in the article?
  - Does it give only one perspective?
  - Does it expose the whole truth?
  - Whose truth is this?

5 Explain your opinion in 5 or 6 sentences.

6 To get you started, read the short model on the next page and then try to answer the *Talk About It!* questions with a partner.

"I fear three newspapers more than a hundred thousand bayonets."

– Napoleon

A Media Literacy Portfolio

A media literacy portfolio is a **collection of articles** from newspapers, magazines or the Internet.

Each article is included to illustrate a specific element essential to establishing **objectivity** and **truth**. These elements are analyzed and then commented upon.

The goal of organizing and building a media literacy portfolio is to make you aware of the techniques the media uses to express its points of view and influence you. Understanding how the media uses these techniques will help you form your **critical judgment** and guide you in a lifelong quest for the truth. ❖

A Squeegee Kid

Everybody knows that being on the street is no easy life. "Danny," who prefers to remain anonymous, is reacting to the recent government regulations about panhandling. He tells us that he is nervous about tomorrow's application of the new legislation that prohibits panhandling on city streets.

"I dropped out of school at 14," he says. "There are so many jobs for guys like me, you know..." he jokes. "What will I do now?"

The new law will make it difficult for street people. They need help, not tickets! Fighting poverty is a major issue that should be tackled by the government, but social programs have decreased over time in favour of military spending. If nothing is done, worse is to come. What will it take to draw attention to this open sore? An open war in our streets?

My comment: *This article doesn't give an objective point of view. We don't know what the government's arguments are or what will happen to the panhandlers. It clearly demonstrates a left-wing opinion since it promotes social programs. There is also an allusion to war. This could be a trigger for a right-wing government that gives importance to military values.* ❖

> **to panhandle:** to approach strangers and beg for money or food.
>
> **to tackle:** to deal with; to treat.

Talk About It!

a) What is this text about?

b) Do you agree with the comment? Explain why or why not.

Think About It!

a) Do you think that in real life there are issues that people are not ready to discuss or about which they cannot "handle the truth"? Which ones? Why?

b) Are all truths good to tell? Should we remain silent on some subjects? Why or why not?

Culture

"You can't handle the truth!"

Perhaps you know this quote. It was said by Jack Nicholson in the climax of the movie *A Few Good Men*.

It comes in response to Tom Cruise, who, portraying an interrogator in a military court, says, "I want the truth!"

Nicholson angrily retorts: "You can't handle the truth!"

From the occurrence of an event to the breaking of the news, media production implies a series of decisions and manipulations. It's as important to know who is writing the news as it is to understand who the target audience is and what the message is. You will soon realize that knowing the hows and whys behind media production can be quite an eye-opener!

ACTIVITY 1

Getting to the Sources

In this activity, you will look at media ownership and citizen journalism and reflect on the impacts they have on objectivity.

1 Team up with a partner and read and discuss one of the two articles on the handout together.

2 Pair up with two other students who read the other article.

3 Explain and share your thoughts about the article you read.

4 Answer the *Talk About It!* questions.

5 Complete the handout.

"Everyone has the right to freedom of opinion and expression; this right includes freedom to hold opinions without interference and to seek, receive and impart information and ideas through any media and regardless of frontiers."

– Article 19 of the Universal Declaration of Human Rights.

to seek: to look for.
to impart: to transmit.
regardless: in spite of.

Culture

Universal Declaration of Human Rights

The *Universal Declaration of Human Rights* is a document that outlines the rights guaranteed to all peoples. It was adopted by the United Nations General Assembly in 1948. It is available in more than 300 languages.

Cues

In this discussion, you might want to use the Six-Hats strategies from **Unit 1**.

The conversation cues on p. 18 could also be helpful...

 Talk About It!

a) What are the positive and negative impacts concerning objectivity in the article you just read? Explain.

b) What connections can you make with Article 19 of the *Universal Declaration of Human Rights*?

A Spin on the Truth

In this activity, you will become acquainted with PR.

❶ Look at the illustration. Notice the photographer in the foreground.

❷ Read the *Culture* box below.

❸ Try to imagine what the text will be about.

❹ Listen to the text *Once Upon a Time: When Things Started Spinning*.

❺ Answer the *Talk About It!* question below.

Culture

PR stands for public relations. PR people often have a background in journalism and they dominate the media business in all fields: government, industry and show business. They're sometimes called "spin doctors" because they are paid to weave words around the truth in order to deliver their message.

spin: a particular point of view, emphasis or interpretation.

to weave: to connect by interlacing (interweaving).

💬 Talk About It!

What's the difference between what the men thought about the railroad company and what actually happened after the crash?

ACTIVITY 3

The World of PR

In this activity, you will learn how PR people "operate."

1. Read the text *The World of PR*.
2. Answer the *Talk About It!* questions on the next page on your handout.

The World of PR

What PR Experts Do

Nowadays, if a company, politician or celebrity is caught in a big crisis, public relations people, PR experts, are called to the rescue! These "spin doctors" will analyze the situation carefully and present both reporters and the public with the facts. However, they will put emphasis on the positive points and give a spin to favour their side of the story. For example, the information they don't want you to notice might be written in very small letters or buried in a lot of other information.

PR people write the press releases that are sent to newspapers and radio and TV stations. These press releases are an important source of information for journalists. Pressured by deadlines, a journalist doesn't always have time to research the issue or make phone calls to verify the information before publishing. Thus, the public will only get the version of the truth that was most important to the PR agent's client.

Occasionally, "a spin doctor" will leak a piece of information prior to an event. The journalist with the scoop will enhance his or her reputation. The newspaper owner will also be pleased because more papers will be sold. Best of all, the PR agent will have served the interests of his/her client by attracting public attention to the information, which will be talked about twice as much when the real news report comes out afterwards.

Companies and government spokespersons often take courses with PR specialists. Mastering interviewing techniques helps them get their message across and deflect any sensitive questions that might put them at a disadvantage in the public eye.

press release: a text about a piece of news.
to leak: to reveal information that was supposed to be kept secret.
spokesperson: a representative who speaks on behalf of a group.
to deflect: to dodge, to turn aside.

How They Avoid the Issues

There are many ways of diffusing problematic issues during interviews. Here are some of the techniques used by PR people:

- Talking in detail and at great length about the good things their clients have been doing
- Leaving out any bad things they might have done!
- Distracting people by giving vivid descriptions of the situation
- Giving a lesson on a related subject or omitting incriminating details in the press release
- Offering an incomplete or selective history of the event or exaggerating certain points
- Creating emotions by means of the message
- Using abridged quotes or quotes out of context

Most people in PR believe that truth is 50% perception and 50% fact. Their goal is to convince you that their interpretation of an event is the best one. Journalists depend on the PR crowd for their information. You must learn to see through the subterfuge and understand how to deflect PR interviewing techniques if you want to find your way through the "mist of words" and get to the whole truth. ❖

Culture

The Master of Spin: Edward Bernays

In the late 1920s, Edward Bernays combined psychology and "spin" to manipulate people.

At the time, only men smoked in public. Yet, using a carefully planned strategy, he convinced young women that smoking in public was an act that would liberate them from male dominance. Cigarettes were referred to as "torches of freedom."

What he did was very clever. He sent letters inviting several young ladies from New York City to attend the Easter Parade in Central Park and smoke in public in order to show the world that they were liberated. Of course, journalists were informed and naturally, they spread the news. As a result, thousands of women hopped on the bandwagon and became hooked on smoking.

The American Tobacco Company reaped huge profits and made Bernays a very rich man.

By the way, Bernays was also the nephew of the most famous psychiatrist of all time: Sigmund Freud.

 Talk About It!

a) What is a "spin doctor"? What's his/her role?

b) What is the truth for a PR person?

c) What is meant by a "mist of words"?

diffusing: dispersing; making seem less important.
abridged: a shortened version.
to tailor: to make or adapt for a particular end of purpose.

ACTIVITY 4

Behind the Scenes

Do you think reporters only write what they want to write? That they only report on what they've received first-hand? Have you ever wondered whose interests are being served by an article you read? (Think back to the text on bottled water at the beginning of this unit...) In this activity, you will learn how news reports come to be written.

❶ Read the commentary *Who Holds the Pen?*

❷ Find the main idea of each paragraph.

❸ Write your answers in the graphic organizer on your handout.

❹ Answer the *Think About It!* question on the next page on your handout. Then answer the questions about strategies.

Strategies

Before reading:
What strategies can you use in order to help you understand the text?

After reading:
What strategies worked best for you?

Who Holds the Pen?

A journalist's job is to seek the truth with as much accuracy and reliability as possible. The problem is that there are often too many points of view to consider. Why is one particular piece of information chosen and another rejected? Who decides what to publish?

First of all, everybody knows that powerful interests are involved when we talk about the media. We often hear that money runs the world. Why should it be any different with the media?

Newspapers, TV channels and radio stations belong to giant corporations and rich magnates who have shares in various other businesses. It would take quite a lot of guts for a journalist to publish an article praising a rival or denouncing the owner's deficiencies. Most newspapers also have strong political allegiances. A journalist would be walking on eggs if he wanted to express opposing views. Furthermore, in this dog-eat-dog world, some advertisers will do just about anything to get the best advertising spots. Isn't it naive then to think that a journalist is free to write what he chooses? After all, who needs a job?

first-hand: direct; from the original source or personal experience.
magnate: a rich, influential person.
share: a part ownership in a company.
dog-eat-dog: ferocious, merciless.

Second, there is another way to make money in the media world – by increasing the audience or readership. And nothing sells better than gossip, sex and celebrity. Novelty and sensationalism are all the rage. Some tabloids thrive on selling pure lies. Truth is not their goal; making money is what it's all about. Even serious newspapers are not immune to this trend and present many more "light," "short," "crusty" articles than in the past, because that's what sells. But is it journalism? What happened to rigour, objectivity and ethics?

Journalists must now focus on finding the short anecdote that will fit anywhere and draw attention. As a result, fewer facts will be posted, fewer opinions published and fewer viewpoints mentioned. Bigger "holes" will be left in news stories.

The government also adds to the pressure. They have the best PR personnel available and publish press releases that promote their political orientations and viewpoints.

Why bother with interviews anyway? Why not just copy and paste the press releases? How long can a reporter swim against the tide? Indeed, who is really holding the pen? ❖

bother: to take care.
to swim against the tide: to act or do something against current or usual practices.

Vocabulary Builder

Here is a list of media-related words:

– altered	– defamatory	– falsified	– prejudice	– slant
– biased	– distorted	– fraudulent	– propaganda	– spin
– deceit	– doctored	– genuine	– scam	– truthfulness
– deceitful	– faithful	– objective	– scoop	
– deception	– fake	– perspective	– slander	

- Look up the meaning of six unfamiliar words.
- Exchange answers with a partner.
- Which words are adjectives? Which ones are nouns?
- Which words have a positive connotation in journalistic practice?

Culture

The *Calgary Herald* paid dearly for posting a two-year-old picture of a giant wave that did not, in fact, represent the actual 2004 tsunami.

 Think About It!

How long can a reporter *swim against the tide*?

 Write About It!

Why do you think the *Calgary Herald* may have published the old picture?

ACTIVITY 5

Your Media Literacy Portfolio, Take 2

You have read and learned quite a lot of things so far, haven't you? Are you closer to the truth now? You don't think it'll stop there, do you? In this task, you'll apply some new notions as you work on your *Media Literacy Portfolio*.

1 Read *How to Conduct an Open-minded Inquiry* on the next page.

2 Read the article provided by your teacher or pick an article from an English newspaper or magazine, or the Internet.

3 Try to conduct an open-minded inquiry. Answer the question, "Who holds the pen?" and then explain your opinion in 5 or 6 sentences.

4 Refer to the model below for help.

5 This will be the second document in your *Media Literacy Portfolio*.

My comment: I think this article is based on sensationalism. People are attracted to this kind of news because it's about a piece of hair that was sold for a lot of money. It is an unusual piece of information that isn't very important (for me at least) except for people who knew who Che Guevara was! I actually did some research on him and it was quite interesting to learn about his life!

A Future Hair-itage?

A Texas bookseller, Bill Butler, paid over $100,000 for a lock of Ernesto "Che" Guevara's hair. The hair was collected by a former CIA agent who helped hunt down and bury Guevara 40 years ago. There is no proof of its authenticity. Included in the purchase were various other artifacts.

Focus on...

Question Tags

- We use question tags to confirm information or ask for agreement.
- With an affirmative sentence, we use a negative question tag.
- With a negative statement, we use a positive tag.

Examples:

- *It is interesting, isn't it?* - *You worked hard on your assignment, didn't you?*
- *It's not your opinion, is it?* - *You don't think it is a lie, do you?*

Practise!

Write seven question tags related to this unit. Vary the verb tense and use both the negative and affirmative.

Refer to p. 269 if you need more help.

Conduct an Open-minded Inquiry

Six questions to ask yourself before and while reading an article:

1 | **Are you emotionally involved in the topic?**
- You are more likely to accept a message if you like what it says.
- You might find one article more truthful than another because your opinion is biased.

2 | **What is the purpose?**
- To inform?
- To persuade or try to convince?
- To sell something?

> See p. 229 in the Toolkit on how to determine the validity of a website.

3 | **Who has ownership?**
- If the newspaper you read at home and the TV news channel you watch are owned by the same group, don't expect to get a different perspective.

4 | **Is the source really an independent source?**
- Remember that independent and activist outlets also depend on sponsors. They may not be as freethinking as they would like you to believe.

5 | **Where did you find the information?**
- Editors are most likely to put what they value the most on the front page and give it more coverage.
- What did a competitor put on its front page?
- Check for information buried in the back of the newspaper.

6 | **What type of data do you consult?**
- Vary your sources: personal blogs, e-zines, scientific publications, PR releases, international and local editions covering the same event...
- Be suspicious of call-in shows and online polls. They can lead to misinterpretations.

> e-zine: contraction for "electronic magazine."

ICT

Check on the Internet for the latest on "Who Owns What" in the world of media.

💬 Talk About It!

a) Do you think that it is always necessary to consult more than one source? Why or why not?

b) How many sources do you think you should consult before forming an objective opinion on a given subject?

c) Are blogs reliable sources of information? Explain.

Media logic is the art of persuading a mass of people by means of language manipulation. In this task, you will learn some techniques used to handle words and reasoning in a sophisticated manner. You will also see how photo presentation can be a form of manipulation.

ACTIVITY 1

Alleged Lies

It is easy for an expert to manipulate language. The messages they deliver may be persuasive, but the reasoning behind them invalid. They may seem like the truth but, in fact, be lies – or the other way around. Not everybody uses his tongue or his pen like a sword, but many media communicators are particularly adept at this sport.

❶ Read the definition of the word **fallacy** in the *Vocabulary Builder* box.

❷ Read examples a) to g) on the next page.

❸ Match each example with the correct type of fallacy.

❹ Complete the handout.

---

alleged: supposedly, without proof.
adept: skilful.

Vocabulary Builder

A **fallacy** is a statement or argument based on false or invalid reasoning. It often involves jumping to incorrect conclusions.

For example:

Fact A: This article is about a real event.

Fact B: This journalist is a very good journalist.

Conclusion: Therefore, this report must be the truth.

Synonyms: misconception, falsehood, untruth.

Antonyms: fact, certainty, reality, truth.

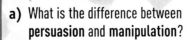 **Talk About It!**

a) What is the difference between **persuasion** and **manipulation**?

b) Why is the reasoning used in the example in the *Vocabulary Builder* box invalid? What makes that example a fallacy?

c) In the cartoon, why is the pig's reasoning invalid?

d) What other examples can you come up with?

e) How can spotting fallacies help you become more media literate?

Recognizing Fallacies

Fallacies are arguments based on arguments that are not valid. Politicians, advertisers and other people in the media often use fallacies to distort, hide or turn attention from the truth.

Knowing the names is not important, but learning to spot these types of arguments will help you become more media literate.

a "Track star Jamie Saunders only takes Relief™ for her headaches."

b "He's not a good negotiator for this job. He has a big nose."

c "Either you oppose building a new community centre or you accept a high increase in taxes."

d "Everyone in your neighbourhood is against the mayor's position on this issue."

e "Hiring teenagers will decrease sales and keep important customers away."

f "It is a well known fact that people who watch the news are right-wing."

g "What's your opinion about higher education and the price of gas?"

COMMON FALLACIES	
Fallacy	**Definition**
1 Ad hominen	Discrediting someone's opinion because of a personal flaw that has nothing to do with the issue. This Latin phrase means "against the man."
2 Alleged certainty	Claiming that a statement is true without verification or proof.
3 Appealing to authority	Using a celebrity to endorse a product or an idea for which he or she is not an expert.
4 Appealing to fear	Persuading people that if something is or isn't done, the consequences will be very negative.
5 Bandwagon	Persuading people to believe or do something because everybody else believes or does it.
6 Complex question	Combining two unrelated elements in the same question and asking for a single answer.
7 False dilemma	Forcing people to choose between two issues when there might be other options.

flaw: a weak element; a weak point in someone's character.

ACTIVITY 2

The Hidden Portrait

Nothing beats a picture when you want to grab attention. The media is very aware of the power of images on the public. Recognizing fake pictures requires a lot of expertise, as techniques and equipment improve every day.

In this activity, you'll see that just by angling the pictures differently or zooming in or out, media can make us believe what they want us to believe.

1 Read the *Think About It!* questions.

2 Listen to the text *Hand Me the Newspaper!*

3 Look at the four pictures below.

4 Identify the four categories of photos that are most frequently used in newspapers by listening to their descriptions.

Culture

Some of the most powerful pictures of tragedy, conflict, disasters and hope depict children. They have a great impact on sales.

In some cases, where identities were divulged, the children ended up missing or dead. As a result, some editors have put a ban on these pictures, but others continue the practices.

UNICEF has published a document called *Media and Children's Rights*, which is now used in more than 20 countries around the world.

UNICEF: agency of the United Nations responsible for programs to aid education and the health of children and mothers in developing countries.

Think About It!

a) What kind of pictures on the front page of newspapers attract your attention?

b) Would you buy a magazine or a newspaper because of one picture?

c) For you, what makes a good picture?

Your Media Literacy Portfolio, Take 3

You're getting the gist of this, aren't you? For this task, you'll need to pay careful attention to the words you read and the photographs you look at.

1 Use the article given to you by your teacher or find yourself another article in an English newspaper or magazine, or the Internet.

2 Ask yourself the question: "What techniques are being used to persuade or manipulate?"

3 Highlight the elements directly on the article and use arrows to explain your points. This will be the third document in your *Media Literacy Portfolio*.

4 Look at the model for help.

CLOSE-UP SHOT: DOESN'T GIVE MUCH INFORMATION

FALSE DILEMMA

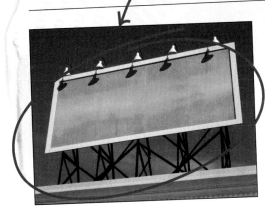

by glamour and top models! No matter that the Clean City Law was officially heralded as a move to end pollution by a mayor who was no doubt seeking political clout and... publicity. Too bad that the streets will be less safe at night without all the lights from the advertisements. Good luck to the wandering tourist as he attempts to find his hotel without any publicity markers or the portable GPS he would have purchased had he seen one advertised.

APPEALING TO FEAR

IRONY

The citizens of São Paulo are rejoicing. Gone are the billboards and neon signs that once cluttered their city! Down have come the panels and signs of opulence and prosperity! What a pleasure it is to behold the squalid reality of inner-city life once masked

All the people of São Paulo love their city's new identity. And, everything, including freedom of speech, comes with a price. Times Square beware! You may be next.

IRONY

ALLEGED CERTAINTY

"If it was so, it might be; and if it were so, it would be; but as it isn't, it ain't. That's logic."

– Lewis Carroll

to get the gist: to understand the main idea; to catch on.

Completing Your Media Literacy Portfolio

Media literacy is something you will exercise for the rest of your life. Your portfolio is well underway, but it requires one final touch before you go on by yourself into the jungle of life. What you need is a practical instrument to refer to: a personal checklist. In the FINAL TASK, you will create your own checklist and try it out.

What to Do

Establish Your Standards

1 Review the entire unit and make a list of elements to be aware of when reading or listening to a media product.

2 Compare lists in your group.

3 Read *How to Make a Checklist* on the next page.

4 Create your personal checklist for evaluating a media text. Use the handout to help you structure your ideas.

5 Revise and edit your checklist. Then make a polished copy of it for your *Media Literacy Portfolio*. It will be the fourth document.

Complete Your Media Portfolio

6 Use the article provided by your teacher or choose one from an English newspaper or magazine, or the Internet.

7 Read the article through the lens of your checklist. Use markers to highlight all the important information in your article. This will become the fifth document of your *Media Literacy Portfolio*.

8 Use the handout to evaluate your work and your checklist. Include this sheet as the final document of your *Media Literacy Portfolio*.

9 Hand in your portfolio. Don't forget to include a presentation page!

How to...
Make a Checklist

1 | **Title**
- Include a short title.

2 | **Purpose**
- Briefly state the purpose of the checklist.

3 | **Content**
- Include at least 12 elements.
- Be precise.
- Provide examples where necessary.

4 | **Structure**
- Use the same format throughout the checklist (check marks, bullet points, numbers or letters).
  - Each point should describe only one element to watch for.
  - Each point should start with the same type of word (a verb, a noun, a question word, etc.) or in the same way.
- Group similar items or ideas together into categories.
- Separate categories with a line or space.
- Call attention to important information. (Box, centre, underline or highlight it.)
- Highlight (in bold) negative words or contractions such as **not**, **no**, **doesn't**.

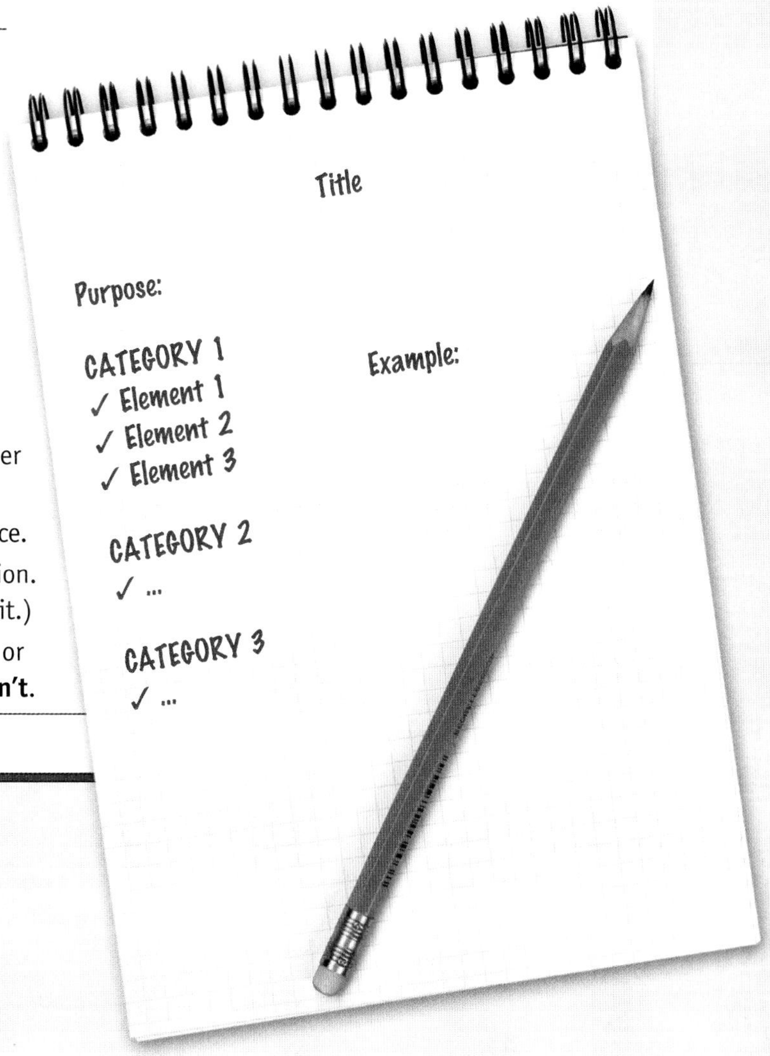

Title

Purpose:

CATEGORY 1
✓ Element 1
✓ Element 2
✓ Element 3

Example:

CATEGORY 2
✓ ...

CATEGORY 3
✓ ...

"In the spider-web of facts, many a truth is strangled."

– Paul Eldridge

5 UNIT

Wrap-up

Look Back

- Look at the pictures on the opening pages.

- You should now be able to explain why each of them is there.

- You should be able to answer the Guiding Questions.

Think About It

- Think about all the things you have learned about media.

- Think about how your checklist can help you recognize objectivity or bias when reading or listening to a media text.

- You should be able to distinguish a good source of information on the Internet from a bad one.

Now What?

- What will you do with your portfolio?

Select some of your work for your portfolio!

3 Name three things you learned about the media in this unit.

2 List two new words that have a positive connotation in journalism.

1 Find one idea that you will remember next time you read an article.

Was Clark Kent a good reporter?
First take a stand on the qualities needed to be a good reporter. Then answer the question.

Unbiased News Reports
Write and record a news report of an accident presenting different points of view (fellow worker, victim, union activist, contractor, town council, etc.).

Fake News
Do some research on the Internet and present your favourite fake news item to the class. Explain how it was produced and presented.

Role play
Some people (mayor, journalist, homeowner, farmer, CEO from local industry, etc.) are meeting at the town council to take a stand on an environmental issue. In groups, develop the different points of view in a role play.
(*Example: local beach shut down because of blue-green algae*)

Refer to **Project 2** on pp. 208-219.

Petrified Man

by Mark Twain

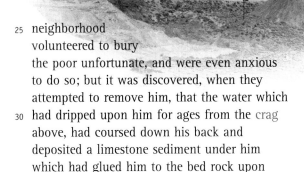

1 A petrified man was found some time ago in
the mountains south of Gravelly Ford. Every
limb and feature of the stony mummy was
perfect, not even excepting the left leg, which
5 has evidently been a wooden one during the
lifetime of the owner – which lifetime, by the
way, came to a close about a century ago,
in the opinion of a savant who has examined
the defunct. The body was in a sitting posture,
10 and leaning against a huge mass of croppings;
the attitude was pensive, the right thumb
resting against the side of the nose; the left
thumb partially supported the chin, the
forefinger pressing the inner corner of the left
15 eye and drawing it partly open; the right eye
was closed, and the fingers of the right hand
spread apart. This strange freak of nature
created a profound sensation in the vicinity,
and our informant states that by request,
20 Justice Sewell or Sowell, of Humboldt City,
at once proceeded to the spot and held an
inquest on the body. The verdict of the jury
was that "deceased came to his death from
protracted exposure," etc. The people of the

25 neighborhood
volunteered to bury
the poor unfortunate, and were even anxious
to do so; but it was discovered, when they
attempted to remove him, that the water which
30 had dripped upon him for ages from the crag
above, had coursed down his back and
deposited a limestone sediment under him
which had glued him to the bed rock upon
which he sat, as with a cement of adamant, and
35 Judge S. refused to allow the charitable citizens
to blast him from his position. The opinion
expressed by his Honor that such a course
would be little less than sacrilege, was
eminently just and proper. Everybody goes to
40 see the stone man, as many as three hundred
having visited the hardened creature during
the past five or six weeks.

Reprinted from *The Works of Mark Twain; Early Tales & Sketches, Vol. 1, 1851–1864*
(Univ. of California Press, 1979), p. 159.

Culture

Mark Twain (1835–1910) is a
pseudonym for Samuel Langhorne
Clemens, who was a very popular
American writer. He was called "the
father of American literature" and was
known for his sense of humour. As an example, in 1897,
an editor apparently got confused with the death notice
of his cousin and announced Twain's death. His answer was:
"The reports of my death have been greatly exaggerated."

Early in his career, Twain wrote a story for a newspaper
about a petrified man supposedly found in the area of
Virginia City. He was extremely surprised that people
could be so credulous. For him, it was obviously just
a satire of a topic that was very popular at the time.

Question

*Why would people believe
this story?*

---

defunct: a person who is deceased.
croppings: cultivated plants or grass.
protracted: lengthy; prolonged.
crag: a mass of protruding rock.

Media Madness

Information, Please!

There's so much information out there just for the asking! Newspapers, TV, blogs, podcasts, the Internet... Modern technology has made access to information a piece of cake. Getting information has never been easier, but at the same time, being well informed can be a real challenge. It's often difficult to know what to believe. Therefore, it's not surprising that at one moment or another, nearly all of us fall victim to misinformation, hoaxes, scams or downright lies proliferated (on purpose or by accident) by the media.

A Case in Point

Have you ever heard of dihydrogen monoxide (DHMO)? Would you know that it is, in fact, water?

Back in 1994, as a hoax, Craig Jackson created a webpage on the dangers of the chemical, and in 1997, Nathan Zohner, a high school student from Idaho, did an award-winning science project based on a petition he circulated to have DHMO banned. He wanted to show how gullible people are. In 2004, two Canadian students from Calgary, Kate Dalgleish and Mikael Sydor, circulated a similar petition to ban the chemical under a fake Hazardous Chemical Act as part of a high school film festival. Their film won the festival. These are but a few of the many examples of how the dihydrogen monoxide hoax haunted and continues to haunt the news.

With hindsight, it may be easy to detect the hoax, but have a look at some of the facts presented:

Dihydrogen monoxide:
- is the major component of acid rain
- contributes to the "greenhouse effect"
- accelerates corrosion and rusting of many metals
- may cause electrical failures and decreased effectiveness of automobile brakes...

It is used:
- as an industrial solvent
- in nuclear power plants
- in many forms of cruel animal research
- in the distribution of pesticides
- as an additive in certain "junk foods" and other food products...

In a world where more and more emphasis is placed on the use and abuse of chemicals and their adverse effects on the environment, it is easy to see how unsuspecting individuals believed what they read and were ready to take a stand against dihydrogen monoxide. Would you have been one of them?

The Bandwagon Effect

Not all information mistruths are so blatant – or so harmless. But the message is the same. Before jumping on the bandwagon, it is essential to "do your homework" and double-check your sources, or you, too, may fall prey to "media madness."

> **Question**
>
> *What is meant by the title?*

---

downright: total; absolute; blatant.
gullible: credulous; easily fooled.

blatant: obvious; deliberate.
prey: a victim.

Men of Truth

Joseph Pulitzer (1847–1911) was a Hungarian-American journalist and publisher who didn't mince his words. He denounced political corruption and promoted democracy. He spoke for the people and against any kind of monopoly. At his death, Joseph Pulitzer left some money to Columbia University in order to establish a foundation for literary achievements, musical composition and journalism. Every April since 1917, prizes are awarded in many categories. The most prestigious one is the gold medal, which is always awarded to a newspaper. The **Pulitzer Prize** is considered to be the highest American literary honour.

Joseph Pulitzer

Michael Moore (1954–) is an American author who has a journalistic approach to movies. He is well-known for his controversial documentaries. Moore gathers facts, interprets them and then organizes ideas in order to persuade people and shake the establishment. Therefore it doesn't come as a surprise that some right-wing detractors think Moore isn't a real journalist! What a case of "ad hominem" fallacy! (See cartoon.)

In his movies, Michael Moore denounces corruption and hypocrisy. He represents average working-class people. Among his favourite themes are the health care flaws in America (*SiCKO*), the opposition to Bush's invasion of Iraq (*Fahrenheit 9/11*), the duplicity of the National Rifle Association (*Bowling for Columbine*), the exploitation of car-industry workers (*Roger and Me*) and media manipulation (*Canadian Bacon*).

Michael Moore

Question

What do the two men have in common?

The case against Mike Moore

WHAT DO YOU THINK OF MIKE MOORE'S POLITICS?

HE'S TOO FAT

HE'S A SLOB

BLOATED

UNSHAVEN

NIK SCOTT

---

to mince (one's words): to hold back out of politeness; to be restrained in speech.

This picture was taken by Oded Balilty in 2006. It won the Pultizer Prize in 2007. It represents a Jewish woman alone trying to prevent Israeli security forces from demolishing her home. Chaos and emotion are both strong features of the photograph.

Humour

"You have a major fiasco at 10:30, followed by a shocking scandal at 2:15."

6 UNIT

Beyond Reality

IN THIS UNIT...

You will learn about science fiction. You will read about the history of this genre and look at different themes that can be exploited. You will also explore different media in which science fiction is present. As a **FINAL TASK**, you will make a storyboard, which you could use to produce your own science fiction adventure.

- What is science fiction?

- What is it about science fiction that makes it so popular, especially with teens and young adults?

Extravagant Fiction Today . . . Cold Fact Tomorrow . . . .

In TASK 1, you will begin exploring the world of science fiction. You will take a quiz to test your knowledge of science fiction, watch a video about the history of science fiction and read four excerpts from various types of science fiction.

ACTIVITY 1

Test Your Knowledge

Are you a science fiction buff or a newbie? Take the following quiz and see where you stand.

❶ Before listening to the quiz, take a couple of minutes to think about what you know about science fiction.

❷ Jot down your ideas down on the handout.

❸ Listen to the quiz and answer the questions.

❹ Compile your answers and read the interpretation.

❺ In your group, answer the *Talk About It!* questions.

❻ Finish completing the handout.

INTERPRETATION

1 to 5

Watch out for the aliens!
You still have a lot to learn about the fabulous world of science fiction!

6 to 10

Your spaceship is preparing for takeoff.
You know a lot about science fiction, but this unit will teach you even more!

11 to 15

You're out of this world!
You'll love this unit! Be prepared to share your expertise.

"Anything you dream is fiction, and anything you accomplish is science, the whole history of mankind is nothing but science fiction."

– Ray Bradbury

 Talk About It!

a) When you think of science fiction, what comes to mind?

b) Are you an avid SF fan? Why or why not?

c) What does the quotation by Ray Bradbury mean?

Culture

Did you know that...?

• The term *sci-fi* has a negative connotation. Most authors and fans of science fiction limit its use to referring to flimsy entertainments, such as monster movies about aliens.

• Science fiction scholars prefer the term *SF*, but it may cause confusion for the general public, which also uses this abbreviation to designate San Francisco.

flimsy: weak, inadequate, without substance.

ACTIVITY 2

A Brief History

Has science fiction always been around? Which authors originated the genre?

❶ Read the capsules about some science fiction icons on the following pages.

❷ Answer the questions on your handout.

❸ In your group, answer the *Talk About It!* questions on p. 145.

Culture

Pulp Magazines

Pulp magazines (whose content was known as "pulp fiction") were inexpensive magazines published from the 1920s to the 1950s. The term comes from the cheap wood-pulp paper they were printed on.

The cover page was usually very cheesy or sensational.

Although considered cheap at first, many respectable science fiction authors once wrote for the "pulps."

"The best way to predict the future is to invent it."

– Alan Kay

> **cheesy:** of poor quality or in bad taste (informal).

Culture

Predictions

Many science fiction authors are known for having made accurate scientific predictions and defining society's vision of the future. Here are a few of the most famous ones:

- **Jules Verne** correctly predicted the use of self-propelled submarines travelling at high speed underwater, as well as submarine warfare and space travel.

- **H.G. Wells** predicted the portable TV, automatic doors, light globes that change night into day, air conditioning and many other inventions.

- **Hugo Gernsback** correctly predicted television, mass transmission of entertainment programs to the home, synthetic milk and food, etc. By the way, the Hugo Awards were named after him.

SCIENCE FICTION ICONS

 Jules Verne
(1828–1905)

This French author is often referred to as the father of science fiction. He is also known for giving prophetic details of future inventions. His most famous works include *Around the World in Eighty Days*, *A Journey to the Centre of the Earth* and *Twenty Thousand Leagues Under the Sea*. Many of his novels were later made into movies.

 Isaac Asimov
(1920–1992)

Asimov was born in Russia, but raised in the United States. He wrote works in many different genres, but is most famous for his science fiction stories and novels, as well as his popular science books. Asimov's three laws of robotics, which were introduced in the 1942 short story *Runaround*, revolutionized the world of science fiction and influenced many subsequent authors who adopted them.

> *"Science fiction reflects scientific thought; a fiction of things-to-come based on things-on-hand."*
>
> – Benjamin Appel

 A.E. Van Vogt
(1912–2000)

He was a Canadian author. His first published story, *Black Destroyer*, was highly acclaimed and became the inspiration for many science fiction movies. *The World of Null-A* and *The Book of Ptath* are among his most famous novels. Van Vogt is known to have said that most of his inspiration came from his dreams and he arranged to be woken up every 90 minutes in order to write them down.

Culture

Asimov's Three Laws of Robotics

1. A robot may not injure a human being, or through inaction, allow a human being to come to harm.

2. A robot must obey orders given to it by human beings, except where such orders would conflict with the first law.

3. A robot must protect its own existence as long as such protection does not conflict with the first or second laws.

 icon: a famous person or thing considered as representing a set of beliefs or way of life.

 Stanley Kubrick
(1928–1999)

He is considered one of the greatest American movie producers of the 20th century. Although he successfully directed and produced movies in other genres, such as *Spartacus* and *Dr. Strangelove, or: How I Learned to Stop Worrying and Love the Bomb,* many admire him for his excellent science fiction movies. One of his most famous, *2001: A Space Odyssey,* was released in 1968 and although it lacked commercial success at first, it later became a cult movie.

 H.G. Wells
(1866–1946)

Along with Jules Verne, this English author is considered to be one of the founding fathers of science fiction. His most famous works are *The War of the Worlds, The Time Machine, The Island of Dr. Moreau* and *The Invisible Man.* Many of his novels were also made into movies.

 **Mary Shelley**
(1797–1851)

This British author wrote *Frankenstein*, which is considered the first SF novel. It was first published anonymously in 1818. The second edition, published in 1823, was credited to her, but it wasn't until the third edition in 1831 that her name appeared on the cover.

Culture

Women and Science Fiction
Did you know that...?

- In the early days of SF, many science fiction stories were in fact written by women, but published under male pseudonyms.

- Clare Winger Harris (1891–1968) is credited as the first women to publish stories under her own name in SF magazines.

- Octavia Butler (1947–2006) is one of very few Afro-American SF authors. She wrote 12 novels and a book of stories and won both Hugo and Nebula awards.

- Well-known Canadian author Margaret Atwood (1939–) writes in a number of genres, including science fiction.

 Talk About It!

a) Had you heard about any of these *Science Fiction Icons* before? If so, which ones?

b) Do you know any others?

c) Do you think that science fiction is a "guy genre"? Explain.

Think About It!

a) Did you notice that all but one of the icons are male? Why do you think this is so?

b) Do you know any female science fiction authors?

pseudonym: a fictitious name, especially a pen name.

ACTIVITY 3

Defining the Genre

In this activity, you will read (or listen to) excerpts of four different types of SF.

❶ Read about *Science Fiction Genres* below.

❷ Follow along in your book on pp. 148-149 as you listen to the four excerpts.

❸ Match each excerpt with its science fiction genre. Find evidence in the text to justify your answers.

❹ Compare answers with a partner.

❺ Discuss the texts in your group using the questions on the handout.

❻ Finish completing the handout.

Science Fiction Genres

Science fiction may be defined as a speculative story that expands on a known scientific fact. It often encompasses other related genres that incorporate imagination. These include:

Fantasy

- It uses magic and other supernatural elements as the main element of the plot or setting.
- Fantasy is often associated with the European Early Middle Ages (500–1000 A.D.).

Fantastic

- It introduces the supernatural or the unexplained into a real-life context or setting.
- This causes ambiguity or what might be called an eerie feeling.

Horror

- It plays on fear.
- Its main intention is to scare the audience.

Adventure

- It tells a heroic tale.
- The characters are constantly being placed in dangerous situations.

speculative: theoretical rather than demonstrable; based on guesswork.
eerie: strange and frightening; suggesting the supernatural.

 Can You Do It?

1. Find other examples of the four listed genres.
2. Classify the other texts in the unit using these four categories.

How to...
Read Science Fiction

There are many different types and subgenres of science fiction, but here's what they all have in common:

The themes:
- *Alternative timelines*
- *A setting in the future*
- *A setting in the past that contradicts known historical facts*

The action:
- *Takes place in outer space or on other worlds*
- *Involves aliens*
- *Sometimes includes flashbacks*

Language:
- *Uses made-up words and technical* jargon
- *Descriptive words create atmosphere*

Most science fiction stories:
- *Contradict the laws of nature (such as gravity)*
- *Involve the discovery of new scientific principles (such as time travel or new technology)*
- *Include faster-than-light travel or robots*
- *Describe new and different political or social systems*

Although science fiction stories may be enjoyed purely for their creativity and imagination, many are, in fact, **social commentaries**.

Culture

AWARDS

The Nebulas

They are voted by the Science Fiction Writers of America and celebrate excellence in science fiction writing. The first Nebula Award was presented to Frank Herbert in 1965 for his novel *Dune*.

The Hugos

Named after Hugo Gernsback, a famous SF author and publisher of *Amazing Stories*, the Hugos are given out annually to honour the best science fiction or fantasy works of the year. The first award was presented in 1953.

jargon: speech used by a particular group.

"The function of science fiction is not always to predict the future but sometimes to prevent it."

– Frank Herbert

Excerpts

The Black Cat
by Edgar Allan Poe

1 One night, returning home, much intoxicated, from one of my haunts about town, I fancied that the cat avoided my presence. I seized him; when, in his fright at my violence, he inflicted a slight wound upon my hand with his teeth. The fury of a demon instantly possessed me. I knew myself no longer. My original soul seemed, at once, to take its flight from my body; and a more than fiendish malevolence, gin-nurtured, thrilled every fibre of my frame. I took from my waistcoat-pocket a pen-knife, opened it, grasped the poor beast by the throat, and deliberately cut one of its eyes from the socket! I blush, I burn, I shudder, while I pen the damnable atrocity.

When reason returned with the morning – when I had slept off the fumes of the night's debauch – I experienced a sentiment half of horror, half of remorse, for the crime of which I had been guilty; but it was, at best, a feeble and equivocal feeling, and the soul remained untouched. I again plunged into excess, and soon drowned in wine all memory of the deed.

Edgar Allan Poe, "The Black Cat," *United States Saturday Post,* August 1843

Edgar Allan Poe

waistcoat: a vest.
feeble: weak; lacking vigour or force.

The Princess and the Goblin
by George MacDonald

2 Now in these subterranean caverns lived a strange race of beings, called by some gnomes, by some kobolds, by some goblins. There was a legend current in the country that at one time they lived above ground, and were very like other people. But for some reason or other, concerning which there were different legendary theories, the king had laid what they thought too severe taxes upon them, or had required observances of them they did not like, or had begun to treat them with more severity, in some way or other, and impose stricter laws; and the consequence was that they had all disappeared from the face of the country. According to the legend, however, instead of going to some other country, they had all taken refuge in the subterranean caverns, whence they never came out but at night, and then seldom showed themselves in any numbers, and never to many people at once. Those who had caught sight of any of them said that they had greatly altered in the course of generations; and no wonder, seeing they lived away from the sun, in cold and wet and dark places.

George MacDonald, *The princess and the Goblin,* published by Strahan & Co., 1872

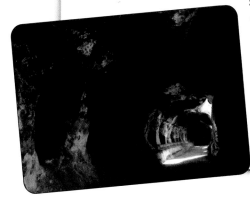

Black Man

by Richard Morgan

(3)

One hundred years from now and against all the odds, Earth has found a new stability; the political order has reached some sort of balance, and the new colony on Mars is growing. But the fraught years of the 21st century have left an uneasy legacy.

Genetically engineered alpha males, designed to fight the century's wars have no wars to fight and are surplus to requirements. And a man bred and designed to fight is a dangerous man to have around in peacetime. Many of them have left for Mars but now one has come back and killed everyone else on the shuttle he returned in.

Only one man, a genengineered ex-soldier himself, can hunt him down and so begins a frenetic man-hunt and a battle survival. And a search for the truth about what was really done with the world's last soldiers.

Richard Morgan, *Black Man*, Victor Gollancz, an imprint of The Orion Publishing Group

Richard Morgan

Robinson Crusoe

by Daniel Dafoe

(4)

Thus years and years passed away. Although I had, to some extent, become contented with my solitary lot, yet at times a terrible sense of loneliness and desolation would come over me. Many times I would go to the top of a hill where I could look out to sea in hopes of catching sight of a ship. Then I would fancy that, at a vast distance, I spied a sail. I would please myself with the hopes of it, and after looking at it steadily, till I was almost blind, would lose it quite, and sit down and weep like a child, and thus increase my misery by my folly. But one day I saw a sight which turned my thoughts in a new channel. It was the print of a naked foot upon the sand near the shore. It filled me with fear, for it showed that the island must sometimes be visited by savages. One morning, going out quite early, I could see the light of a fire about two miles away. I went to the top of the hill and looked in the direction of the fire. I saw that five canoes were drawn up on the shore, while a swarm of naked savages were dancing about the fire. Presently they dragged two poor wretches from the boats. One of them was knocked down at once, and several of the savages set to work to cut him up. They were evidently cannibals, and were going to hold one of their horrible feasts on their captives. The other captive was left standing for a moment, and seeing a chance to escape, started to run. I was greatly alarmed when I saw that he was coming directly toward me, but when I saw that only two pursued him, and that he gained upon them, I made up my mind to help him. When they were near enough, I took a short cut down the hill, and placed myself between pursuers and pursued. Then I advanced on the foremost, and knocked him down with the stock of my gun. The other took his bow and was going to shoot me, when I fired at him and killed him. Then I made signs to the poor runaway to come to me, and he did so in fear and trembling, kneeling at my feet and setting my foot upon his head, as a sign that he was my slave.

Daniel Dafoe, *Robinson Crusoe*, published by W. Taylor, 1719

Strategies

The last text is longer.
Don't try to understand every word. Go for the general meaning.
Try to visualize what is happening.

---

fraught: causing distress.
to weep: to cry.
wretch: a miserable or mean person.
to pursue: to try and overtake or capture something or someone.

Focus on...

Direct and Indirect Speech

Direct Speech

1. Is what someone says word for word.
2. Uses quotation marks.
   Example: He said, "Today's movie is about UFOs."

Indirect Speech (Reported Speech)

1. Isn't necessarily word for word.
2. Doesn't use quotation marks.
   Example: He said that today's movie was about UFOs.

In indirect speech, the verb tense changes from the **present to the past** (Obviously, the person who made the original statement made it sometime in the past).

As a rule, when you report something that was said (indirect speech), you go back a tense. Look at the following chart:

Direct Speech	Indirect Speech
Simple present: He said, "I <u>love</u> this book!"	**Simple past:** He said that he <u>loved</u> that book.
Present continuous: He said, "I <u>am watching</u> a science fiction film."	**Past continuous:** He said that he <u>was watching</u> a science fiction film.
Present perfect: He said, "I'<u>ve been</u> a SF buff for five years."	**Past perfect:** He said that he <u>had been</u> a SF buff for five years.
Present perfect continuous: She said, "I'<u>ve been reading</u> this book for two days."	**Past perfect continuous:** She said that she <u>had been reading</u> that book for two days.
Simple past: She said, "I <u>read</u> the book last week."	**Past perfect:** She said that she <u>had read</u> the book last week.
Past continuous: She said, "We <u>were reading</u> earlier."	**Past perfect continuous:** She said that they <u>had been reading</u> earlier.
Past perfect: He said, "The film <u>had</u> already <u>started</u> when she arrived."	**Past perfect:** NO CHANGE He said the film <u>had</u> already <u>started</u> when she arrived.
Past perfect continuous: She said, "It <u>had</u> already <u>been playing</u> for five minutes."	**Past perfect continuous:** NO CHANGE She said it <u>had</u> already <u>been playing</u> for five minutes.

Note: In reported speech, the pronoun often changes. Notice the pronouns highlighted in the above examples.

Practise!

1. Transform the direct speech in the following sentences to indirect speech:
   a) "I use my time machine every day," he said.
   b) She said, "The president wasn't at his desk yesterday when I called. Apparently, he had left the planet on his private spaceship."

2. Transform the indirect speech in the following sentences to direct speech:
   a) She said that *The Blob* was her favourite science fiction adventure when she was young.
   b) Barbara said that there was an alien in her basement and a spaceship in her backyard.

Can You Do It?

Take three statements in the first person from *Robinson Crusoe* and write them as direct quotes.

Example: He said, "I think I spy a sail."

Then, exchange papers with a partner and rewrite his/her statements as indirect quotes.

Example: He said that he spied a sail.

ACTIVITY 4

Common Terms

Since science fiction is based on hypothetical situations and things that have not been invented (at least not yet...), it is normal that the genre possess its own vocabulary. In this activity, you will become acquainted with some of the words and expressions that have become part of SF jargon.

❶ Read the *SF Jargon* box below.

❷ Make a list of SF jargon you come across in the texts you read in this unit. Use the graphic organizer on your handout. Feel free to add any other SF words or expressions you know.

❸ Compare lists with a partner and then in your group.

❹ Share your thoughts on the question in the *Talk About It!* box.

SF JARGON

Science fiction buffs also have their own "language," which is known as *fanspeak*. **Fanspeak** includes terms such as *gafiate* (getting away from it all), *fanzine* (short for "fan magazine"), *BEM* (bug-eyed-monster) and *trekkie* (a fan who is primarily into *Star Trek*).

Science fiction jargon often includes terms that are made up. This includes *technobabble*. **Technobabble** is the fusing of the words technology and babble. It is used to give the reader the impression that the author has genuine scientific knowledge.

In addition, there are many words and expressions that are commonly used in science fiction writing. These include:

- **cyborg:** a human who has certain physiological processes aided or controlled by mechanical or electronic devices [cyb(ernetic) +org(anism)].
- **dalek:** a robot-like creation that wants to take over the universe. Daleks resemble human-sized salt and pepper shakers.
- **droid:** a kind of highly intelligent robot that was popularized in *Star Wars*.
- **FTL:** faster than light.
- **rejuv:** shortened form of "rejuvenation," which refers to medical technology capable of reversing ageing.
- **sentient:** an alien possessing human-level intelligence.
- **tachyon:** any hypothetical particle that travels at speeds faster than light.

 ## Talk About It!

How does this special vocabulary add to the genre? Does it make it more interesting and believable or confusing?

Although science fiction stories cover a wide variety of topics, some themes are recurrent. In TASK 2, you will learn more about the most common ones.

ACTIVITY 1

A Different Time, a Different Place

Time travel and space travel are themes that are repeatedly exploited in science fiction stories. In this activity, you will read all about them.

❶ Read the text *Space and Time Travel*.

❷ Before you write, discuss the *Write About it!* questions in your group.

❸ Complete the handout.

Strategies

- If this text seems long, break it up into chunks.
- Read one section at a time.
- After each section, stop and think about what you have just read.
- Check your comprehension by answering the corresponding questions on the handout.

Culture

The Philadelphia Experiment or Project Rainbow

– It is said to be a military operation in which a ship is rendered invisible for a short period of time.

– According to different versions, the ship was in fact teleported to another dimension, met up with aliens, didn't actually disappear but was invisible to radar, or travelled to another time.

– Although it is considered a hoax by many, some conspiracy theorists still regard it as true.

hoax: a trick; something untrue.
far-fetched: improbable; not easily believable.

Space and Time Travel

Space Travel

Many science fiction stories have the characters flying off to space, or aliens from space coming to Earth either to peacefully explore or invade. There are many variations on the theme of space travel.

Jules Verne first explored the possibility in 1865 in *From the Earth to the Moon*. No one had actually travelled in space at that time, and although the story has the characters flying in space, they don't actually land on the moon. Using the scientific knowledge of his era, Verne figured out that there would be no gravity, oxygen problems, etc.

Then, NASA was created in 1958 and man landed on the moon in 1969, so that great leaps and bounds were made in space travel in a short period. Science fiction writers had to figure out a way to overcome the boring mechanics of space travel within the cramped quarters of a spaceship, the long time frame required to travel to other planets, and various problems related to gravity. Thus the space opera was born.

The Space Opera

The space opera violates some of the rules of science fiction because both the science and technology are often far-fetched and sometimes seemingly impossible, even if they don't go as far as fantasy does. Although the alien characters are purely imaginative, their existence is still a remote possibility, unlike the magical characters in fantasy novels or stories.

A space opera is always set in outer space or on a distant planet. The characters have arrived there by using "warp speed," which is faster than light speed and of course, technologically speaking, impossible. The aliens have many human characteristics and often the communication barrier doesn't exist; aliens and humans being able to understand each other easily. There are lots of space battles as the theme of good versus evil is explored once again.

In the classic space opera, humans must battle aliens in order to save their planet, or their civilization as they know it. The same goes for aliens travelling to Earth. It is usually to conquer Earth and the highly evolved beings often end up returning to their planet, having been beaten by the earthlings. Other species come to Earth and snatch humans in their sleep, in order to perform experiments on them, and then bring them back again, without anyone being so much the wiser.

Space operas also sometimes include a romantic element – a forbidden interspecies relationship or humans leaving behind the love of their life or their family to go save the world from the evil aliens. As in a fairy tale, the story finishes when all is well and everyone is reunited.

Classic examples of the space opera are *Star Wars*, *Star Trek* and *Dune*.

Time Travel

A counterpart to space travel is time travel. There are many variations to the theme of time travel. In one instance, a character returns to the past to change the future and make it more like he wants it to be. In another variation, a time traveller goes back to fix catastrophes of history, such as the fall of Rome or the plague. Sometimes, an object mistakenly gets stuck in the past or the future and the hero of the story sets out to rescue it.

Most of the time travellers use a time machine, which is often a mechanical contraption of some sort. One can often choose the date one wishes to go to, but, time machines being imperfect, mistakes are just as often made.

Almost all time-travel stories agree: the past must not be disturbed because it could lead to dire consequences. The writer René Barjavel first talked about the **grandfather paradox** in his 1943 book, *The Imprudent Traveller*. The grandfather paradox is a powerful argument against time travel. It says this: What would happen if a man travelled back in time and killed his biological grandfather before he actually met the time traveller's grandmother? As a result, one of his parents would never have been born, nor would he. This would imply that he could not have travelled back in time to kill his grandfather after all, which in turn implies that the grandfather would be alive after all, and the traveller would be alive also, allowing him, in fact, to travel back in time and kill his grandfather after all! So, each possibility seems to imply its own negation: a type of logical paradox.

Classic time-travel stories include the movies *Back to the Future*, *Planet of the Apes*, Ray Bradbury's *A Sound of Thunder* and the cartoons *Buck Rogers* and *Futurama*. ❖

✏️ Write About It!

a) Would you prefer to travel ahead in time or back in time? Why?

b) Do you think we're the only species in the universe? Do you believe in aliens? Explain your answers.

plague: an epidemic disease.
dire: dreadful, terrible.

Culture

Grey Aliens make up about 75% of alien sightings in the U.S.

They are described as short with long arms, almond-shaped eyes and grey skin.

They started to appear in science fiction stories as early as the 1900s.

One of the first references to **Time Travel** is in H.G. Wells' *The Time Machine*.

From a scientific point of view, using the theory of special or general relativity, time travel to the future is indeed a possibility. But it has yet to be proven that time travellers are a reality. Maybe time will tell!

ACTIVITY 2

What if...?

Some science fiction authors create a setting in which they alter history. They take real events and change the outcome. *What if Hitler hadn't existed?* Or *what if Hitler had won the Second World War?* They choose a premise and explore different possibilities.

Can you imagine a world where historical or scientific facts have been modified?

❶ Read the *Hypothetical Situations* below.

❷ Brainstorm with a partner and make a list of at least five other possibilities.

❸ Share your list with your group.

❹ Individually, choose one of the hypothetical situations.

❺ On the handout, write one paragraph explaining your answer to the following questions using the past unreal conditional:
  • What consequences might the change have had?
  • How might society have evolved?
  • Who or what might have been affected?

❻ Finish completing the handout.

❼ Share your work with the class.

Hypothetical Situations

What would have happened if...

① Women had never been given the right to vote?

② Humans and dinosaurs had always cohabitated?

③ Electricity had never been invented?

④ Scientists had maintained that Earth was flat?

⑤ Scientists had implanted bacteria on the moon that would permit life there?

Can You Do It?

Here are two movies with alternate endings:

• *The Butterfly Effect*
• *Back to the Future*

How many others can you think of? Do you know of any examples from video games?

Think About It!

a) Do these situations meet the criteria of science fiction? Why or why not?

b) Do you agree that yesterday's past is tomorrow's future?

The Past Unreal Conditional

The Past Unreal Conditional is used to speak about **imaginary situations in the past**.

- Use it to describe:
  - What you would have done differently.
  - How something could have happened differently if circumstances had been different.
- Use the following form:
  - **If + Past Perfect..., ... would have + past participle...**

Example: **If** they **had not invented** the car, society **would have evolved** in a different way.

Using the Past

	Active Voice	**Passive Voice**
Present Perfect		
Affirmative	Aliens **have visited** Earth many times.	Earth **has been visited** by aliens many times.
Negative	Aliens **haven't (have not)** visited Earth.	Earth **has not (hasn't)** been visited by aliens.
Simple Past		
Affirmative	Aliens **visited** Earth in the 1950s.	Earth **was visited** by aliens in the 1950s.
Negative	Aliens **didn't (did not)** visit Earth.	Earth **was not (wasn't) visited** by aliens.
Past Perfect		
Affirmative	Aliens **had visited** Earth several times.	Earth **had been visited** by aliens several times.
Negative	Aliens **had not (hadn't)** visited Earth before that time.	Earth **had not (hadn't) been visited** by aliens before that time.

Refer to the Toolkit at the back of your book for more help on verbs or on writing a paragraph.

THREE STEPS TO WRITING A PARAGRAPH

1. Introduce the main idea of the paragraph in a topic sentence.
2. Write facts and information to support the main idea.
3. Restate the main idea using different words.

ACTIVITY 3

Different Angles

In this cooperative activity, you will be working first in an expert group, then returning to your base group.

1 In your group, each choose one of the four topics: *society*, *culture*, *politics* or *religion*.

2 Read the text on the handout provided by the teacher.

3 Answer the questions.

4 Form an expert group with three other people who chose the same text you did. Together discuss what you read and validate your ideas.

5 Return to your base group. In your own words, explain your text to your teammates.

6 Complete the handout together.

Culture

Visual **Art** artists are an important part of the science fiction world. Their illustrations appear in magazines and on book covers. It has also become the trend to hang sci-fi pictures on walls.

What do you think about sci-fi art?

"For me science fiction is a way of thinking, a way of logic that bypasses a lot of nonsense. It allows people to look directly at important subjects."

– Gene Roddenberry, creator of *Star Trek*

Montage of Outer Space and Other Science Fiction Scenes by Anton Brzezinski

In the Media

Science fiction is all around us. In TASK 3, you will listen to a famous science fiction radio play, learn about comic strips and read about sound and special effects in movies.

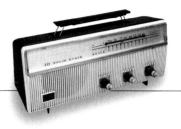

 ACTIVITY 1

The Great Hoax

Radio dramas are plays acted out on the radio. In the 1930s, they were very popular. On October 30, 1938, Orson Wells adapted the novel *The War of the Worlds*, written by H.G. Wells, as a radio drama.

The first 60 minutes of the show was presented as a series of news bulletins, causing a great uproar, as people actually believed that Earth was being invaded by aliens. Although there were at least two announcements made during the show to the effect that it was merely a play, many people failed to hear them and started to panic.

> *"Science fiction works hand-in-glove with the universe."*
>
> – Ray Bradbury

❶ Listen to parts of the 1938 broadcast of *The War of the Worlds*.

❷ Answer the *Talk About It!* questions in your group.

❸ Complete the handout.

Talk About It!

a) In Unit 5, you explored truth in the media. One of the points made was that people often have a tendency to believe what they want to hear. How does this tie in with *The War of the Worlds* radio show?

b) Would you have believed an invasion was taking place? Why or why not?

c) Could something like this happen on TV today?

Culture

Science Fiction and Radio

- Science fiction on the radio has been around since the 1930s, when plays were adapted from comics, books and short stories.

- Science fiction dramatizations on the radio still exist in some cities. Classic stories are adapted or new ones presented.

uproar: a heated controversy.

ACTIVITY 2

Comic Strips and Video Games

Along with *Buck Rogers*, *Flash Gordon* is one of the most famous science fiction comic strips. In this activity, you will take a closer look at the first strip from 1934. You will also discuss how SF has come to video games.

① Look at the *Flash Gordon* comic strip on the next page and read a summary of the plot. What makes this comic strip science fiction?

② With a partner, think about other science fiction comic strips that you know. How are they different from *Flash Gordon*?

③ Answer the *Talk About It!* questions with a partner.

④ Complete the handout about science fiction in comic strips and video games.

ICT

Go on the Internet and find out more about *Flash Gordon* or look into other early science fiction comic strips.

Share your findings with the class.

Vocabulary Builder

Choose the Right One

Even for native speakers, some words are easily confused.

- Here are a few of them:
  - weather, whether
  - they're, there, their
  - who's, whose
  - loose, lose
  - than, then
  - its, it's
  - affect, effect
  - advice, advise

Can you distinguish between each of them and use them correctly?

Work orally with a partner and try to come up with a sentence using each one correctly.

 Think About It!

a) How are heroes and heroines depicted in science fiction comic strips and video games?

b) What connections can you make with body image and Unit 4?

The story begins with Earth being bombarded by meteors believed to be from outer space. A mad scientist, Dr. Zarkov, kidnaps Flash and Dale, and the three travel to the planet Mongo.

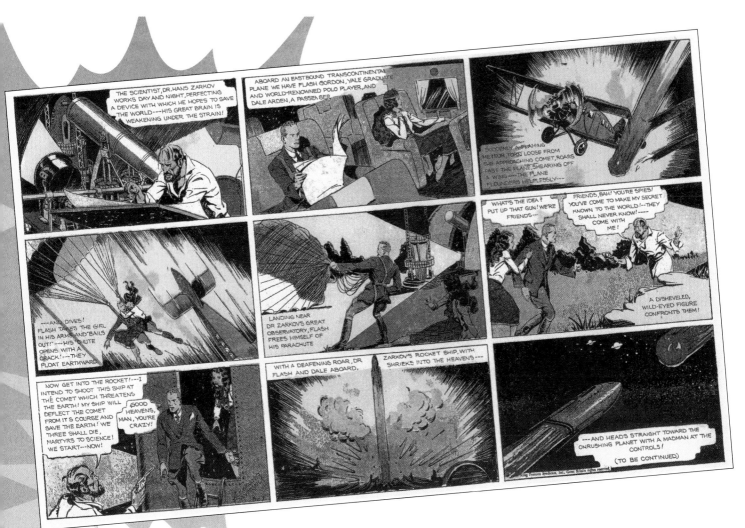

Culture

Did you know that...?

- Many of the first video games were based on science fiction.
- Technology has greatly evolved and today, the graphics are so amazing that you can actually confuse computer-generated characters with real-life people.

Talk About It!

a) Do you read SF comic strips?

b) Do you know of any science fiction comic strips in English?

c) Do you think that SF comic strips and video games are for kids or adults? Explain your thinking.

ACTIVITY 3

Movies

Science fiction movies are known for their spectacular special effects. Although many of these effects are created by computers nowadays, some are still done by humans. In this activity, you will read about how some special effects are produced.

1 With a partner, look at the pictures and decide which ones are man-made and which ones are computerized.

2 Write your answers on the handout.

3 Read the three texts about special effects.

4 What new information did you learn?

5 Read the *Think About It!* questions on the next page and complete the handout.

Special Effects

You can't talk about science fiction movies without bringing up special effects: one doesn't go without the other. Although most special effects are computerized today, it wasn't always so. Camera tricks that now seem really basic to us used to amaze people. You would have been awestruck the first time you saw Scotty being beamed up in *Star Trek*. And, did you know that the spaceship in the first *Star Wars* movie was built completely by hand? It's the way the scene was filmed that made it seem real to the audience.

There are many different kinds of special effects, but generally they can be divided into two distinct categories: **man-made** and **computerized**. ❖

Culture

- **B movies** were originally movies made on very low budgets, presented as part of a double-bill with a major motion picture (the A movie).

- Many people still believe the B stands for bad.

- Titles include *Attack of the Killer Tomatoes*, *The Swamp*, *The Rocky Horror Picture Show*, the original *King Kong*...

- And did you know that the first *Star Wars* was considered a B movie? Do you know why?

Man-made Effects

Latex

The use of latex revolutionized the special effects industry. You can do many things with it: create monsters out of humans, add scars, make young people old, etc. A good example of this was provided by Jim Carrey as the Grinch in the movie *How the Grinch Stole Christmas*.

Rain/Snow/Wind/Fire

Producing a movie is very costly. Producers can't wait for the right weather to occur. They take matters into their own hands and create their own weather using snow and rain machines. If it's a windy, snowy day, they add giant fans and they're in business.

As for fire, well you probably know that a movie scene can be shot many times before it is perfect. Setting fire to the whole set just isn't feasible, so professionals are brought in. They usually set up big tubes in which fire can be turned on or off at the press of a button.

Explosions

They can be computer generated, but the result never seems to be as good as when pyrotechnic machines are used. These machines can create any kind of explosion, from the shattering of a window to the blowing up of an entire building. ❖

Computerized Effects

The Blue Screen

This allows the actors to find themselves in imaginary situations, like flying a bike in the sky or standing on top of the Brooklyn Bridge. The actors are shot acting in front of a blue screen. The background is put in afterwards. Green and red are also sometimes used, but blue is the colour that works best because it is the complementary colour to flesh tone. Since the most common colour used is flesh tone, using the opposite is the logical choice. Another reason is that the background colour will often reflect on the foreground, creating a slight tinge around the edge. Blue is the colour that shows least.

Computer Animation

A series of cartoon frames is put together in the classical manner, but physical models can also be used. They are positioned and the image recorded. Then, using computers, the models can be made to move in any way desired.

Compositing

This is when one shot is superimposed on top of another, giving the illusion that two things are present at the same time, when in fact they are not. A good everyday example of this is the weather person on your local TV news. The person is superimposed on a computerized map. ❖

Think About It!

a) Why do you think special effects are so important?

b) Would science fiction movies still be so popular if the special effects were removed?

Talk About It!

In Unit 2, you explored how music influences the mood of a scene from a film. In a science fiction film, what is more important: special effects or music?

The Adventure

Now that you have learned a lot about science fiction, it's time to plan, and perhaps create, your own science fiction adventure. In the FINAL TASK, you will write a synopsis and create a storyboard for an original science fiction adventure. Afterwards, your storyboard could be turned into a story, video or comic strip... Or, it could be chosen for a role play in front of the class.

What to Do

Step 1

❶ Find an idea for a science fiction adventure. Scan the unit for inspiration.

❷ Look at the synopsis and storyboard on the next page. What do you notice?

❸ Answer the *Talk About It!* questions with a partner.

Step 2

❹ Write the synopsis of your science fiction adventure.
- Only a short description of the action is required.
- It should answer the five Ws: Who? What? Where? When? Why?

❺ Make your storyboard:
- In the first column on the left, write a short summary of the action for each scene.
- In the second column, write or draw what we see in each scene.
- If you wish, you may add a third column with what we hear in each scene.

Step 3 (optional)

❻ Follow the steps of the **Production Process** on p. 247 and produce your science fiction adventure using the medium of your choice. You can produce the entire storyboard or choose just one frame.

OR

As a group, choose one of the storyboards and turn it into a role play, following the guidelines in Project 2 on pp. 208-219.

Invaders from Within

Synopsis: *In the year 2136, humans who have colonized the planet Mars come back to Earth after a break in communication with the planet. They are shocked by what they discover.*

Storyboard:

What Happens	How I Imagine It
① The spaceship is in space, about to enter Earth's atmosphere.	
② The spaceship lands and the passengers get out in their protective suits, noticing that not a sound can be heard, but there are ants everywhere.	
③ The men exploring the planet discover dead bodies everywhere. There is not a sign of human life anywhere. Humans and animals alike have all been killed.	
④ The visitors from Mars discover that ants, who have always outnumbered humans by millions, have suddenly ganged up and taken over the entire planet. The visitors barely make it back to their ship.	
⑤ The visitors return to Mars.	

Reminder:
Refer to your Toolkit for help with verbs.

 Talk About It!

a) Do you think the storyboard is truly representative of the story?

b) What would you change?

Wrap-up

Look Back

- Look back at the pictures in the opening pages. You should now be able to say what each represents and why they were chosen.

- You should be able to answer the Guiding Questions.

Think About It

- Are you more apt to read or watch science fiction now that you've learned about it in the unit?

- Do you think science fiction is intended for a specific audience, or can anyone enjoy it?

Now What?

- Who or what would you like to know more about?

Select some
of your work for
your portfolio!

3 Name three authors you didn't know before doing the unit.

2 List two things you have learned in this unit.

1 Name one science fiction movie you would like to watch.

OTHER THINGS TO DO

Choose an author and find out more about him or her. Read something he/she wrote. Share with the class.

Create a Webquest, puzzle or game based on science fiction.

Make a poster promoting the story you created in the FINAL TASK.

Watch either *Bicentennial Man* or *I, Robot*. Find an original way to share your feelings and opinions about the film you watch.

They're Made out of Meat

by Terry Bisson

(This story originally appeared in Omni Magazine *in April 1991 and was nominated for the Nebula Award. It is taken from the collection* Bears Discover Fire.*)*

1 "They're made out of meat."

"Meat?"

"Meat. They're made out of meat."

"Meat?"

5 "There's no doubt about it. We picked up several from different parts of the planet, took them aboard our recon vessels, and probed them all the way through. They're completely meat."

"That's impossible. What about the radio signals? The messages to the stars?"

"They use the radio waves to talk, but the signals don't come from them. The signals come from machines."

10 "So who made the machines? That's who we want to contact."

"They made the machines. That's what I'm trying to tell you. Meat made the machines."

"That's ridiculous. How can meat make a machine? You're asking me to believe in sentient meat."

"I'm not asking you, I'm telling you. These creatures are the only sentient race in that sector and they're made out of meat."

15 "Maybe they're like the orfolei. You know, a carbon-based intelligence that goes through a meat stage."

"Nope. They're born meat and they die meat. We studied them for several of their lifespans, which didn't take long. Do you have any idea what's the lifespan of meat?"

"Spare me. Okay, maybe they're only part meat. You know, like the weddilei. A meat head with an electron plasma brain inside."

20 "Nope. We thought of that, since they do have meat heads, like the weddilei. But I told you, we probed them. They're meat all the way through."

"No brain?"

"Oh, there's a brain all right. It's just that the brain is made out of meat! That's what I've been trying to tell you."

25 "So... what does the thinking?"

"Thinking meat! You're asking me to believe in thinking meat!"

"Yes, thinking meat! Conscious meat! Loving meat. Dreaming meat. The meat is the whole deal! Are you beginning to get the picture or do I have to start all over?" "Omigod. You're serious then. They're made out of meat."

30 "Thank you. Finally. Yes. They are indeed made out of meat. And they've been trying to get in touch with us for almost a hundred of their years."

"Omigod. So what does this meat have in mind?"

"First it wants to talk to us. Then I imagine it wants to explore the Universe, contact other sentiences, swap ideas and information. The usual."

35 "You're not understanding, are you? You're refusing to deal with what I'm telling you. The brain does the thinking. The meat."

"We're supposed to talk to meat."

"That's the idea. That's the message they're sending out by radio. 'Hello. Anyone out there. Anybody home.' That sort of thing."

40 "They actually do talk, then. They use words, ideas, concepts?"

"Oh, yes. Except they do it with meat."

"I thought you just told me they used radio."

"They do, but what do you think is on the radio? Meat sounds. You know how when you slap or flap meat, it makes a noise? They talk by flapping their meat at each other. They can even sing by squirting
45 air through their meat."

"Omigod. Singing meat. This is altogether too much. So what do you advise?"

"Officially or unofficially?"

"Both."

"Officially, we are required to contact, welcome and log in any and all sentient races
50 or multibeings in this quadrant of the Universe, without prejudice, fear or favor.
Unofficially, I advise that we erase the records and forget the whole thing."

"I was hoping you would say that."

"It seems harsh, but there is a limit. Do we really want to make contact with meat?"

"I agree one hundred percent. What's there to say? 'Hello, meat. How's it going?' But will this work?
55 How many planets are we dealing with here?"

"Just one. They can travel to other planets in special meat containers, but they can't live on them.
And being meat, they can only travel through C space. Which limits them to the speed of light and
makes the possibility of their ever making contact pretty slim. Infinitesimal, in fact."

"So we just pretend there's no one home in the Universe."
60 "That's it."

"Cruel. But you said it yourself, who wants to meet meat? And the ones who have been aboard
our vessels, the ones you probed? You're sure they won't remember?"

"They'll be considered crackpots if they do. We went into their heads and smoothed out
their meat so that we're just a dream to them."
65 "A dream to meat! How strangely appropriate, that we should be meat's dream."

"And we marked the entire sector unoccupied."

"Good. Agreed, officially and unofficially. Case closed. Any others? Anyone interesting on
that side of the galaxy?"

"Yes, a rather shy but sweet hydrogen core cluster intelligence in a class nine star in G445 zone.
70 Was in contact two galactic rotations ago, wants to be friendly again."

"They always come around."

"And why not? Imagine how unbearably, how unutterably cold the Universe would be
if one were all alone..."

The End

Question

What is made out of meat?

The Special Effects of "2001: A Space Odyssey"

by George D. DeMet

1 More than 30 years after its initial release, Stanley Kubrick's *2001: A Space Odyssey* still inspires those who see it. Like a piece of fine art or a classical symphony, its appeal has only
5 grown over time. A strikingly unique film, it captivated a generation of young people in the late 1960s, who accepted its visual message with religious fervor. Initially rebuffed by leading film critics, *2001* is today considered
10 one of cinema's greatest masterpieces.

An epic story spanning both time and space, *2001* begins 4 million years ago, in a prehistoric African savanna, where mankind's distant ancestors must learn how to use the first
15 tools in order to survive. The film cuts to the technological utopia of the early 21st century, where life in outer space is an everyday reality. The story then takes us to the first manned space mission to Jupiter, which consists of two
20 human astronauts and a super-intelligent computer named HAL. The final segment of the film contains a fantastical 23-minute light show of special effects and a mystifying conclusion designed to make its audience question
25 themselves and the world around them.

Director Stanley Kubrick, first approached science fiction writer Arthur C. Clarke in early 1964 to collaborate on what both hoped would be "the proverbial good science fiction film."
30 They spent a year working out the story, and Kubrick began pre-production in the mid-1965.

On the recommendation of Clarke, Kubrick hired spacecraft consultants Frederick Ordway and Harry Lange. Lange was responsible for designing
35 much of the hardware seen in the film.

Every detail of the production design, down to the most insignificant element, was designed with technological and scientific accuracy in mind. Senior NASA Apollo administrator George
40 Mueller and astronaut Deke Slayton are said to have dubbed *2001*'s Borehamwood, England production facilities "NASA East" after seeing all of the hardware and documentation lying around the studio. Even today, most audiences and critics
45 still find *2001*'s props and spaceships more convincing than those in many more recent science fiction movies. While earlier science fiction films had aimed for a streamlined
50 "futuristic" look, *2001*'s production design was intended to be as technically credible as possible.

Production designer Anthony Masters was responsible for making Harry Lange's design concepts a reality. More than 100
55 modelmakers assisted him and the other members of the art crew in this task. For greater authenticity, production of many of the film's props, such as spacesuits and instrument panels, was outsourced to various
60 aerospace and engineering companies. Everything had to meet with Kubrick's approval before it could be used in the film.

Kubrick's unrelenting perfectionism was evident when it came to designing the mysterious alien
65 monolith, which appears at various points throughout the film. Originally envisioned as a tetrahedron, none of the models were impressive enough. Kubrick then commissioned a British company to manufacture a 3-ton block
70 of transparent lucite, which also lacked the necessary visual impact. The black slab finally used was constructed out of wood and sanded with graphite for a completely smooth finish.

It was not unusual for the crew to go to great
75 lengths to create the film's unique sets. The film's' most impressive set is that of the interior of the spaceship *Discovery*. To compensate for the weightlessness of outer space, the ship's crew compartment was envisioned as a centrifuge that
80 would simulate gravity through the centripetal force generated by its rotation. A 30-ton rotating ferris wheel set was built by Vickers-Armstrong Engineering Group, a British aircraft company at a cost of $750,000. The set was 38 feet
85 in diameter and 10 feet wide. It could rotate at a maximum speed of 3 miles per hour, and was dressed with the necessary chairs, desks and control panels, all firmly bolted to the inside surface. The actors could stand at the bottom

90 and walk in place, while the set rotated around them. Kubrick used an early video feed to direct the action from a control room, while the camera operator sat in a gimbaled seat. *2001*'s special effects team was supervised by Kubrick himself,

95 and included Con Pederson, Wally Veevers and Douglas Trumbull, who went on to create effects for other science fiction movies such as *Close Encounters of the Third Kind* and *Blade Runner*. Work on the film's 200+ effects scenes

100 had begun even while Kubrick and Clarke were working out the script; Kubrick had used a reel of experimental effects shot in an abandoned New York corset factory to help "sell" the film to studio executives. Kubrick's crew hoped to set a

105 new standard for quality in visual effects. As Kubrick put it, "I felt it was necessary to make this film in such a way that every special effects shot in it would be completely convincing – something that had never before been accomplished in

110 a motion picture."

2001 was one of the first films to make extensive use of front projection, a technique where photography is projected from the front of the set onto a reflective surface. The prehistoric Africa

115 scenes were actually filmed in the Borehamwood studio, with second unit photography projected behind the actors onto a screen measuring 40 feet by 90 feet to provide the illusion of an outdoor scene. Front projection was also used for some

120 of the film's outer space effects scenes. The more traditional technique of rear projection was reserved mainly for the many video displays and computer monitors that appeared in the film.

Although most of the visual effects techniques

125 used in *2001* had been used before, there was one sequence that broke new technical and artistic ground. The "Star Gate" seen in the final segment of the film, where whirling lights and colours streamed around amazed theatre

130 audiences, was created using a "Slit Scan" machine developed by Douglas Trumbull, which allowed the filming of two seemingly infinite planes of exposure. Additional effects for the sequence were created applying different

135 colored filters to aerial landscape footage and filming interacting chemicals.

Other effects were achieved through a combination of creative camerawork, hard work and dedication. To make a stray pen "float"

140 in a weightless environment, it was attached to a rotating glass disk. The illusion of astronauts floating in space was created by hanging stunt performers upside down with wires from the ceiling of the studio, often for hours at a time.

145 The achievements of *2001*'s effects, which were all done without the benefits of computer technology, are nothing less than amazing. Kubrick held his crew to the highest standards to insure that the film's effects were designed

150 to be as realistic-looking as possible. To insure that every element of an effects scene was as sharp and clear as a single-generation image, he ruled out the use of many techniques that would have been much faster and less expensive.

155 $6.5 million of his $10.5 million budget ended up going toward effects alone, and it was nearly two years after the end of principal photography that film was finally finished.

When audiences first saw *2001* in the spring

160 of 1968, many were baffled. The film lacked a traditional plot structure, contained almost no dialogue and had an ending that many found confusing. Leading film critics, like Andrew Sarris and Pauline Kael, panned the film,

165 arguing that Kubrick had sacrificed plot and meaning for visual effects and technology. Young audiences soon discovered the film, however, and it became a huge commercial success. The film inspired many, who have said

170 they became filmmakers, engineers or scientists as a result of seeing *2001*.

Even today, *2001* continues to be a part of people's lives. Films and television commercials consciously evoke its imagery, countless fans

175 post their thoughts about it on the Internet and articles like this one continue to be written about it. It is a testament to the genius and dedication of Kubrick and his crew that the future they so meticulously constructed still

180 looks so convincing.

George D. DeMet. "The Special Effects of 2001: A Space Odyssey" *palantir.net [online]* Orginally published in *DFX*, July 1999.

Question

What makes the special effects in this movie so impressive?

7 UNIT
WONDERING ABOUT WONDERS

IN THIS UNIT...

You will discover the Seven Wonders of the Ancient World, as well as other wonders from around the world. You will also explore why people leave traces. Throughout the unit, you will think about and discuss what a "wonder" means to you. As a **FINAL TASK**, you'll choose your own wonder for future generations to marvel at.

Beauty

Guiding Questions

- What is a wonder?
- Why do humans leave traces by building such outstanding things?

Wonder

MAJESTY
Grandeur

In TASK 1, you will explore the Seven Wonders of the Ancient World and the stories behind them. Storytellers are some of the world's first historians. A short video, descriptive texts and some images and maps will help you to start unearthing the past.

ACTIVITY 1

Exploring Ancient Wonders

There are many wonders in our world, both natural and man-made. What are the Seven Wonders of the Ancient World?

1 Look at the photo collage. Which wonders can you identify? Which ones belong to the original Seven Wonders of the Ancient World?

2 Try to list the original Seven Wonders.

3 Listen to the short audio text. You may follow along on the next page.

4 Then, look at the map next to the text and complete your list. Discuss as a class.

Can You Do It?

As you do the activities in this unit, be on the lookout for synonyms for the word **wonder**. How many can you find?

💬 **Talk About It!**

a) What wonders might people make lists about in the future?

b) Imagine 2,500 years from now. What kind of wonders might exist in the year 4510?

What Are These Ancient Wonders?

Have you ever heard of the Seven Wonders of the Ancient World? Most people have, but can you actually name them? Don't worry. Most people can't. There are so many impressive modern monuments, enduring historical relics and spectacular natural wonders to keep track of, that few people can actually list the seven ancient wonders off the top of their heads. To make matters worse, only one of the original seven is still standing.

The earliest known list of the seven ancient wonders was compiled by Callimachus of Cyrene, a poet, scholar and librarian. Although little is known about his life, what we do know is that he was born in North Africa and that he travelled around the Mediterranean.

Each of the Seven Wonders of the Ancient World is a testament to human ingenuity. Each one demonstrates

humankind's ability to create majestic wonders as a way of showing honour and respect.

Most of the wonders were inspired by mythology, religion or art. Ancient civilizations paid homage to their gods, kings and loved ones by accomplishing astounding architectural feats. The time span over which they were built covers about 2,500 years, starting with the Great Pyramid in around 2700 B.C.E. all the way up to the Colossus of Rhodes in the early 200s B.C.E.

Look at the map. Get ready for a whirlwind tour through the Mediterranean and the Seven Wonders of the Ancient World. ❖

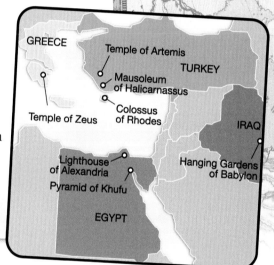

> **relic:** something cherished for its age or historic interest.
> **to keep track:** to remember or keep in order.
> **off the top of your head:** another way of saying to know something by heart, from memory.
> **human ingenuity:** the inventiveness and creativity of the human race.
> **feat:** an achievement or accomplishment.
> **time span:** a period of time.
> **whirlwind:** quick or speedy.

Culture

Counting Years

B.C. stands for **B**efore **C**hrist.

A.D. stands for **A**nno **D**omini, Latin for "in the year of the Lord." It's supposed to refer to the year of Jesus Christ's birth, but many scholars suggest that he was born earlier, around 5 B.C. Since there is **no year 0**, we jump from **1** B.C. to **1** A.D.

Over the last decades, many people have chosen to use the following terms that are more embracing of all cultures and religions.

B.C.E. refers to Before Common Era. (It's the same as B.C.)
C.E. refers to Common Era. (It's the same as A.D.)

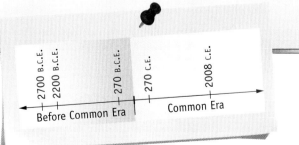

 Think About It!

Throughout the ages, man-made and natural wonders have always amazed us. Think about a place you know and love. Why is it so special to you?

ACTIVITY 2

Why Seven?

1 Take a few minutes to think about the number seven.

2 Read the *Culture* box.

3 In your group, discuss the *Talk About It!* questions.

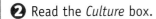

Culture

Why Seven?

Since ancient times, the number **seven** has had special significance. Here are some examples:

1. Seven days in a week
2. Seven virtues
3. Seven deadly sins
4. Seven stars make up the Big Dipper, part of the Ursa Major constellation
5. Seven heavens, according to a Islamic tradition
6. Seven-branched menorah at the temple in Jerusalem
7. Seven Sages of Greece
8. Seven seas, as in "to sail the seven seas"
9. Seven spots on a common ladybug
10. Seven symbolic steps taken by Buddha right after his birth
11. Seven books in the Harry Potter series
12. Seven colours in a rainbow
13. The opposite faces of a die add up to seven.
14. Seven external holes in the human head

> **menorah:** a candelabra; one of the oldest symbols of the Jewish people.

Can You Do It?

1. Can you name all seven items in some of the categories listed in the *Culture* box?

2. Make your own list of seven. Use one of these suggestions or propose your own.
   - Top seven TV shows
   - Top seven songs
   - Top seven movies
   - Top seven pastimes
   - Top seven music groups or artists
   - Top seven dream vacation spots

3. Share and explain your list with a classmate.

 Talk About It!

a) What makes the number seven significant?

b) Is it a lucky number for you? Why or why not?

c) Why do you suppose there are seven wonders?

The Super Seven

In this cooperative activity, you will learn more about each of the Seven Wonders of the Ancient World.

1 Read the text that has been assigned to you and complete the corresponding section of the handout.

2 Find someone who has been assigned a different text and share information. Complete the corresponding section of your handout.

3 Continue moving about the classroom sharing information until you have completed all seven sections.

4 Return to your group and share your information. Identify the Seven Wonders below.

5 Finish completing the handout.

Culture

Maarten van Heemskerck was a 16th-century Dutch artist. He is famous for his paintings of the Seven Wonders of the Ancient World.

The Pyramids of Egypt

1

Built: From about 2650 to 2500 B.C.E.

Location: Giza, Egypt, on the west bank of the Nile River near Cairo

History: The Egyptian Pyramids are the oldest of the ancient wonders and the only one that still exists. There are a total of 10 pyramids at Giza, but the first three are the best known and most acclaimed. The first one, also the largest, was erected for the **Pharaoh Khufu** and is known as the **Great Pyramid**. It rises to a height of about 42 metres. It used to be even taller, but has lost about 9 metres off its top over the years.

It's widely believed that the mammoth Khufu pyramid, which covers a land area of $5^1/_4$ hectares, took about 20 years to build. More than 100,000 labourers dragged or pushed an estimated 2.3 million limestone blocks up mud-slicked ramps to construct the royal tombs. People suggest that the pyramids' shape is an important religious statement. Many scholars think that it may have symbolized the slanting rays of the sun. Others speculate that the sloping sides were intended to help the soul of the king ascend into the sky to join the gods. ❖

Culture

The Great Sphinx of Giza was built almost 100 years after the completion of the Great Pyramid. In Arabic, it's called Abu-al Hawl, which means "Father of Terror."

A hectare is equal to 100 square metres.

Culture

Egyptians believed that the **pharaohs** were direct descendants of the gods and would enjoy eternal life after their mortal death. They also believed that the departed pharaohs would move across the skies watching over their people. Thus, the pharaohs became more important in death than in life.

Hanging Gardens of Babylon

2

Built: About 600 B.C.E.

Location: The ancient city of Babylon in Mesopotamia, which corresponds to modern-day Iraq

History: The gardens were built by **Nebuchadnezzar II** around 600 B.C.E.

Apparently, the elaborate gardens were built to cheer up the king's homesick wife. She missed her homeland with its fragrant plants and trees. She found the flat, dry terrain of Mesopotamia depressing. According to one source, the gardens covered a large area and went up 23 metres into the sky. Since Babylon rarely received rain, the vast gardens needed to be irrigated with water from the nearby Euphrates River. Slaves actually worked in shifts turning wheels to lift water from the nearby river. The water was then used to irrigate the trees, shrubs and flowers. The hanging gardens were destroyed in an earthquake after the 1st century B.C.E. ❖

mud-slicked: wet and slippery, covered with water and mud.
slanting: on an incline.
sloping: on an incline.
fragrant: perfumed and sweet-smelling.
shrub: a woody plant, smaller than a tree; bush.

The Colossus of Rhodes

3

Built: Early 200s B.C.E.

Location: Near the harbour of Rhodes, a Greek island in the Aegean Sea

History: A Greek sculptor and his apprentices worked for 12 years to build a giant bronze statue. It was built primarily in homage to the sun god, Helios. It is believed to have stood on a **promontory** overlooking the water. The bronze Colossus stood almost as high as the Statue of Liberty in New York City. It measured about 37 metres in height. Interior stone blocks and iron bars supported the hollow statue. It was the last of the ancient wonders to be built. It did not stand very long. In fact, of the seven wonders, it was the one with the shortest lifespan. A powerful earthquake destroyed it, only 56 years after it was built! ❖

shore: a riverbank or sea coast.

The Pharos (Lighthouse) of Alexandria

4

Built: About 270 B.C.E.

Location: On a small island off the coast of Alexandria, Egypt

History: The lighthouse was about 122 metres high. It was one of the tallest structures on Earth at the time. It was designed by the Greek architect, **Sostratus.** At its very top, a mirror reflected sunlight during the day. At night, a fire guided sailors to safety. Legend suggests that the mirror was also used to detect and burn enemy ships before they could reach the shore. The lighthouse was also a tourist attraction. Food was sold to visitors on the observation platform at the top of the first level. For 1,500 years, the lighthouse guided sailors into the city harbour. It was the last of the six lost wonders to disappear. Severely damaged by earthquakes in the early 1300s, it fell into the sea. In 1994, a team of archaeological scuba divers working in the Mediterranean found the ruins of the legendary lighthouse. ❖

Vocabulary Builder

Promontory refers to a high point of land or a rock projecting into the sea. Synonyms include: *peninsula, bluff, cape, point, jetty.*

Promontory comes from the Latin word *promonturium,* or *prominēre,* meaning "to project" or "stand out." By looking at where words come from, at their *etymology,* we can discover new connections. Can you think of another word that has a similar Latin root? Use a dictionary to help you.

Culture

The lighthouse of Alexandria was called **pharos** by the Greeks.

This inspired the French word for lighthouse, *phare.* It also inspired the Italian and Spanish word, *faro,* as well as the Portuguese word, *farol.*

The Temple of Artemis at Ephesus

5

History: The Temple of Artemis was one of the largest and most complex temples built in ancient times. It was built in honour of **Artemis,** the goddess of the hunt and the wilds. Artemis is sometimes known as Diana.

The temple had a marble sanctuary and a tile-covered wooden roof. It was conceived by the Greek architect, **Chersiphron,** and his son Metagenes. Inside the temple, there were two rows of at least 106 columns. Each column rose from 12 to 18 metres in height.

The original temple was burned down by a young man in 356 B.C.E. It was an act of arson. The young man proudly took credit for setting the fire, in an attempt to ensure a place in history. Eventually, the temple was rebuilt on its original foundations.

Built: About 550 B.C.E.

Location: In the Greek city of Ephesus, located on the Aegean coast of modern Turkey

A second fire devastated the rebuilt temple in 262 C.E., but its foundations and some debris have survived. Today, some of the second temple's sculptures may be viewed at the British Museum in London. ❖

Culture

Only one of the wonders of the ancient world was commissioned by a woman. All the others were sponsored by men.

Artemisia entered history when she hired architects and sculptors to build an elaborate tomb for her and her husband.

The Mausoleum at Halicarnassus

6

Built: About 353 B.C.E.

Location: In present-day Turkey

History: This enormous white marble tomb was built to hold the remains of **Mausolus,** and his wife, **Artemisia.** Two Greek architects collaborated to design the approximately 41 metre-high tomb. They were commissioned by Artemisia, along with four famous Greek sculptors. The sculptors added an ornamental frieze, or decorative band, around the outside of the structure. Word of the grandeur of the finished monument spread through the ancient world. The word "mausoleum" became synonymous with any large tomb. The building was taken down after an earthquake damaged it in the early 15th century. Only the foundations and a few pieces still remain. However, many of the mausoleum's sculptures may be viewed in the British Museum in London. ❖

The Statue of Zeus

7

Built: About 457 B.C.E.

Location: The ancient Greek city of Olympia

History: In about 450 B.C.E., the city of Olympia built a temple to honour the god **Zeus.** The Doric style of the temple was too simple for some, so a lavish 12-metre statue of Zeus was commissioned for inside. Athenian sculptor Phidias created an ivory Zeus seated on a throne, wearing a golden robe. Zeus had a wreath around his head. He held a figure of his messenger **Nike,** goddess of victory, in his right hand. In his left hand, he held a sceptre.

Some rich Greek citizens eventually decided to move the statue to a palace in Constantinople (present-day Istanbul, Turkey). This gesture prolonged its life because a fire later devastated the temple at Olympia. Sadly, the new location could not keep Zeus safe forever. A severe fire destroyed the statue in 462 C.E. Today, all that remains in Olympia are the temple's fallen columns and the foundations of the building. ❖

Culture

Olympia was the site of the first Olympic Games, held in 776 B.C.E.

Culture

The Greeks developed three architectural systems, which they called orders. Each one was distinct.

The three orders are:

1 Doric
This is the simplest of the three. It is plain looking, but sturdy.

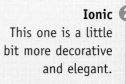

Ionic 2
This one is a little bit more decorative and elegant.

3

Corinthian
This is the most elaborately decorated of all.

lavish: elaborate, fancy.
wreath: a garland or circle of flowers or foliage.

Focus on...

The Placement of Adjectives

- In English, adjectives almost always go **before** the nouns they describe:
  Examples: **seven** *wonders, a* **round** *coliseum, an* **ancient** *ruin...*

- Sometimes, we want to describe a noun with more than one adjective. The general order is:

OPINION	Before	FACT
An opinion is what you THINK about the noun.		A fact is what is DEFINITELY TRUE about the noun.
Example: a **wonderful** *monument*		*Example: a* **natural** *wonder*

- You can also use the word "with" in your descriptions:
  Examples: – a beautiful old coin **with** *Egyptian engravings*
  – a fantastic building **with** *tall Doric columns*

- For a long string of adjectives, here is the usual order:

Determiner or number	Opinion	Appearance (size, shape, condition)	Age	Colour	Origin	Material	Noun
an	*itsy-bitsy*	*teeny-weeny*		*yellow*		*polka-dot*	bikini
two	*wonderful*	*big*	*old*		*Chinese*	*brass*	lamps

(Note, however, that sometimes this order is changed to show emphasis.)

- Look at the following examples. Notice that commas do not always separate the adjectives.
  Examples: – the seven spectacular ancient wonders [number – opinion – age]
  – a big square Egyptian pyramid [appearance – appearance – origin]

> **NOTE**
> We generally use no more than three adjectives preceding a noun.

Practise!

1. String the following adjectives together in order. Explain your reasoning.
   a) [an – marble – white – enormous] tomb
   b) [fantastic – modern – a – Egyptian] wonder

2. Use as many adjectives as possible to describe the following nouns.
   a) a friend   c) a pastime
   b) a type of food   d) a type of music

Can You Do It?

Look back through the texts from this Activity:
1. Find seven examples of nouns with one descriptor.
2. Find seven other examples of nouns with two or more descriptors.

How the Wonders Were Chosen

In this activity, you will learn about and discuss the three main criteria that were used to define the Seven Wonders of the Ancient World.

1 Read the three criteria used to define the Seven Wonders of the Ancient World.

2 Discuss them in your group using the *Talk About It!* questions.

3 Write your answers on the handout.

Grandeur

◆ Impressive or awesome

◆ Exalted in some deliberate way

◆ Prestigious (well-known constructions rather than obscure ones)

◆ Unique (one of a kind or a first of its kind)

Vision *and* Purpose

◆ The construction of each wonder came from "special" inspiration (vision).

◆ Each wonder had an important use or intention (purpose).

Examples of vision and purpose: serving as a tomb, paying homage to a god or bringing beauty into the world

Size, Design *and* Craftsmanship

◆ Unequalled nature of the construction

◆ Imposing, mammoth dimensions

◆ Inventive and skilful configuration

Vocabulary Builder

The word *criteria* is plural. The singular is *criterion*.

A similar example is the plural *phenomena*, which is *phenomenon* in the singular.

---

exalted: revered or sacred; held in high regard.
craftsmanship: skill and fine artistry in building or making things.

 Talk About It!

a) What do you think about the criteria that were used? Can these criteria still be used to describe wonders today? Explain why or why not.

b) What other ways of defining a wonder could you add?

Write About It!

Which of the Seven Wonders of the Ancient World would you choose to visit? Why? In your text, use at least two strings of adjectives.

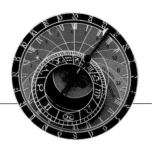

In this task, you will uncover two disciplines that dig into the past. History explores the stories of people and places. Historians dig mostly through books and archives. On the other hand, archaeologists actually excavate hidden or buried information.

ACTIVITY 1

Caring About the Past

The study of history provides a window into the past. Peering through this window can help you understand the present. In short, the past provides us with chapters of the human story. In this activity you explore the question: Why does history matter?

to peer: to look.

❶ Read the quotations.

❷ Watch the interview with Gabriel Tordjman.

❸ Read the text *Why Should We Study History?*

❹ Write down your thoughts about why history might be important on the handout.

❺ Share your thoughts and ideas with a partner.

"... to converse with [people] of other centuries is almost the same as [travelling]."

– René Descartes "Father of Modern Philosophy"

Why Should We Study History?

There are many different reasons to study history. First of all, it's fun. It includes heroes from sports, music and entertainment. Peacemakers and warriors, men and women, are all represented in stories that move us through time and take us on journeys around the world. History can be humorous as well as serious. Read the five reasons to study history presented below. Think about them. Your opinion about history just might change. History:

- Helps you uncover how the world of today has come about.

- Exercises your critical thinking skills, teaching you to ask the right questions and providing you with good reasons for your own opinions. It teaches you to think.

- Lets you travel in time by examining stories from the past, showing you that our way of thinking and living is not the only way.

- Teaches you about human behaviour and shows you how amazing and inspiring people can be, as well as how terrible and destructive.

- Enables us all to become better citizens of our ever-expanding global village, allowing us to make better decisions about our future.

"Those who cannot learn from history are doomed to repeat it."

– George Santayana American philosopher, poet and novelist

Reading or Digging

Have you ever wondered what archaeologists really do? How does their work overlap and intersect with that of historians? Let's find out.

❶ Read the *Fact Sheet* with a partner.

❷ Look for the similarities and differences between historians and archaeologists,

and create a Venn diagram together with your partner.

❸ Compare your Venn diagram with another pair.

Fact Sheet

- **Archaeology**, like **history**, may be defined as the study of the past.

- Both disciplines interpret the past but they use different tools.

- A major difference between the two is that **archaeology** deals with *concrete evidence* more than *written records*. Archaeologists search for clues about ancient cultures. They try to understand how these cultures developed, lived and died.

- We have not been able to examine the written clues of some ancient civilizations because:
  - They followed an oral tradition or their records were destroyed.
  - Their records have not yet been discovered.

  In these situations, **archaeologists** must study and reconstruct the past using evidence they uncover.

- *Artifacts* are the heart of **archaeology**. Artifacts are *remnants* of the past and range from *buildings* and *cities*, to *clay pots* and *tools*, to *mummies* and *tombs*.

- **Historians** do a lot of *research* and *reading*. They look for connections and new interpretations of *existing sources*, but **archaeologists** must uncover and piece together hidden clues from the past. **Historians** may study artifacts, too, but only those that are easily accessible. They may go to *museums*, *antique stores* or even *people's homes* to consult primary sources.

- **Archaeologists** search for primary sources that are *buried*. They conduct careful *excavations* and document their findings. *Digging, collecting, labelling* and *analyzing data* are activities at the core of this discipline. ❖

ICT

1. Do you recognize your "cousin" at the top of this page?

2. How old do you think she is?

Don't know the answers? Try doing an Internet search. Use "Lucy" as your keyword. Don't forget the quotes around her name.

A Heritage to Discover

In TASK 3, you will think about what heritage means to you and what is being done to protect world heritage.

ACTIVITY 1

A World to Discover

In this activity, you will explore what heritage means to you and others. You will share a part of your heritage with some classmates and learn about their heritage, too.

1 Consult the *Vocabulary Builder* box.

2 Read the text about heritage below.

3 Think about what heritage means to you.

4 Think about some words to describe heritage.

5 Answer the *Talk About It!* questions.

Vocabulary Builder

Synonyms for heritage include:

- *ancestry*
- *birthright*
- *patrimony*
- *legacy*

Can you find at least four others? Use a thesaurus.

heirloom: a piece of property that has been in a family for one or more generations.

HERITAGE

*H*eritage may be many things, but in this unit, heritage refers to something that is passed down from one generation to another. It can be something material, like a house, or something immaterial, like a tradition or a story. It depends on the context. It includes your grandmother's special recipe, your dad's high school pictures and the songs your family sings on holidays. You might be amazed; it also extends to old churches and majestic mountains.

Heritage is where you and your family come from. Remember, it can be about both places and customs. So an actual region, like the Gaspé region, may be part of your heritage, and traditional folk dances, too.

Heritage is about your ancestors, both your blood relations and the entire human family. Think about the places and things that surround you. Is there a building or monument that comes to mind? What about a lake or forest? Heritage includes places that have significance because of the stories behind them or because of the beauty they manifest. World heritage is something that extends beyond your family. It touches the global community.

Read on to discover more about our shared world heritage. ❖

Talk About It!

a) What place or tradition would you want to share and protect? Explain.

b) What heirloom would you like to bring to class? (Remember, you may include concrete items or intangible traditions.) Explain your choice.

c) What connections can you make with wonders?

Go to pp. 194-195 to learn about Canada's World Heritage Sites.

ACTIVITY 2

United as Nations

The United Nations is an organization of independent states that was formed in 1945. Its main goal is to promote international peace and security. UNESCO was created that same year.
Read on to discover UNESCO's role in protecting world heritage.

❶ Read the text below.

❷ Answer the questions about Canada's World Heritage Sites on the handout.

UNESCO
and World Heritage

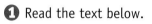

In 1972, a convention concerning the protection of World Cultural and Natural Heritage was held. Certain places were deemed of "outstanding universal value," forming part of the common heritage of all humanity. Protecting world heritage is a concern for us all. It's the responsibility of the entire international community. That means you and me. Monuments, natural sites and a range of cultural expression (referred to as intangible culture) are waiting to be explored. The World Heritage List now boasts more than 851 entries. Information and education are both key issues, so get informed. A global legacy is waiting to be discovered. Go and consult UNESCO's World Heritage list. The sites are listed by country. Explore a legacy from the past. Learn about the wealth we have to pass on to future generations. ❖

Culture

UNESCO stands for the **U**nited **N**ations **E**ducational, **S**cientific and **C**ultural **O**rganization. It's based in Paris, but has more than 50 field offices, and many specialized institutes and centres all over the world.

The main goal of UNESCO is to contribute to global peace and security by encouraging international collaboration through education, science and culture.

to deem: to form or have an opinion; think or judge.
to boast: to proudly display.

Culture

Did you know that...?

• Canada has 14 sites on UNESCO's World Heritage list.

• The historic district of Old Quebec, including the Château Frontenac and the Citadel, is on the list.

• Miguasha National Park on the Gaspé Peninsula and the Rideau Canal in Ottawa are the most recent Canadian additions to the list.

Talk About It!

a) Do you believe that UNESCO plays an important role in the world? Explain why or why not.

b) Do you think that collaborating to protect world heritage can help break down cultural borders? Why or why not?

ACTIVITY 3

From Then 'til Now

Now it's time to learn about a new list with new wonders and how one man is working to inform and protect world heritage.

❶ Read the following short text.

❷ Read the *Think About It!* questions aloud with your group. Take a few moments to reflect.

❸ Now share your thoughts and discuss the *Talk About It!* questions with your group.

❹ Use your handout to guide your discussion and help you keep on track.

SEVEN NEW WONDERS

July 7, 2007 marked the official declaration of the New Seven Wonders of the World in Lisbon, Portugal. This contest encouraged people to nominate and then vote for a wonder of their choice. It was the brainchild of Swiss-born Canadian Bernard Weber a filmmaker, museum curator, aviator and explorer.

Weber's foundation organized the contest to "protect humankind's heritage across the globe." The poll attracted almost 100 million votes. Despite its good intentions and the generally positive response, the competition met with some criticism. UNESCO, which administers the World Heritage sites program, Bernard Weber suggested that the competition would change very little in the long run. UNESCO issued a statement saying, "This initiative cannot, in any significant and sustainable manner, contribute to the preservation of sites elected by [the] public." ❖

Bernard Weber

 Talk About It!

a) What do you think? Do you agree with the statement by UNESCO?

b) Discuss the benefits of an Internet poll. Would you participate in such a survey? Do you think it could make a real difference?

 Think About It!

Imagine travelling back in time to visit the ancient wonders and then back to the present day.

a) How would these wonders compare with today's achievements?

b) What modern wonders would you choose to compare them with?

brainchild: an original idea or plan.
poll: a survey.

My Wonder

What is a wonder to you? What single wonder will you choose? What media will you use to create your sales pitch and sell your wonder to the rest of the class? Get ready to choose, describe and defend your wonder. That's your FINAL TASK!

In Preparation 📋

❶ In preparation for the FINAL TASK, read the text below. It will help you choose and define your wonder.

❷ Answer the questions on the handout, then move on to the next page.

Different Wonders, Different Intentions?

The modern world is evolving so quickly. The structures and monuments that humankind is now able to create certainly surpass those of the past, according to certain criteria. But what about context? The original seven wonders were certainly remarkable for their time. Do you think that the time frame or context should be considered when discussing wonders? Remember that the criteria from the distant past reflected an early world of kings and queens, and pharaohs and mythical gods. So, do the criteria of **grandeur, vision and purpose, size, design,** and **craftsmanship** still apply? Can you think of any criteria you might add?

In addition, if the categories have evolved, then we must redefine or expand the notion of a wonder. Different wonders may necessitate different criteria. Think about natural wonders, such as Percé Rock for example. Located just off the tip of the Gaspé Peninsula, it is one of the largest and most spectacular natural arches in the world. It certainly

satisfies the criterion of size. Its beauty and splendour make it one of the most important tourist attractions in Quebec. What do you think? Is it a wonder?

The Canadian Broadcasting Corporation (CBC) conducted its own Internet poll. More than 25,000 wonders were nominated and over 1 million votes cast. Nominations included natural wonders, modern constructions and even the Montreal bagel!

Now it's your turn to propose a wonder in the existing category of ancient wonders or in a new category. You might choose a technological wonder, an artistic masterpiece or something else. The choice is yours. In this FINAL TASK, you will choose, categorize and defend your wonder. ❖

My Wonder

What to Do

1 In your group, discuss different potential wonders. List them on the handout.

2 Share your thoughts about criteria and how to choose a wonder.
Write your criteria on the handout.

3 Share your ideas about a medium, too.
- Do you think a poem or short text would be effective?
- Would you prefer to create a poster or a PowerPoint presentation?
- What about a brochure or an advertisement?

4 Choose your wonder and your medium.

5 Put it all together and sell your wonder.
Follow the steps of the **Production Process** on the next page.

Production Process

GETTING READY TO CREATE

- Take the time to review the handouts you have completed throughout this unit.
- Use the checklist on the handout to make sure you know the requirements of the task.
- Define the criteria you will use and choose your wonder.
- Do any necessary research.
- Select and organize your ideas.
- Decide which medium you will use.

CREATING YOUR SALES PITCH

- Create your rough draft.
- Don't forget to express the reasons you chose your wonder.
- Remember, you're out to sell it!
- Use your creativity.
- Try to think of a catchy slogan.

REVISING

- Read your text to see if the ideas are complete, coherent and well organized.
- Vary your vocabulary.
- Pay special attention to adjective placement.
- Ask someone for feedback.
- Make any necessary changes to your text.

EDITING

- Use resources to help you correct any grammar and spelling errors.

PUBLISHING AND/OR PRESENTING

- Make sure that your final copy is neat and clear.
- If you are presenting your work orally, practise your sales pitch.
- Be dynamic. If you want people to "buy" your wonder, then you need to convince them.

You might want to make a series of memo cards. You learned how to do this in **Unit 2**. Refer to the Toolkit in your book.

Look Back

- You should be able to recognize the images in the opening pages.

- You should be able to explain why the title was chosen for this unit.

Think About It

- Think about the future for a moment. Can you imagine anything that could be considered a future wonder?

- Think about life in ancient times. If you could travel in time, is there a period and place you would like to visit?

Now What?

- Answer the Guiding Questions at the beginning of the unit.

- Is there something or someone in the unit you would like to know more about?

Select some of your work for your portfolio!

3 Name three things you have learned.

2 List two new vocabulary words or expressions you have learned.

1 Name one good reason to preserve world heritage.

OTHER THINGS TO DO

Explore an interactive archaeological website. Try the keywords archaeology + interactive sites. Then go and explore different sites and places.

Represent one of the ancient wonders through art. Let your creative side shine. You might make a model of the Great Pyramid, a "papyrus" scroll with hieroglyphic writing, a drawing or painting of the Hanging Gardens of Babylon, etc.

Many dramas and documentaries have been made about historical events. Find a film that interests you. Watch history come alive. Write a film review and share it with a friend.

Write a myth or legend about one of the wonders.

The Epic of Gilgamesh is perhaps the oldest written story on Earth. It comes to us from Mesopotamia, known as the "cradle of civilization," which broadly corresponds to modern-day Iraq and Syria. The epic was originally written on 12 clay tablets in cuneiform script. It is about the adventures of the historical King of Uruk (somewhere between 2750 and 2500 B.C.E.).

The Story of Gilgamesh

(retold by Elisa Shenkier)

1 Gilgamesh was the King of Uruk. His father was mortal and his mother was a goddess. However, because he was part mortal, Gilgamesh would eventually die. Throughout the legend, Gilgamesh battled with his own mortality.

In the beginning, Gilgamesh was a bad ruler. His subjects were terribly unhappy and they asked the
5 gods for help. So the gods created a man, Enkidu. Enkidu came from the wilderness. He was covered with hair, wild like the wilderness. He ate grass with the gazelles and drank water with the animals. A young man, frightened by the sight of Enkidu, asked his father what to do.

His father advised him to go to Uruk and tell Gilgamesh. Then he told his son to find a woman to help them lure Enkidu to civilization. The son did what he was told.

10 A woman came and taught Enkidu the ways of human beings and civilization. Then she spoke about King Gilgamesh and his strength. Enkidu also heard stories about Gilgamesh's bad behaviour as ruler of Uruk. He decided to challenge Gilgamesh to a fight in order to force him to behave properly. When they met, they struggled long and hard, but finally Gilgamesh won. Enkidu then recognized Gilgamesh as a true king and the men became the best of friends.

15 Gilgamesh longed to perform great deeds, so that his name would be remembered. He was always seeking immortality. He wanted to go to the cedar forest and kill the guardian monster, Humbaba. Enkidu was terrified because he knew the monster. Gilgamesh insisted; Enkidu finally agreed, and they prepared for the journey.

When they entered into the cedar forest, Enkidu's hand became paralyzed as he touched the gate.
20 Gilgamesh helped his friend. They had terrible nightmares while in the forest, but still continued their search for Humbaba. When the monster finally appeared, the friends fought him and emerged victorious.

Gilgamesh Represented In Chaldean Seal

---

cuneiform: an ancient form of writing that uses wedge-shaped letters.
lure: to charm, attract or captivate.
deed: an achievement or accomplishment.

After the battle, Gilgamesh bathed and put on clean clothes and his crown. He was a very handsome man. He was so attractive that Ishtar, the goddess of love, wanted to marry him. He rudely refused.
25 This hurt and angered Ishtar. She went to her father and demanded that he punish Gilgamesh. Soon after, Gilgamesh's best friend fell ill. Enkidu got sicker and sicker and then died. When he was sick, he cursed the woman who had led him to civilization, Gilgamesh and death itself. However, he forgave everyone just before dying. He had decided that the joy of his friendship with Gilgamesh was worth any cost.

30 Gilgamesh was distraught with grief and denial of death. He despaired over the loss of his best friend, but also feared for his own death. He now understood that his day would come. Seeking to avoid death, Gilgamesh set out on a quest for Utnapishtim, the only human being who had been granted eternal life by the gods. He wanted to learn the secret of how to avoid death.

Eventually, Gilgamesh came to the entrance of the land of the gods, an otherworld guarded by a man-
35 scorpion and his mate. Gilgamesh was able to impress the scorpions with his strength and courage, and so they let him pass. He continued his quest for the secrets of life and death. On his way, he met a divine winemaker, Siduri. She offered him shelter and advice. She encouraged him to accept his human fate and enjoy life, but he still insisted on continuing his journey. Siduri took pity on Gilgamesh and pointed him to the island where Utnapishtim lived with his wife, protected by the Waters of Death.

40 When Gilgamesh arrived, Utnapishtim told him his story. It was the story of a flood (remarkably similar to the flood story in Genesis). Utnapishtim said that he had received a warning before the flood because he was a good man. He had been instructed to build a great ark, to gather his family and to collect each kind of animal and plant. After the flood, the gods descended and bestowed immortality on Utnapishtim and his wife. Gilgamesh was deeply saddened when he realized that he would never be
45 immortal. Utnapishtim felt bad for Gilgamesh and told him about a sea plant that could make him young again, if not immortal. Gilgamesh dove into the sea to pick the plant, only to lose it later. While resting on his journey home to Uruk, a snake slithered up and ate the plant of youth. Gilgamesh returned to Uruk a changed man. He had become a good friend and just ruler. The immortality he sought was achieved through the city he had built, the courage he had shown and the good he had
50 done. When death finally came for Gilgamesh, he was mourned by all the people of Uruk.

Question

Why do myths and legends exist?

---

to curse: to put a malediction on someone or something.
to bestow: to give a special gift or privilege.
to mourn: to feel sadness when someone dies, to miss and remember someone who died.

Canada's World Heritage Sites

The following map shows the names and geographical locations of all 14 of the existing Canadian World Heritage sites. They cover a huge land area, touching most of the provinces and territories. Take a moment to look at the map. Notice how both natural wonders and human constructions are included. Read on to discover an incredible wonder that resides on an archipelago *in western Canada. Then, continue across the country for an introduction to some of the other sites.*

Canada's Existing World Heritage Sites

SGang Gwaay

This incomparable specimen of Haida culture endures on a remote island beach in British Columbia's Gwaii Haanas (*Place of Wonder*) National Park Reserve. It's an extraordinary example of Haida ingenuity, art and culture dating back 10,000 years.

There's an unforgettable collection of 28 memorial and mortuary poles in this village, as well as the remains of large cedar longhouses dating back to the mid-19th century. The village was occupied until shortly after 1880. This collection of poles, the largest assemblage of its kind in North America, pays silent homage to past Haida chiefs and their decision not to use preservatives on these sacred objects. "The site commemorates the living culture of the Haida, based on fishing and hunting, and their relationship with the land and sea, and offers a visual key to their oral traditions. What survives is unique in the world, a 19th-century Haida village where the ruins of houses and memorial or mortuary poles illustrate the power and artistry of Haida society."

---

archipelago: a group or chain of islands, as in the Queen Charlotte islands off the northwest coast of British Columbia.

longhouse: a building constructed by a variety of native peoples in different parts of North America. It sometimes extends over 100 metres in length, hence its name.

Nahanni National Park

This park, located in the Northwest Territories, is home to the Nahanni River, one of the most spectacular wild rivers in North America.The undisturbed natural area displays deep river canyons cutting through majestic mountain ranges, in addition to huge waterfalls and complex cave systems. The geomorphology of the park is remarkable, demonstrating a wide range of form and the complex nature of evolution.

Canadian Rocky Mountain Parks

These Albertan mountain parks are renowned for their scenic splendour and biological diversity. They include Banff, Jasper, Kootenay and Yoho national parks as well as Mount Robson, Mount Assiniboine and Hamber provincial parks. They provide classic illustrations of glacial geological processes that are found throughout the area, including icefields, remnant valley glaciers, canyons and prime examples of erosion and deposition.

Wood Buffalo National Park

The park, located in northeastern Alberta and southern Northwest Territories, includes some of the largest undisturbed meadows left in North America. It is the largest national park in Canada. It provides a crucial habitat for the world's largest herd of wood bison, a threatened species. It's also the only place in North America where the predator-prey relationship between wolves and wood bison has continued, unbroken, over time.

Dinosaur Provincial Park

This park contains some of the most important fossil specimens discovered from the period of Earth's history known as the "Age of Dinosaurs." Thirty-nine dinosaur species have been uncovered here and more than 500 specimens have been taken out for exhibition in museums around the world.

Historic District of Quebec City

Quebec City was founded by French explorer Samuel de Champlain in 1608. July 3, 2008 marked the celebration of its 400th anniversary. Almost half the buildings in the Historic District were built prior to 1850 and many date back to the initial founding of the city. Old Quebec is unique; it's the only walled city in North America. This beautiful example of a fortified city is comprised of two parts: the Upper Town and the Lower Town.

L'Anse aux Meadows National Historic Site

This remarkable archaeological site is located at the northernmost tip of Newfoundland. These excavated remains of an 11th-century Viking settlement are virtually identical to similar traces found in Greenland and Iceland from the same time period. This site provides a unique glimpse into human history and migration, showing evidence of the earliest known European presence on the American continent.

UNESCO Convention Concerning the Protection of the World Cultural and Natural Heritage
World Heritage Committee, Thirtieth Session, Vilnius, Lithuania, July 8-16, 2006

Question

Which site on the map would you like to learn more about?

geomorphology: the study of the characteristics, origin and development of landforms.
meadow: a grassland or prairie.

What's in a List?

The ancient Greeks loved making lists. People today still make lists. Not only are things easier to remember when organized into groups, but the simple act of organizing can be psychologically satisfying. Apparently it was so to the ancients, and it still is to us. One of the most enduring lists ever written is that of the "Seven Wonders of the World." Compiled as a list of architectural and artistic marvels, it represents nearly 2,000 years of ancient Mediterranean culture.

People often refer to the list of wonders that occurs in a poem by **Antipater of Sidon**, a Greek epigrammatist who lived around 100 B.C.E. Others assert that the most famous classical list comes from **Philon of Byzantium**, an obscure writer who lived from around 280 to 220 B.C.E. His short account called *The Seven Sights of the World* was essentially a travel guide for fellow Athenians. However, the earliest known list was actually compiled by the scholar Callimachus of Cyrene, who lived from 305 to 240 B.C.E. He was the Chief Librarian in Alexandria, Egypt and he wrote A *Collection of Wonders Around the World*. He is thought to have written more than 800 books during his 20 years as Chief Librarian. Sadly, everything was lost when a series of fires ravaged his works and innumerable other manuscripts.

Culture

An **epigram** is a short poem. It is supposed to be witty and concise. Originally, epigrams were found on statues of athletes, funeral monuments and in sanctuaries. The following example demonstrates the epigrammatist's clever, narrative approach:

You're rich and young, as all confess,
And none denies your loveliness;
But when we hear your boastful tongue
You're neither pretty, rich, nor young.

– Martial (Latin poet)

Question

What kind of lists do people make today?

---

boastful: bragging, pretentious, egotistical.

Ancient Egyptian Bird

The Canteen of the Gods.

Culture

According to Greek mythology, **Mount Olympus** was home to the Greek gods and Zeus was their supreme ruler. The gods lived in palaces surrounded by clouds. Everyday, they would go to the Great Hall and feast. They would eat **ambrosia** and drink nectar. The word **ambrosia** comes from two Greek words: *a* meaning "not" and *mbrotos* meaning "mortal". So ambrosia was the delectable food of the immortals, non-humans who could live forever.

Question

Which of these cartoons do you like best? Explain your choice.

IT'S DEBATABLE!

IN THIS PROJECT...

You will learn all about debates: what they are and when they're used. You will learn how to go about debating effectively and... how to win your case.

Pick a subject, prepare your arguments and bring out the gavel. The jury is ready. The issue is sizzling! It's debatable!

"I think debating in high school and college is most valuable training whether for politics, the law, business, or for service on community committees. (...)
A good debater must not only study material in support of his own case, but he must also, of course, thoroughly analyze the expected argument of his opponent. The give and take of debating, the testing of ideas, is essential to democracy."

– John F. Kennedy, August 22, 1960

GOAL

To organize and carry out a class debate on the topic of your choice or on one provided by your teacher.

People debate each and every day. Debates take place in Parliament, during meetings at school and even in your house! Yes, that argument you had with your parents over your allowance is a debate... when you are being polite, are well prepared and have convincing arguments, of course!

Where, when, how, with whom we debate and on what subject might vary, but in the end, debating is always used for the same reason: **to try to change someone else's mind about something.** We debate to **convince** and **persuade**.

If you learn how to debate, the benefits will be endless. It will make you a better writer, speaker and negotiator. It might prepare you for a career in law or politics... and it will certainly help you be more convincing with your parents when it comes time to negotiate your curfew or use of the car!

Vocabulary Builder

Do you know the difference between these words?

- *Discuss, argue, debate, dispute:* They all mean to talk with others in an effort to reach an agreement, to ascertain the truth or to convince.

- *Discuss* involves close examination and a sharing of opinions.

- *Argue* emphasizes the presentation of opposing opinions.

- *Debate* involves formal, organized argumentation, often in public.

- *Dispute* implies differences of opinion and confrontation.

So, what exactly is a debate?

A formal debate is like a game. Two sets of participants face off against each other in a verbal duel. Each team tries to convince an audience that their point of view is better. That's how they "win" the debate. As in every game, there are rules to follow. In this project, you'll be learning these rules and preparing for a class debate.

Learning to debate properly can help you everywhere, anywhere and at any point in your life! Voicing an opinion by basing it on facts makes all the difference between a complainer and someone who just might convince us of his or her point of view!

1. **Decide** on the topic of the debate.

2. **Brainstorm** about the topic and list as many arguments as possible for both sides.

3. **Research** your side of the issue.

4. **Prepare** your arguments.

5. **Organize** your information in preparation for the debate.

6. **Give it your best shot.**

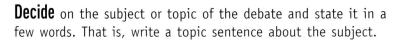

STEP 1

Decide on the subject or topic of the debate and state it in a few words. That is, write a topic sentence about the subject.

If your topic is imposed by your teacher, you still need to formulate your position in a topic sentence.

Here's an example:

Topic	Topic Sentence
Voting age	The voting age should be changed to 16.
	The voting age should remain at 18.

Tips
- It doesn't matter which side of the issue you're on. A good debater can argue anything... and win!
- A good debater uses **facts, not emotions.** Personal feelings should be left out of a debate.

Brainstorm about your topic.

Try to find as many **pros** and **cons** as possible.
- **Pros** are arguments in favour of the topic sentence.
- **Cons** are arguments against it.

Here are some possible arguments regarding the voting age:

a) *Teenagers are more intelligent than adults.*

b) *Teenagers are interested in politics.*

c) *Teenagers are allowed to drive at the age of 16.*

d) *Teenagers rarely read newspapers.*

e) *Teenagers are immature at 16.*

f) *Some teenagers work and pay taxes.*

g) *Teenagers use public services, such as public transportation and hospitals.*

h) *At 16, teenagers are dependent on parents.*

i) *Teenagers can legally quit school at 16.*

Talk About It!

a) Which of the examples given above are **pros** and which ones are **cons**?
   Are they all facts?

b) What other arguments could you propose for either side?

Tips
- Write down EVERYTHING that crosses your mind.
- Think about all the possible arguments, on both sides, so that you'll be ready for anything.

Research your side of the issue.

You need to back up your ideas with examples, statistics, quotes from public figures and, in fact, anything that proves your point. This is really the most important part of the debate and your guarantee of success.

PLAGIARISM

All of the following are considered plagiarism:

- Turning in someone else's work as your own
- Copying words or ideas from someone else without giving credit
- Failing to put a quotation in quotation marks
- Changing words but copying the sentence structure of a source without giving credit
- Copying so many words or ideas from a source that it makes up the majority of your work, whether you give credit or not

Most cases of plagiarism can be avoided by citing sources. Acknowledging that certain material has been borrowed and providing your audience with the original sources is usually enough to prevent an accusation of plagiarism.

RELIABLE SOURCES

It is extremely important to make sure that the source you are using is reliable. To evaluate the reliability of your information, you need to check up on the author and the publication. They need to be credible. Just because someone is an expert in the field of biology does not mean that his/her opinion on politics is credible.

Who is the person? Can we trust what they say? What is their background?

Remember, anybody can create a website and write an opinion! It does not mean they are credible!

Tips

Make sure your sources are reliable and avoid plagiarism!

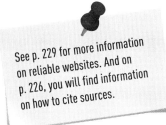

See p. 229 for more information on reliable websites. And on p. 226, you will find information on how to cite sources.

Prepare your arguments carefully.

Review your research and take notes.

Tips

Refer back to **Unit 2** on p. 50 to review how to prepare note cards effectively.

Avoid the following when preparing your arguments:

- **Ad hominem remarks**
  Attacking the person who is speaking instead of their arguments
- **Getting on the bandwagon**
  Saying something is true because everybody is saying it
- **Restatement**
  Repeating the same opinion over and over using different words

The Roles

As a class, you will need to choose a moderator and a timekeeper.

MODERATOR

The moderator introduces the topic of the debate and presents the team members at the beginning of the debate. He/she also introduces each speaker during the debate. The moderator may intervene during the debate and call the debaters to order. The moderator is neutral.

TIMEKEEPER

The timekeeper makes sure everybody respects the time limits. He/she warns speakers when they have one minute left and when their time is up. The timekeeper is also neutral.

As a team, you will need to decide who holds the following positions. If there are not enough members to assume <u>all</u> the positions, one person can do two jobs.

Here are the "job openings" for the debate:

LEAD DEBATER

The lead debater presents the team's point of view, as well as the points and the proof found during the research.

QUESTION ASKER

The question asker interrogates the other team about <u>their</u> points of view.

QUESTION ANSWERER

The question answerer responds to the questions asked by the other team.

CLOSER

The closer summarizes the team's position, responds to any new issues that are raised during the debate and ends the debate.

Organize your information in preparation for the debate. There is no need to memorize anything. To be convincing, you must know what you are talking about, not read from a sheet!

Give it your best shot!

No, they don't make toasters...

Toastmasters International is a non-profit organization that helps members develop communication skills.

Most clubs have approximately 20 members who meet regularly to practise public speaking techniques and leadership skills.

Each meeting is structured, and includes an evaluation session where feedback is given in a positive manner.

Toastmasters International also sponsors a Youth Leadership Program.

What It Takes to Be a Great Debater

1. Be prepared.
2. Take good notes.
3. Don't speak too loudly or too softly.
4. Take your time. Don't speak too fast.
5. Stand up straight. Don't fidget.
6. Use your hands. Be dynamic.
7. Move around. Don't just stand there!
8. Don't chew gum or on a pen. We need to hear you clearly!
9. Use your note cards. Don't read from a sheet.
10. Practise, practise, practise!

The Rules

When debating, the main rule is: <u>Be respectful!</u>
1. Address your opponents with respect.
2. Never attack a person, only their arguments.
3. If your opponent's argument is flawed, show it! That's how you win a debate.
4. Be quiet when others are speaking.
5. Wait your turn to speak. It might be tempting to respond to something they are saying, but wait. You will get your chance!

Tips

Remember, you are being judged at ALL times! Your behaviour during the debate is just as important as your arguments!

How a Debate Works

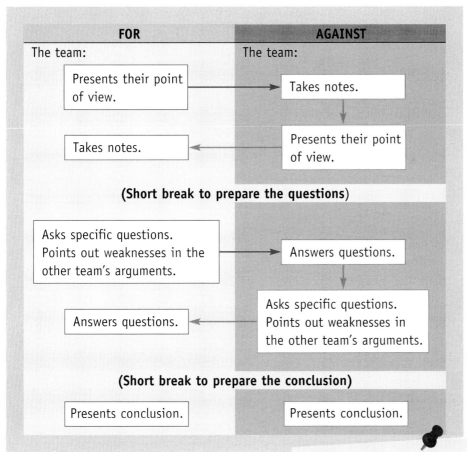

FOR	AGAINST
The team:	The team:
Presents their point of view.	Takes notes.
Takes notes.	Presents their point of view.
(Short break to prepare the questions)	
Asks specific questions. Points out weaknesses in the other team's arguments.	Answers questions.
Answers questions.	Asks specific questions. Points out weaknesses in the other team's arguments.
(Short break to prepare the conclusion)	
Presents conclusion.	Presents conclusion.

> **Tips**
> - When your team is not presenting, it is important to pay close attention and take notes.
> - What the other team is saying can help you! It might build your case and give you good ideas.
> - Your notes will come in handy when it comes time to ask questions and present your conclusion.

> Your conclusion is your last chance to shine! Summarize your position, remind everyone of your arguments and, again, be convincing!

Winning

The team that has presented the strongest case will win the debate. But, how do we determine who has presented the strongest case?

That will be up to your classmates to decide. They will be THE JURY!

Jurors

The jurors will vote for the side that they believe was most convincing.

They will look for the team that:

- has shown the greatest understanding of the issue
- has provided the best evidence, examples and statistics
- has asked the best questions, ones that exposed the other team's weaknesses
- has answered the questions with the most conviction
- presented the best overall debates, including the way they spoke, moved around and used gestures, as well as the way they showed respect

2
PROJECT

In the Limelight!

IN THIS PROJECT...

You will learn how to do a role play and step informally into the limelight!

"With any part you play, there is a certain amount of yourself in it."

– Johnny Depp

"All the world's a stage, and all the men and women merely players.

They have their exits and their entrances and one man in his time plays many parts."

– William Shakespeare
(*Much Ado About Nothing*)

Culture

Did You Know...?

Limelight was used as stage lighting in theatres and music halls before electric lighting. This lighting was created by an intense flame directed at a cylinder of calcium carbonate (called limestone).

Even though limelight is not used anymore, the expression "in the limelight" has survived. It means "in the public eye" or "in the spotlight."

GOAL

To organize and carry out a role play on the topic of your choice, or on one provided by your teacher.

What is a role play?

As young children, you may have played games like cops and robbers or cowboys and Indians. This was a form of role-playing. And surely you played house, store or doctor! This, too, was role-playing. Without calling it role-playing, many of us continue to use some form of role play in our daily lives. When we are faced with a dilemma, it sometimes helps to practise different scenarios by ourselves (in front of a mirror perhaps) or with a friend. That's also a form of role-playing. Job interviewers, first-aid instructors and the military all use simulation activities, which are still other forms of role-playing.

Putting yourself in another person's shoes can give you an entirely new perspective and help you understand the other person's point of view. It can also allow you to be someone else for a moment and do things you might not normally do. It helps develop creativity, problem-solving and social skills.

In role-playing activities in the classroom, each student assumes the role of a specific character and every character is involved in a specific situation. A role-playing activity may involve preparation and practice or it might be more spontaneous. Whatever the case, it involves you acting out a part and interacting with other characters. In other words, it's you, stepping into the limelight!

But... I hate speaking in front of people!

Role-playing is very different from giving a speech or a theatrical performance. There are no scripts to learn by heart and no rehearsals. It's done in small groups and is more like participating in a discussion than giving a performance! When you "role-play," you become someone else. You put yourself in someone else's shoes. It's not about you! Therefore, you cannot be judged on what you say, because you are not saying it: your character is!

Culture

- There are many types of role-playing games. A lot of them are based on fantasy. One of the most popular was created in the 1970s and is still very popular today. Can you guess which game it is?

- There are also lots of role-playing games on the Internet. Do you know any of them?

Role-playing has been around for a very long time. It was used by ancient Romans and medieval Europeans who organized enactments of past events.

💬 Talk About It!

a) How many other examples of role-playing games or activities can you think of?

b) Do you or any people you know engage in any role-playing games?

c) Why do you think role-playing games are popular?

d) Do you think role-playing can be useful? If so, when and how?

① **Get to know** your character.

② **Look** at the situation of the role play.

③ **Put it all together.**

④ **Present** your role play.

⑤ **Evaluate** your participation and **reflect** on the role play.

Role-playing will help you become a better story writer. By putting yourself in your character's shoes, you will create more interesting characters with greater depth. You can take the skills you learn in this role-playing project and use them the next time you have a story to write!

STEP 1

Get to know your character.

Sometimes, the character you will be impersonating is a real person or a character from a story; at other times, you'll have to create an entire persona. Whether you have a lot of time to prepare or just a few minutes, you can still get to know your character. The more you know about your character and what makes him/her tick, the better prepared you will be.

So, how do I do this?

1. If you were given a character card, begin by reading the information it contains. If you don't have one, consider making your own.

2. Take a few minutes to jot down everything you know about your character.

3. Read and answer the questions on the next page.

4. Define your character's personality by making a list of his/her character traits. There is a list on p. 214 to help you.

You may be given a character card with basic information about the person you will pretend to be:

Character Card

Name: Jenna Smith

Information: Jenna is a 16-year-old teenager. She is in Secondary IV and works part-time in a grocery store. She wants to be a doctor one day.

Tips

Make your character come alive.

- Practise gestures and facial expressions he/she would use.
- Think up simple accessories to complement your character's personality: a briefcase and tie for a businessman; a cane and glasses for an old woman, etc.

If your character is a real person and you are given some preparation time:

- Research your character in books, magazines and on the Internet. Find out about his/her life.
- Interview the person if you can. Get to know him/her as much as possible. (Refer to the list of questions on the next page to help you.)

what makes someone tick: what someone is like; what a person does and how he/she acts.

Character Questionnaire

Here are some questions to consider about your character.

1. How old is your character?
2. How and where did your character grow up?
3. What is your character's nationality or ethnic group?
4. What languages does your character speak?
5. Does he/she have a family?
6. What is his/her profession?
7. What are your character's particular likes and dislikes?
8. What are your character's fears?
9. To whom is your character loyal?
10. Does your character have any enemies?
11. Does he/she have friends?
12. What are your character's ambitions or goals?
13. What are your character's deep, dark secrets?
14. How does your character present himself/herself publicly (as compared to privately)?
15. Is your character a happy person?

Feel free to add any other questions you think might be relevant!

Tips

If your character is fictional, then all your research will come from your head! Be creative!

Culture

- Many actors spend weeks, even months, preparing for their role in movies or in a play. When he was asked to play the role of Rubin "Hurricane" Carter in the movie *The Hurricane*, Denzel Washington spent hours with Carter getting to know him and seeing how he talked, moved and thought.

- In the movie *Boys Don't Cry*, actress Hillary Swank played the role of a man. Since this obviously was not something that she was used to, she spent months dressing, walking and talking like a man. She walked around the city where she lived as a man to see what it was like.

LIST OF EMOTIONS

- aggressive
- amused
- angry
- annoyed
- awkward
- bored
- calm
- crushed
- disappointed
- excited
- frustrated

- furious
- happy
- hysterical
- indifferent
- intrigued
- irritated
- nervous
- overwhelmed
- quiet
- sad

- scared
- stressed
- surprised
- suspicious
- terrified
- tired
- touched
- uncomfortable
- upset
- etc.

CHARACTER TRAITS

- affable
- ambitious
- arrogant
- bossy
- charming
- clever
- clumsy
- cold-hearted
- conservative
- cooperative
- courageous
- cowardly
- creative
- curious
- daring
- demanding
- determined

- disagreeable
- dishonest
- dynamic
- easygoing
- efficient
- fun-loving
- generous
- glamorous
- gullible
- hard-working
- honest
- humble
- humorous
- imaginative
- immature
- independent
- intrepid

- jealous
- kind
- laid-back
- lazy
- loyal
- mean
- meticulous
- negative
- obedient
- obnoxious
- open-minded
- outspoken
- peaceful
- pious
- polite
- positive
- predictable

- quiet
- rebellious
- respectful
- rigid
- rude
- self-confident
- serious
- stubborn
- studious
- successful
- theatrical
- thoughtful
- timid
- unpredictable
- uptight
- vivacious
- wild
- etc.

Can You Do It?

Find at least three actions that would most likely be in character, and three that would be out of character for each of the people below. Use the following structure:
He/she would be (emotion) *if...*

1. A young child who adores animals
2. A rebellious teenager
3. Santa Claus

Vocabulary Builder

"In character" is an expression used to signify that how a person acts and what he/she says is in line with his/her personality. For example, a lazy person will not act the same way as a "go-getter."

Tips

To impersonate your character:

- Define his/her personality traits. For example, maybe he/she is honest, intelligent and hard-working...
- Determine how he/she will react to the situation. What will his/her emotions be?
- Characterize his/her attitude. How the person stands, talks and walks says a lot about who the person is.

All of these will help you stay "in character."

Look at the situation of the role play.

Now that you know who your character is and how he or she thinks, you need to familiarize yourself with the situation that your character must face. This situation may be based on a story read in class or an issue that you have been discussing, or it may be a situation "pulled out of a hat." Often the situation will include a problem that needs solving.

1. You may receive a situation card. If so, read it.

2. Validate your understanding of the situation with the other participants in the role play.

3. Think about how your character will react. Use the *Think About It!* questions to help you.

4. Make a T-chart with what the person says and what he/she does.

5. Discuss your ideas in your group and take notes.

Culture

Improvisation, which is also called improv, is a form of role play in which the actions are usually directed by the audience. They are the ones who choose the setting or situation. Sometimes, they also decide on the characters and the tone. Also, in improv, there is no prep time per se.

per se: as such.

The Situation

The Characters:
Jenna Smith (teenager)
Karen Thompson (Jenna's mother)
Gary Holmes (owner of the grocery store and Jenna's employer)
Ouzill (tattoo artist)

Jenna wants to get a butterfly tattoo on her shoulder. Tattoo artists will not tattoo anyone under 18. Jenna needs to get permission from her mother to get the tattoo, but everyone around her seems to have an opinion.

Will Jenna get her tattoo?

Think About It!

a) What is my character's point of view about the situation?

b) Has my character ever faced a similar situation?

c) Is there anything in my character's background (past history, education, family, affiliations, etc.) that might affect how he/she reacts?

d) What emotions will my character show? Refer to the list on the previous page for ideas.

Put it all together.

Now that you understand your character and know what the situation is, it's time to put the role play together. If everyone involved has a basic idea of what is going on, the role play will be more interesting and the conversation will flow more smoothly.

1. In your group, plan the basic scenario of your role play.

2. Use the checklist on the next page to help you.

3. Work together to complete the graphic organizer on the handout.

4. Individually, note a few keywords and expressions your character will say and validate them in your group.

5. Find some simple props to use.

6. Make any necessary signs or posters.

PROPS

A prop is an accessory used to help you impersonate your character. It also provides visual support.

Props do not have to be elaborate. One or two objects can help set the scene. For example, a waiter might carry a tray and have a towel draped over his arm or a toddler could hold a blanket and carry a teddy bear.

Props can also help define the situation of the role play. For example, chairs may be arranged to form a waiting room or set up to model seats on a bus.

Present your role play.

1. Read the situation card to the class or very briefly explain the situation, then present each of the characters. You may choose a narrator to do this.

2. As you do the role play, keep in mind the hints for interacting in a role play that are given on p. 218.

3. Try to stay in character and, above all, have fun *walking in someone else's shoes and stepping into the limelight!*

Checklist

Individually

1. I have prepared by learning about my character.
2. I have referred to the **Character Traits** and determined at least four character traits of my character.
3. I have read the situation.
4. I have referred to the **List of Emotions** and found those that best explain how my character will feel and react to the situation.

With the other participants in the role play

5. We have validated our understanding of the situation.
6. We have each explained our characters and together found ways for them to interact.
7. We have established a general sequence of events.
8. We have noted any essential cues or questions we don't want to forget.
9. We have come up with simple props to make our role play more interesting.
10. We have decided who will present the role play and the characters and how it should be done.

"Acting is something different to everybody. I just know that if you watch an actor or actress getting better and better, I think that's them just understanding themselves better and better."

– Cameron Diaz

Refer to the functional language cues in the Reference section at the back of the Student Book for suggestions.

How to Interact During the Role Play

Having a conversation is not that difficult
if you follow some basic rules.

1. **Listen!** This is the most important rule in any conversation. Of course, talking is very important, too, but if you don't listen, it won't be a conversation; it'll be a soliloquy or a speech!

2. **Practise active listening.** Listening shows the other persons involved that you are paying attention to them. Make eye contact. Use gestures and facial expressions.

3. **Ask questions and make comments.** Asking questions shows that you are interested and that you are listening to what the other person is saying. Getting your two cents worth in is another way of reacting. Agreeing with everything can kill a conversation just as easily as disagreeing with everything.

4. **Paraphrase what the other person says.** Make sure you understand what the other person is saying by repeating what they have just said. Use sentences like: *So, if I understand correctly, what you said was...* or *So, what you mean is...*

5. **Don't panic if there is a pause.** If there is a pause or a lull in the conversation, don't panic! If the topic seems to have run out of steam, use this short moment to think of other questions or topics to discuss. Is there something that someone said that could start the discussion up again?

soliloquy: a monologue.
to get your two cents worth in: to give your opinion.
lull: a break or pause; moment of silence.
to have run out of steam: to have lost momentum or energy.

Tips

Try not to interrupt the other person in the middle of a sentence. Let the person finish, wait your turn and then express your point of view. You don't want people to think you're rude, unless of course, that's part of being "in character"...

Evaluate your participation and **Reflect** on the role play.

Once your role play is finished, it's important to look back at how it went and how you and your group did when you were in the limelight.

1. Use the handout to evaluate your strengths and weaknesses.

2. Then, take a few minutes to think about the situation itself and how your character handled it.

3. Make connections with your character by answering the *Think About It!* and *Talk About It!* questions.

 Think About It!

a) In what ways are you and your character alike?

b) In what ways are you different?

 Talk About It!

How would you have reacted in the same situation?

"The play was a great success, but the audience was a disaster."

– Oscar Wilde

Reference

TOOLKIT

Strategies

Strategies are specific actions or techniques used to help you solve problems or learn more effectively. Being able to select and use the right strategy in a given situation can help you know what to do if you are having difficulty.

Here is a list of common strategies, divided into categories. In addition, you may have some personal strategies that work for you.

COMMUNICATION STRATEGIES
These strategies will help you interact more effectively.

STRATEGY	WHAT IT MEANS
1. GESTURE	*Using body and facial expressions to help you get your message across.*
2. RECAST	*Repeating what you've just heard.* *Use it to check comprehension.*
3. REPHRASE	*Using other words to say the same thing.* *Use it when you feel your message has not been understood.*
4. STALL FOR TIME	*Hesitating when you need time to think about what to say next.*
5. SUBSTITUTE	*Replacing more difficult words with ones that are easier to understand.* *Use it to make your message clearer.*

LEARNING STRATEGIES
These strategies are grouped into three categories: **metacognitive**, **cognitive** and **social/affective**.

Metacognitive strategies involve reflecting about your work and your learning.

STRATEGY	WHAT IT MEANS
6. DIRECT ATTENTION	*Concentrating on the task without being distracted.*
7. PAY SELECTIVE ATTENTION	*Focusing on specific things or details.*
8. PLAN	*Thinking ahead.* *Use this strategy to be prepared.*
9. SEEK OR CREATE PRACTICE OPPORTUNITIES	*Watching TV or surfing on the Internet in English...* *Finding ways to practise and use English outside the classroom.*
10. SELF-EVALUATE	*Reflecting on your work.* *For example, identifying strong points and ways to improve.*
11. SELF-MONITOR	*Checking and correcting your own language while speaking.*
12. SET GOALS AND OBJECTIVES	*Fixing personal objectives that are both short-term and long-term.*

Cognitive strategies involve the material you use to learn and its contents.

STRATEGY	WHAT IT MEANS
13. ACTIVATE PRIOR KNOWLEDGE	*Thinking about what you already know about a subject and making links with personal experience.*
14. COMPARE	*Looking for similarities and differences in two or more texts.*
15. DELAY SPEAKING	*Taking time to listen and then speaking when you feel ready to speak.*
16. INFER	*Using the clues and information available to make intelligent guesses or draw conclusions.*
17. PRACTISE	*Doing an exercise to apply and use what you have learned.*
18. PREDICT	*Guessing what a text is about or what will happen.*
19. RECOMBINE	*Putting elements together from different parts of a text or from different sources.*
20. SCAN	*Looking at a text quickly for specific information.*
21. SKIM	*Reading through a text quickly in order to grasp the general idea.*
22. TAKE NOTES	*Writing down keywords or things you want to remember.*
23. TRANSFER	*Applying what you have learned to a new context or situation.*
24. USE SEMANTIC MAPPING	*Organizing your ideas into categories.*

Social/Affective strategies involve communicating and working with others.

STRATEGY	WHAT IT MEANS
25. ASK FOR HELP, REPETITION, CLARIFICATION, CONFIRMATION	*Getting information from others when you need help.*
26. ASK QUESTIONS	*Asking others for feedback or correction.*
27. COOPERATE	*Working together to carry out a task or reach a common goal.*
28. DEVELOP CULTURAL UNDERSTANDING	*Communicating with someone who speaks the language you are learning and finding out as much as you can about that culture.*
29. ENCOURAGE YOURSELF AND OTHERS	*Showing a positive attitude.*
30. LOWER ANXIETY	*Finding ways to relax before listening to a text or talking in front of an audience.*
31. REWARD YOURSELF	*Acknowledging that you did a good job.*
32. TAKE RISKS	*Daring to say something without worrying about making mistakes.*

Competencies

In this section of the Reference Toolkit, you will find step-by-step procedures to help you develop particular aspects of both cross-curricular and ESL competencies.

How to...
Cite Sources and Make a Bibliography

Citing Sources

There are general rules to follow when citing sources:

1 **When you copy something word for word**
- Use quotation marks
- State the source

2 **When you borrow ideas that are NOT general knowledge, without copying them word for word**
- **Don't** use quotation marks
- State the source

Making a Bibliography

A bibliography is a list of sources used when doing research. The purpose of a bibliography is to give credit to the authors and allow the reader to consult the sources for additional information.

How to List Sources

Source	Required Information and Order	Example
Book	Author (last name, first name). *Title: Subtitle*, Place of Publication: Publisher, Date.	Gleason, Simon. *Revisiting Aliens*, New York: Winston Publishing, 1999.
Magazine or newspaper article	Author (last name, first name). "Title of Article." *Title of Periodical*, Volume # (Date): Pages.	Tangor, Isabel. "Looks that Kill," *Mirror*, Vol. 14 (Jan. 2008): pp. 16-19.
Website	Author (if available). "Title of Page." Editor (if available). Institution. URL. [date accessed] **(Omit any information not available.)**	"Truth or Lies in Journalism." http://www... [accessed on Oct. 17, 2001]
Article from an encyclopedia	Author (last name, first name). "Title of Article." *Title of Encyclopedia*. Date.	File, Caroline. "History of Pop Music." *New World Encyclopedia*. 1979.
Person	Person interviewed (last name, first name). Occupation. Type of Interview. Date.	Bellows, Andrew. Songwriter. Personal Interview. May 2002.
Advertisement	Company. Advertisement. *Source*. Date: Page.	PermaLook. Advertisement. *The Daily Press*. Feb. 21, 2004: p. 19.
Film	*Title*. Director. Distributor, Year.	*Reaching Out*. Dir. Daniel Burton. JYL Productions, 1996.
Photograph	Subject. Person who took the photograph. Date.	Great Wall of China, Beijing, China. Personal photograph by Olga Justin. July 27, 2006.

The abbreviation for **page** is **p.** For **pages**, it's **pp.**

Keep an Information Log

An information log is a way of keeping track of information from your research.

There are **three keys** to keeping a good information log:

1 **Selection**
- Don't write everything.
- Choose only the most **interesting** and **pertinent** information.

2 **Recording**
- Don't copy word for word.
- Go for **keywords** and ideas.
- Use point form, not complete sentences.
- Pay special attention to **dates** and the **spelling** of proper nouns.
- Write down the sources.

3 **Organization**
- Write each new entry on a separate page.
- Use a system in order to find your information easily.
  - Highlighting and underlining
  - Colours
  - Symbols like "*" and "→"

Keep your log up to date. It will only be useful if it is complete.

The easiest way to search on the Internet is to use a search engine.

Follow these tips to make your search easier and more efficient:

For a simple search

- Identify **keywords** and **phrases**:
  - Play with your search terms
  - Identify synonyms, distinctive terms and alternative spellings
- Type your word into your search engine.

For a more precise search

Use **AND**, **OR** and **NOT**:

- **AND** narrows the search results.
  Example: survival and avalanches
  A search using these words will return documents that contain only both words.
- **OR** broadens the results.
  Example: rap or music
  A search using these words will return documents that contain one of the words or both words. Only one of the words needs to be present to bring up a document.
  In this case, you will get **all** the documents that contain the word <u>rap</u> or the word <u>music</u>!
- The **NOT** operator drops any documents that contain the excluded term.
  Example: Olympics boycott not 2008
  This will return documents about Olympic boycotts not related to the year 2008.

Use "+ ...":

- *rap + music* will return documents that contain **both** words.
- Putting a word in quotation marks will return only documents containing **exactly** what you put in the quotation marks:
  Example: "rock music of the 60s"

How to...
Determine the Validity of Information on the Web

Since anyone can put anything on the Web, how do you know if the information you find is true? Use these guidelines to help you.

1 Look at the **ending** of the URL (Web address).

.gov or .gouv	These are government websites.
.edu or .ac	These belong to educational organizations.
These websites are generally considered to be reliable sources.	

.org	These websites belong to organizations. The information they provide is considered reliable, but it may be biased in order to promote a cause.

2 Addresses that anybody can buy **may** be less reliable. Validity depends on the **author's credibility** and whether or not it is possible to check the veracity of the information. You should be able to answer **"YES"** to the following questions:

1. Is there a mission statement describing the purpose of the site?

2. Is the author identified?

3. Are sources listed and documented?

4. Does the site attempt to be objective?

5. Does it present facts and/or both sides of an issue?

6. Does the site "look" professional and not have too much distracting advertising?

7. Is the site without spelling and grammatical errors?

8. Is the date of the most recent site update indicated?

9. Is it easy to navigate around the site? Do the links work?

10. Are you able to contact the owner or the webmaster of the site?

In addition, the answers to these other questions can provide clues to the reliability of the website:

11. Who sponsors the site?

12. What information is given about the author or the organization?

How to...
Communicate Effectively

BEFORE presenting:

- **Prepare a short introduction and closing.** This will contextualize your presentation.
- **Practise** your presentation until you feel comfortable with your material.
- **Prepare support material and visual aids.**
- **Know how your equipment works** and **test it!**

WHILE presenting:

- **Make eye contact** with the audience.
- **Don't read.** Use note cards instead.
- **Vary the tone of your voice.**
- **Have a backup plan** if something quits working in the middle of your presentation.
- **Relax!** Remember, you are the expert who has something to share with your audience.
- **Don't forget to smile!**

AFTER presenting:

- **Ask for feedback.**
- **Self-evaluate** and **set goals** for future presentations.
- **Reward yourself!**

To interact orally in English, which means to carry on a spontaneous conversation with one or more persons, you must:

❶ Initiate

- Make a comment or ask a question.

❷ React

- Use gestures and facial expressions.
- Answer the question or respond with a pertinent comment.

❸ Maintain

- Ask another question related to the subject.
- Ask someone for his/her opinion.
- Give your opinion on the subject.
- Change subjects and start over again.

❹ End

- Make a polite remark or comment:

  Thanks for the idea!

  Great! Let's do it.

- Take your leave:

  Bye! See you later!

Strategies you can use:
- Stall for time
- Ask for help or clarification
- Use gestures and substitute words
- Take risks

Functional Language

For Initiating Interaction

SHARING YOUR OPINION

- *In my opinion, ...*
- *According to me, ...*
- *I think that... (I don't think that...)*
- *I believe that... (I don't believe that...)*
- *I feel that... (I don't feel that...)*
- *It seems to me that...*
- *It doesn't seem likely that...*
- *I wish that... would...*
- *I wonder if... will/would...*
- *I realize that...*
- *I prefer that...*
- *...*

USUAL GREETINGS

- *Hello!*
- *Hi!*
- *Howdy!*
- *Good morning*
- *Good afternoon*
- *Good evening*
- *Greetings!*
- *...*

EXPRESSING ASPIRATIONS

- *I would like.../I wouldn't like...*
- *I really hope that...*
- *It's my dream to...*
- *It's my life goal to...*
- *I wish I could...*
- *I am willing to sacrifice* (my free time) *for* (a dancing career).
- *I would give up* (chocolate for a year) *to* (meet him).
- *I would rather* (be rich and famous) *than* (poor).
- *If I could, I would* (travel all year long).
- *It's not important to me that* (you come with me to the show).
- *I don't care if...*
- *I have no desire to...*
- *...*

MAKING REQUESTS

- *Can you help me?*
- *May I help you?*
- *Could you please* (turn the volume down)*?*
- *Would you please* (listen to me)*?*
- *Would you mind if* (I sat down)*?*
- *Do you mind* (me taking off my shoes)*?*
- *Is it okay if* (I call my mom)*?*
- *May I* (borrow your pencil)*?*
- *...*

Toolkit ■ Competencies

For Reacting and Maintaining Interaction

AGREEING AND DISAGREEING

- I agree/I don't agree.
- I believe you're... (mistaken/right).
- I don't think that's (correct).
- I think so, too.
- On the other hand, ...
- According to (him), that's not true.
- That's impossible because...
- ...

ANSWERING
(besides yes or no)

Affirmatively	Negatively
• Right on!	• No way!
• Okay/OK.	• Never.
• Sure!	• Never ever.
• Fine.	• Not on your life.
• Perfect!	
• Sweet!	• Under no circumstances.
• No problem!	
• No sweat!	• Absolutely not!
• All right.	• Of course not.
• You bet.	• Nope.
• Of course.	• I don't think so.
• Absolutely.	
• Definitely.	• I doubt it.
• Why not?	• Forget it!
• That's it!	• Impossible!
	• I'd rather not.

REASSURING

- It doesn't matter.
- It's not important.
- It's okay.
- Don't worry about it.
- Take it easy.
- Don't sweat it.
- Stay cool.
- Keep calm.
- Don't panic.
- So what?
- The same thing happened to me...
- You're not alone.
- You can count on (me).
- ...

REACTING

- I can't believe it!
- No kidding!
- I've got to admit, ...
- Wow! That's...
- Huh? I don't get it.
- Come again. (when you want someone to repeat)
- Are you sure?
- What's the point?
- So what?
- ...

WARNING

- Watch out!
- Watch it!
- Be careful!
- Look out!
- Stand back!
- Watch your step!
- Don't touch.
- Keep out!
- ...

SHOWING UNCERTAINTY OR POSSIBILITY

- I'm not sure.
- I don't know...
- In a way...
- Sort of...
- Maybe.
- Really?
- Perhaps.
- Possibly.
- It's possible.
- I guess so.
- ...

Functional Language

For Reacting and Maintaining Interaction (*continued*)

INTERRUPTING

- *Excuse me for interrupting, but...*
- *May I please add something? (...)*
- *I'd like to add something, if you don't mind. (...)*
- *There's something I'd like to mention. (...)*
- *Excuse me, but the point is...*
- *That's not the point.*
- *...*

POSSIBLE ANSWERS

- *Of course!*
- *Go ahead.*
- *By all means.*
- *Be my guest.*
- *Please do.*
- *Please feel free to jump in.*
- *...*

ASKING FOR PRECISION

- *I'm sorry, but I don't understand...*
- *I'm sorry. I didn't catch that./I didn't get that.* (Could you repeat what you said?)
- *Could you please explain* (how that works)?
- *What are you referring to?*
- *What are we talking about here?*
- *What do you mean?*
- *What was that again?*
- *How do you spell that?*
- *Can you put it another way?*
- *Can you be less vague?*
- *...*

POSSIBLE COMMENTS OR ANSWERS

- *Hold on a sec!*
- *Wait a minute, please.*
- *Just a minute.*
- *Not so fast!*
- *Give me a minute here.*
- *Let me think about it.*
- *Come again.*
- *Hmm... Let me see...*
- *Well...*
- *...*

For Reacting and Maintaining Interaction (continued)

MAKING POLITE CONVERSATION

- *How are you?*
- *How's everything going?/How's it going?*
- *How's your ...* (mother, father, sister)*?*
- *How was...* (your trip, the party, the weather)*?*
- *What's up?*
- *What's new your way?/What's new with you?*
- *How are things?*
- *...*

SOCIAL CONVENTIONS

- *Bless you!* (when someone sneezes)
- *Pleased to meet you./How do you do?*
  (when you meet someone for the very first time)
- *May I please speak to...?* (when you want to speak with someone else, not the person who answered the phone)
- *May I please be excused?* (when you want to leave the table after a meal)
- *No, thank you. I'm just looking.* (when a clerk in a store asks you if you need help and you don't)
- *Never mind.* (when you don't need someone's help after you asked for it)
  (Be careful though, this can be impolite...)
- *Best wishes* (when someone is sick or when you want to wish someone well)
- *Congratulations!* (when someone tells you some great news)
- *I'm sorry to hear that.* (when someone tells you some sad news)
- *That's too bad.* (when someone tells you some sad/bad news)
- *...*

> Use *How do you do?* only when you have been introduced to someone. It is incorrect to use it to mean *How are you?*

LEAVE-TAKING

- *Goodbye!/Bye!/Bye for now!*
- *See you later/See you* (tomorrow).
- *Catch you later!*
- *Talk to you soon.*
- *Ciao.*
- *Take care!*
- *Say hello to* (your sister) *for me.*
- *See you later, alligator.*
- *After while, crocodile.*
- *Have fun!*
- *Good luck!*
- *Have a nice day!*
- *Nice talking to you!*
- *...*

> **Good night** is used when someone goes to bed or when someone leaves at night.
> Don't use it as a greeting.

Functional Language

For Doing Group Work

GETTING ORGANIZED

- What do we have to do?
- How do we do this?
- What should we do first?
- How should we separate (the work, the task)?
- Who wants to do (Part A)?
- Let's start with...
- Let's read (the instructions).
- ...

ENCOURAGING

- Good job! Fantastic! Great!
- You've got it!
- You did it!
- Yippee!
- You're the best!
- You're a genius!
- Come on, you can do it.
- We're with you all the way.
- Go for it!
- Almost!
- You're getting there.
- Next time will be better.
- Don't give up.
- Hang in there!
- We deserve a pat on the back!
- We're doing...
- ...

WORKING TOGETHER

- Let's do it together!
- Whose turn is it?
- It's (my) turn. It's (Carolyn's) turn.
- Who's next?
- Oops! Let's get back on task!
- Is everybody ready?
- ...

RELFECTING TOGETHER

- What were our strong/weak points?
- We did great on (respecting the time limits).
- (Kenny), you did a great job (on the poster)!
- We need to improve on (speaking only English).
- We could do better at (sharing the work).
- Good! But I think we can (share ideas even more).
- Next time, we'll (plan more carefully).
- Let's try to (finish on time).
- ...

PLAYING GAMES

- It's (my, your) turn.
- You start.
- Roll the dice.
- Move ahead (4 squares).
- Change places with (Rob).
- Go back to square (17).
- Take a chance.
- Take a risk!
- Lose a turn.
- Free turn!/Free spin.
- Play again.
- Shuffle the cards.
- Cut!
- Deal the cards.
- Draw (pick) a card.
- Lay down your cards.
- Winner/loser
- You win!
- ...

"TIME IS MONEY..."

- Hurry up!
- Let's go.
- Come on!
- Shake a leg.
- Time!
- ...

To reinvest understanding of texts, you must:

❶ Read, listen to and watch a variety of authentic texts in English.

(Stories, fairy tales and legends, poems, newspaper and magazine articles, songs, movies...)

❷ Construct the meaning of the texts and show what you understand by:

- Asking questions
- Answering questions
- Completing graphic organizers
- Discussing with classmates, etc.

❸ Adapt or use the information and ideas from one text or several texts in a new way.

❹ Reflect on your learning and set new goals.

Strategies you can use:

Before reading, listening to or watching a text:
- Activate prior knowledge
- Predict
- Direct or focus your attention

While reading, listening to or watching a text:
- Pay selective attention
- Skim or scan a written text
- Take notes
- Ask yourself questions and use inference

After reading, listening to or watching a text:
- Ask questions
- Restate what you have understood
- Self-evaluate

The Response Process

Many texts, especially stories and poems, naturally stir up feelings and make us think. One way of exploring these feelings and thoughts is through the Response Process. The Response Process has three phases: exploring the text, establishing personal connections with the text and generalizing beyond the text.

1. When **exploring texts**, you:

Before
• Make predictions about the content of the text.
• Set goals for exploring the text.
• Determine what strategies to adopt to help you understand the text.
• Use guiding questions to help you know what to look for.
While
• Confirm or invalidate your predictions.
• Try to answer the guiding questions.
• Identify key elements that you believe are important.
After
• Answer the guiding questions.
• Jot down any ideas you think are pertinent.
• Support these ideas with direct links to the text.
• Share your ideas with your peers.
• Discuss the text with your peers using the prompts provided.

2. When **establishing personal connections with the text**, you:

 • Relate what happens in the text to your own personal experiences or to those of someone you know.

3. When **generalizing beyond the text**, you:

 • Deal with the issue mentioned in the text on a broader level. You might, for example, discuss how it relates to your school or community, or even decide to make it your cause.

Use these discussion prompts to help you carry out the Response Process

❶ EXPLORING THE TEXT

- *From the title and the illustration, I think this text will talk about...*
- *I already know this about the subject: ...*
- *For me, the most important part of the story is when...*
- *I noticed that...*
- *I learned that...*
- *I understood that...*
- *I had trouble understanding...*
- *To understand the text, I...*
- *I found this idea very interesting because...*
- *That part makes me think of...*
- *I believe the author is trying to...*
- *The text is about...*
- *...*

❷ ESTABLISHING A PERSONAL CONNECTION WITH THE TEXT

- *I experienced something similar when I...*
- *I know how the character feels because I...*
- *The main character is exactly like my sister...*
- *The woman in the story reminds me of my mother...*
- *I find this character very interesting because...*
- *I heard about this before. ...*
- *If I were in the same situation, I would...*
- *...*

❸ GENERALIZING BEYOND THE TEXT

- *We can do something about it...*
- *I think we should...*
- *Maybe we could...*
- *I have an idea. Let's...*
- *What if we all...*
- *...*

Before reading

1 Look at the **title** and **illustrations**.
- What information do they give you about the story?
- Can you make any predictions?
  - *I think this story is about...*

While reading

2 Read for the **general idea**.
- Don't try to understand every word. Pick out words you know.

3 If there is a word you don't know, **keep on reading**. You may get the meaning from the context, or you may be able to understand the text anyway.

4 **Visualize** what's going on, like a film in your mind.
- Let yourself become part of the action. Imagine you are there.

5 Don't try to read the whole thing at once. **Read a section and stop**.
- Just say what you think it means. Do you have any questions?

6 Then, try to **predict** what might happen next.
  - *I think that...*

After reading

7 Try to make sense of the story. Identify:
- The characters
- The setting (where and when)
- The problem or conflict
- The climax (turning point)
- The **resolution** or the **ending**

8 Think about why the author wrote this story:
  - *The message the author wished to convey is...*
  - *I think the author wanted to show that...*

9 **Share** your opinions:
  - *I think this story is... because...*

The Parts of a Story

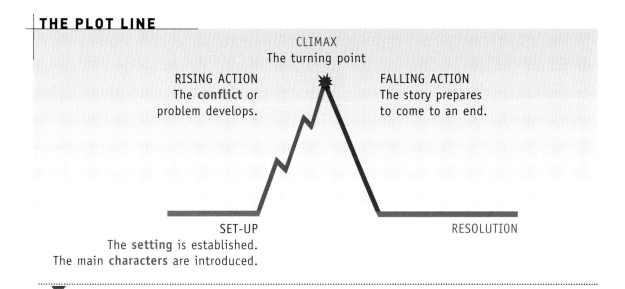

① Setting

When and where the story takes place

② Characters

The people in the story

③ Plot

The **series of events** that make up the action of the story

(The set-up, rising action, climax, falling action and resolution are all part of the plot.)

④ Conflict

The **problem** or sticky situation that the main character must deal with

⑤ Climax

The **turning point** of the story

⑥ Resolution

The conclusion: how the problem is resolved

Non-fiction is information that is presented as being true. It is supposed to be factual information.

Examples of non-fiction include:

- *Documentaries*
- *Biographies*
- *Textbooks*
- *News articles*
- *Scientific papers*
- *Encyclopedia entries*

Magazine articles, articles on the Internet and some articles in the newspaper may or may not be non-fiction, depending on the subject and how it is treated.

Most of time, non-fiction is read in order to obtain specific information about a specific subject.

Four Strategies for Reading Non-fiction

1 | **Inferring information**

- Before you begin reading, look at the **titles**, **subtitles** and **illustrations**.
- Most articles are divided into sections. The **subtitles** will give you an idea about what to expect in that part of the article.

2 | **Note-taking**

- When you find the information you are looking for, **stop and write it down**.
- If you copy word for word, use quotation marks.
- Don't forget to write down the **page number** and the **source**.

3 | **Scanning**

This strategy is useful when you know exactly what you are looking for. Here's how to do it:

- Run your finger (and your eyes!) quickly down the page, looking for the desired information.
- When you spot it, stop and read it to make sure it's what you want.

4 | **Paraphrasing**

Paraphrasing is **putting something that someone else has said into your own words**.

- After you have read a factual article or a section of an article, it can be useful to repeat to yourself what you have just read in your own words.
- If you get stuck, go back and read the difficult section again.

Dateline
(when)

Headline
(It sums up the article.)

Placeline
(where)

Lead
(the beginning of the article)

- It contains the most important information.
- In general, you will find out:
  who
  what
  when
  where

News articles use the *inverted triangle*. All the essential information is given at the beginning. The details are at the end.

Daily Press

Thursday, May 27, 2004

Teens Tackle Thief

New Linton, NB. Late yesterday afternoon, two high school students found themselves the centre of attention. Gillian Carter, 16, and her friend Roxane Malone, 15, were coming out of the mall when they heard a scream. At the same time, a tall man wearing a light grey hooded sweatshirt and navy sweatpants raced past them. "I noticed he was carrying a lady's purse and something just clicked. I stuck out my foot to trip him and Roxie kicked him in the groin. Real hard! He fell to the ground screaming obscenities. I snatched the purse and we hurried back inside the building

for help." A clerk called 911 and the police arrived and took the suspect into custody.

The woman whose purse had been stolen was elated. Thanks to some quick thinking and quick actions by the girls, she recovered everything. "These girls are my lifesavers. My purse had my rent money and grocery money in it, not to mention all my cards," said the 62 year old, who preferred to remain anonymous.

Body
It gives facts about an event that has taken place recently.

Quotes from the people involved add interest and credibility to the article.

Newspapers also contain two other kinds of articles:

- Feature Articles: special, detailed reports on a person or event
- Editorials: articles expressing the opinion(s) of the editor(s) on a specific issue

How to...
Use a Dictionary

1 | **For spelling**

- Dictionaries show how words are written.
- They also specify if a word is invariable or has an irregular form.

2 | **For accuracy**

- Dictionaries give all the definitions of a word.
  - Choose the one that best represents what you want to say.
  - Try replacing it with a synonym to see if it makes sense.

3 | **For creativity**

- Most dictionaries provide synonyms, antonyms and idiomatic expressions.
  - Use them to vary your writing.

4 | **For pronunciation**

- Beside each word, you will find brackets [...] with the correct pronunciation.

Use a **thesaurus** [thi-sôr'es] to find synonyms and antonyms.

To write and produce texts, you must:

1 Write often about different subjects.

2 Explore different types of texts, for different audiences.

3 Follow the Writing and Production Processes.

4 Use strategies like planning, note-taking and semantic mapping.

5 Use resources like dictionaries, thesauruses and checklists.

6 Reflect on your writing to find concrete ways to improve specific points in future texts.

The Writing Process

PREPARING TO WRITE

- Be clear about the purpose and the targeted audience.
- Brainstorm with others.
- If necessary, do more research and take notes.
- Organize your information.

WRITING THE DRAFT(S)

- Put your ideas on paper; don't worry about mistakes yet.

REVISING

Get feedback on:

- The logical sequence of the information presented
- Your choice of words
- The variety of sentence structures used

Make the necessary changes.

EDITING

Get feedback on:

- Punctuation
- Grammar

PUBLISHING

- Add illustrations.
- Make a polished copy.

The Production Process

PRE-PRODUCTION

- Brainstorm about the type of media text you wish to create.
- Determine the techniques you will use.
- Plan the layout or storyboard of your media text.

PRODUCTION

- Create your media text according to your layout or storyboard.
- Use a checklist to make sure you don't forget anything.
- Validate a preliminary version by presenting your work to a sample audience.
- Edit and add final touches, taking feedback into account.
- Present your media text to your intended audience.

POST-PRODUCTION

- Review the whole process.
- Evaluate your work objectively and set new goals for future productions.

How to...
Peer Edit

One good reason for using peer editing or small group editing is to get feedback – helpful feedback! Here's how to go about it.

TO GIVE FEEDBACK ▼

TO RECEIVE FEEDBACK ▼

1

Listen *carefully:*
- *Don't interrupt.*
- *If necessary, take notes.*

Read *your text to your partner.*

2

Give feedback:
- *Use a checklist.*
- *Mention strong points.*
- *Offer suggestions.*

Avoid:
- *Negative comments.*
- *Automatic stamp of approval.*
- *Getting off track.*

Listen *carefully:*
- *Don't interrupt.*
- *Take notes.*

3

Ask for help:
- *Ask for clarification, if necessary.*
- *Ask for help with specific things.*
- *Don't make excuses.*
- *Be open to the possibility of change.*

Remember the goal:
To produce the best text possible

I really like your arguments. They support your opinion... You forgot to write a closing.

Thanks for the feedback!

How to...
Write a Paragraph

A paragraph is a group of sentences that develops one idea or topic. This idea is expressed in one sentence called the topic sentence. All the other sentences in the paragraph explain or support this idea. The concluding sentence restates the topic sentence in different words.

To write a paragraph, follow these steps:

1 | Choose your <u>subject</u>.

2 | **Determine what you want to say** about the subject <u>in general</u>.

3 | **Write the topic sentence. All the other sentences will support or explain this sentence.**

4 | **Support or explain the topic sentence with at least three facts, arguments or examples.**

5 | **Write a concluding sentence. This should repeat what you said in the topic sentence in a different way.**

It was his will to live that kept him alive. Although he couldn't walk, he dragged himself out of the woods to the clearing. He had no food except for a candy bar, so he broke it into little pieces and forced himself to ration it. He knew he mustn't sleep, so he sang and shouted and invented stories. And he thought about his family. When the rescuers arrived three days later, he was extremely weak, but conscious. "I wanted to hold my new baby in my arms," he said. "I made myself the promise I would."

Types of Paragraphs

There are many different types of paragraphs. The type you choose will depend on your purpose.

Different Types of Paragraphs

Type of Paragraph/Purpose	What to Do	What to Include
DESCRIPTIVE • To describe a person, place, event or object	• Create a picture for the reader. • Make him/her feel, smell, see, etc. • Use lots of details. • Choose a mood.	• Vivid language • Lots of adjectives • Adverbs • Strong verbs
NARRATIVE • To tell a story about one event or sequence of events	• Use chronological order. • Use transition words like *first*, *then*, *later*, *finally*, etc. • Make sure there is a beginning, a middle and an end.	The principal elements of a story: characters, setting, conflict, climax and resolution
EXPLANATORY/EXPOSITORY • To give information or to explain something	• Use chronological order. • Or, show the relation between elements (*in between, next to, behind,* etc.). • Support with examples and facts.	• Concrete language and examples
OPINION/PERSUASIVE • To convince the reader	• State your opinion clearly. • Justify it with facts, arguments and examples. • Explain why. • Use transition words like *in fact, furthermore, thus, however,* etc.	• Statistics • Quotations from experts • Reliable sources

Each time you finish writing about one idea, stop.

Start a new paragraph for each new idea. Your writing will be better organized.

How to...
Write a Narrative Essay

The Parts

In a narrative essay, you are basically telling a story. Therefore, you will use the conventions found in any story:

- The **setting** and **characters**
- A **climax**
- An **ending** (how the incident resolved itself)

The Characteristics

- Are based on a **personal experience** (your own or someone else's)
- Communicate a main idea or a **lesson learned**
- Are written in the first person "**I**" or the third person "**he**" or "**she**"

The Structure

- The **INTRODUCTION** states the **importance of the experience**.
- The **MAIN PARAGRAPHS** use **concrete, specific details** to describe persons, scenes and events. You may include dialogue as long as you use proper punctuation.
- The **CONCLUSION** makes a point or **illustrates the importance of the story once again**.

The Steps

1. **Choose an experience** you want to write about.
2. **Think about why it is significant**.
3. **Follow the Writing and Production Processes** to write your essay.

Language

Narrative essays use **descriptive language** to make the reader feel the action and the emotion.

Choose **vivid verbs** and add **adjectives** and **adverbs**.

Examples:

- *We <u>listened</u> to the speaker. → We gave the incredible guest speaker our undivided attention.*
- *The man was <u>walking</u> down the road. → The elderly fellow was hobbling painfully down the narrow, unpaved country road.*

Use a thesaurus to find synonyms and enrich your vocabulary!

Write a Friendly Letter

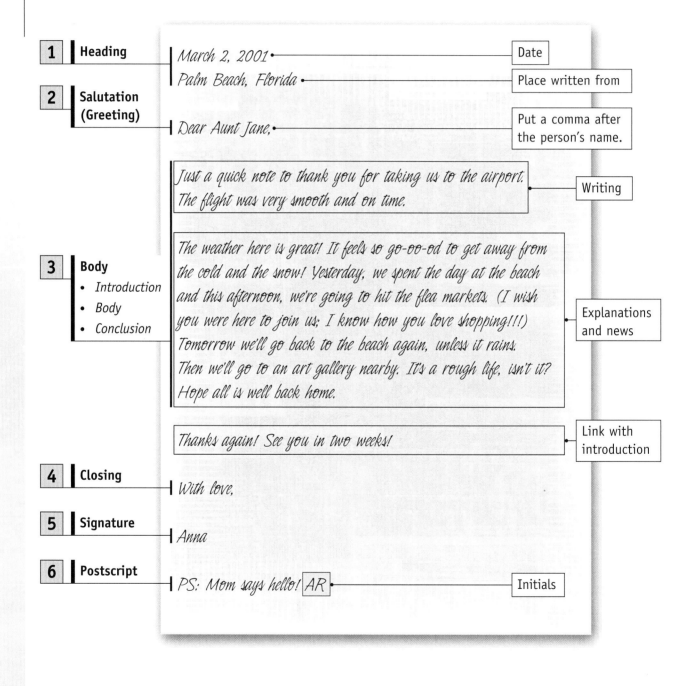

1 | **Heading**

March 2, 2001 •————————————— Date

Palm Beach, Florida •————————— Place written from

2 | **Salutation (Greeting)**

Dear Aunt Jane, •————————— Put a comma after the person's name.

3 | **Body**
- *Introduction*
- *Body*
- *Conclusion*

Just a quick note to thank you for taking us to the airport. The flight was very smooth and on time. •—— Writing

The weather here is great! It feels so go-oo-od to get away from the cold and the snow! Yesterday, we spent the day at the beach and this afternoon, we're going to hit the flea markets. (I wish you were here to join us; I know how you love shopping!!!) Tomorrow we'll go back to the beach again, unless it rains. Then we'll go to an art gallery nearby. It's a rough life, isn't it? Hope all is well back home. •—— Explanations and news

Thanks again! See you in two weeks! •—— Link with introduction

4 | **Closing**

With love,

5 | **Signature**

Anna

6 | **Postscript**

PS: Mom says hello! AR •————————— Initials

Write a Business Letter

A business letter is a more formal type of letter. Often it is written to people you have never met. Here's what to include in a business letter.

1 Heading

62 Légaré Street
Montreal, QC H2C 2Y7
September 16, 2008

- Write your complete address and the complete date.
- Use the official two-letter abbreviation for the province or state.
- Put the postal code on the same line as the city.

2 Inside Address

Mr. Jerry Waterford, Chairman
REACH-OUT Campaign
1902 First Avenue
Melville, NS B1Y 3X9

3 Salutation (Greeting)

Dear Mr. Waterford:

- Put a colon after the greeting.
- If you don't know the person's name, use: *Dear Sir or Madam:*

4 Body
- *Introduction*
- *Body*
- *Conclusion*

I am writing to request information about the use of steroids at the high school level.

As a school project, my classmates and I are preparing a presentation on teens and steroids. In doing research, we came across your excellent website and would appreciate receiving copies of your brochure, "Truth and Consequences: What Teens Should Know," as well as the accompanying DVD.

We appreciate your help in making teenagers aware of the dangers of using steroids and thank you in advance for answering our request.

5 Closing

Sincerely,

- After the closing, put a comma.
- Other examples of closings:
  Sincerely yours,
  Yours truly,
  Respectfully,

6 Signature

David Singh
David Singh

- Type your name four lines below the closing.
- Sign between the two.

Write a Five-paragraph Essay

A five-paragraph essay is a written composition that has five paragraphs. It is about a single subject and usually gives the author's personal point of view.

Parts of a Five-paragraph Essay

1 | **Introduction**
- State what your essay is going to be about.

2 | **Body**
- Identify three distinct points that support or explain your topic.
- Each of these points will be one new paragraph.

3 | **Conclusion**
- Explain what you just wrote and say why.
- Make a link to your introduction.
- Be careful not to include any new information!

The Steps

1. Choose a topic.

2. Find information about your topic.
You will need facts and interesting information to support your ideas.

3. Plan your essay.
Your essay will have three parts. Figure out what you want to say in each one.
Use a graphic organizer or make an outline to help you keep track.

4. Follow the steps of the Writing and Production Processes.

5. Use a checklist to help you remember everything.

Grammar

Numbers

	Cardinal	Ordinal
0	zero	--
1	one	fir<u>st</u> (1st)
2	two	seco<u>nd</u> (2nd)
3	three	thi<u>rd</u> (3rd)
4	four	four<u>th</u> (4th)
5	five	fifth
6	six	sixth
7	seven	seventh
8	eight	eighth
9	nine	ninth
10	ten	tenth
11	eleven	eleventh
12	twelve	twelfth
13	thirteen	thirteenth
14	fourteen	fourteenth

	Cardinal	Ordinal
15	fifteen	fifteenth
16	sixteen	sixteenth
17	seventeen	seventeenth
18	eighteen	eighteenth
19	nineteen	nineteenth
20	twenty	twentieth
21	twenty-one	twenty-first
30	thirty	thirtieth
40	forty	fortieth
50	fifty	fiftieth
60	sixty	sixtieth
70	seventy	seventieth
80	eighty	eightieth
90	ninety	ninetieth
100	a/one hundred	

In english the number zero is followed by a plural noun:
- *two pens*, *one marker*, **zero pencils**.

When writing numbers in a text:

- If the first word in a sentence is a number, write it in full.
  Example: Twenty-five people were present at the meeting.
- Numbers under 10 are written in full; the others are written as numbers.
  Example: There were 25 people at the meeting, but only eight of them were from my school.

Large Number Cardinal	
1,000	a/one thousand
10,000	ten thousand
1,000,000	one million
1,000,000,000	one billion
1,000,000,000,000	one trillion

In British English, **hundreds** and **tens** are separated by **and**; in American English, the **and** is omitted:

123:
- *one hundred* **and** *twenty-three* (British)
- *one hundred twenty-three* (American)

In Canada, we find both forms, but the British form is the official form.

Names of Coins	
One cent	*penny*
Five cents	*nickel*
Ten cents	*dime*
Twenty-five cents	*quarter*
One dollar	*loonie*
Two dollars	*toonie*

Roman Numerals					
I	1	X	10	LX	60
II	2	XI	11	XC	90
III	3	XII	12	C	100
IV	4	XV	15	D	500
V	5	XX	20	M	1000
VI	6	XXV	25	MCM	1900
VII	7	XL	40	MM	2,000
VIII	8	L	50	$\overline{\text{L}}$	5,000
IX	9				

Today, Roman numerals are still used on **clocks, to identify events** like the Super Bowl, for some **page numbers** and for **movie titles**.

Dates	May 25, 2005 or 25 May 2005
Years	2006/1996–1999 or 1996–99/the eighties or the 1980s
Time of Day	6:00 a.m. or 6:00 A.M./11:45 p.m. or 11:45 P.M.
Address	241 Marks Road/4683 42nd Street West
Percentages	70% (seventy percent)/65.5% (sixty-five point five percent)
Large Round Numbers	4 million or 4,000,000/8.5 million or 8,500,000
Fractions	1/2 (one-half)/1/4 (one-fourth, one-quarter)
Prices	$46.34 (forty-six dollars and thirty-four cents)

A Few Other Special Names

- for zero:
  - *nought* (chiefly British)
  - *oh* (when saying phone numbers)
  - *nil* or *nothing* (in sports scores)
    The score is 7-nil or 7 to nothing.
  - *love* (tennis)
  - *zip, nada, zilch, nothing!*
- for twelve: *dozen*
- for thirteen: *baker's dozen*
- for 144 (used in commerce): *gross*
- for 10^{100} (1 + 100 zeroes): **googol**

The popular search engine **Google** took its name from a pun on the number googol. The difference in spelling was due to an error.

Nouns

A noun is a person, place, thing, idea or quality. *Boy, park, pencil, music* and *happiness* are all nouns. Common nouns refer to things like objects, professions and locations, not names of people or places.
They do not start with a capital letter.

Proper Nouns (names of specific persons, places or things)	
• Proper nouns always start with a capital letter.	*Columbo, Africa, Andy Warhol, James A. Naismith, the Underground Railroad*
Possessive Nouns (nouns that show ownership)	
1. Possessive nouns are formed by adding **'s** to nouns in the singular.	• *Lisa's purse* • *A baker's dozen*
2. For plural nouns, an apostrophe (') is added.	• *The neighbours' car* • *the dogs' owner*
3. With words that end in an **s** sound, the possessive is formed by adding **'s** or just **'**.	• *Charles' car or Charles's car* • *the princess' crown or the princess's crown*
4. For family names, the name is pluralized and an **'** is added.	• *the Johnsons' garden*

PLURAL NOUNS
- Some nouns are always plural. *Examples: clothes, sunglasses, pants, scissors, pyjamas*

NON-COUNT NOUNS
- Non-count nouns are ALWAYS <u>singular</u>.
- They are things that <u>cannot</u> be counted.
- They often express qualities, substances, abstract things or collective names for count-nouns like:
  - **furniture** (*tables, chairs, beds, etc.*)
  - **money** (*dollars, euros, quarters, etc.*)

Six general ways to make singular nouns plural:

Rule	Examples	Exceptions
1. For most nouns, add **s**.	*cars, horses, hats*	
2. If a noun ends with **s**, **ch**, **sh**, **x** or **z**, add **es**.	*bus**es**, church**es**, bush**es**, tax**es**, quizz**es***	When **ch** sounds like a **k**, add only **s**. (*Example: stomach**s***)
3. If a noun ends with **f** or **fe**, change the **f** to a **v** and add **es**.	*scar**ves**, loa**ves**, lea**ves**, kni**ves***	*beliefs, chiefs, cliffs, gulfs, proofs, roofs, safes*
4. If a noun ends with **y** preceded by a **vowel**, add **s**.	*toy**s**, birthday**s**, key**s***	
5. If a noun ends with **y** preceded by a **consonant**, drop the **y** and add **ies**.	*bunn**ies**, penn**ies***	
6. If a noun ends with **o** preceded by a **vowel**, add **s**.	*cameo**s**, radio**s***	
7. If a noun ends with **o** preceded by a **consonant**, add **es**.	*tomato**es**, potato**es**, hero**es***	music terms (*pianos, sopranos, altos, tangos, concertos, etc.*) and *zoos*
8. Invariable nouns	*deer, fish, offspring, salmon, sheep*	
9. Irregular nouns	*man/men, woman/women, child/children, foot/feet, die/dice, mouse/mice, tooth/teeth*	

Zero and *volcano* can be written either way in the plural (*zeros/zeroes; volcanos/volcanoes*).

Articles

Indefinite Articles	
Singular	**Plural**
(a/an)	**(–/some)**
Use indefinite articles for objects that are **not specific**.	
Examples: – *She is reading **a** book.* – *Apples are good for you.*	
Use the indefinite article the first time you speak of something: *Examples:* – *She found **a** wallet.* – *He is a busboy in **a** restaurant.*	

a = words that begin with a <u>consonant</u> sound (*a radio, a wonder*)

an = words that begin with a <u>vowel</u> sound (*an elevator, an hour*)

Definite Articles	
Singular	**Plural**
(the)	**(the)**
Use definite articles for objects that are **specific** or **unique**. It is clear which particular objects are being referred to.	
Examples: – *She is reading **the** book I gave her yesterday.* – *May I have **the** green apple?*	
Use the definite article the second time you speak of something: *Examples:* – ***The** wallet contained a lot of money.* – ***The** restaurant is downtown.*	
Use definite articles for: • Names of rivers, oceans and seas • Names of deserts, forests, gulfs, peninsulas and mountains *Examples:* – ***The** Atlantic* – ***The** Rockies*	

Some/Any

• Use <u>**some**</u> for an INDEFINITE number or quantity in an affirmative statement: *I need some help. We want some answers.*

• Use <u>**any**</u> with negative statements: *I don't have any money. They don't want any food.*

Do NOT use articles for:

• Sports
• Hobbies, activities and school subjects
• Names of streets, roads, avenues, etc.
• Languages
• Names of continents

• Names of countries
• Names of provinces and states
• Names of lakes and bays
• Names of individual mountains

Pronouns and Possessive Adjectives

Pronouns are words used to replace nouns. They act like nouns. Possessive adjectives and possessive pronouns are used to show ownership.

1. Here is a list of personal pronouns, possessive adjectives and pronouns and reflexive pronouns:

<table>
<tr><td colspan="2">Personal Pronouns</td><td colspan="2">Possessive Adjectives and Pronouns</td><td rowspan="2">Reflexive Pronouns</td></tr>
<tr><td>Subject Form</td><td>Object Form</td><td>Possessive Adjective</td><td>Possessive Pronoun</td></tr>
<tr><td>I</td><td>me</td><td>my</td><td>mine</td><td>myself</td></tr>
<tr><td>you</td><td>you</td><td>your</td><td>yours</td><td>yourself</td></tr>
<tr><td>he</td><td>him</td><td>his</td><td>his</td><td>himself</td></tr>
<tr><td>she</td><td>her</td><td>her</td><td>hers</td><td>herself</td></tr>
<tr><td>it</td><td>it</td><td>its</td><td>its</td><td>itself</td></tr>
<tr><td>we</td><td>us</td><td>our</td><td>ours</td><td>ourselves</td></tr>
<tr><td>you</td><td>you</td><td>your</td><td>yours</td><td>yourselves</td></tr>
<tr><td>they</td><td>them</td><td>their</td><td>theirs</td><td>themselves</td></tr>
</table>

Be careful not to confuse **it's** (it is) and **its** (possessive adjective)!
- *It's* raining!
- *The dog is chasing **its** tail.*

The possessive adjective always refers to the person who is the owner: *Jane's book = her book.*

2. This is when to use them:

	When to Use Them	Examples
Personal Pronouns (subject form)	To carry out the action of the verb They usually precede the verb.	• *I live in Victoriaville.* • *She comes from Gaspé.* • *They are studying science.*
Personal Pronouns (object form)	To receive the action of the verb They follow the verb.	• *I gave **him** a surprise party.* • *He invited **you** to the beach.* • *We saw **them** on TV.*
Possessive Adjectives	To show ownership They agree with the "possessor," not the object.	• *Angela lost **his** cell phone. (John's)* • *Angela lost **her** cell phone. (Angela's)* • *Someone stole **our** car.*
Possessive Pronouns	To show ownership They replace a possessive adjective and the noun it modifies.	• *That cell phone is **hers**. (Angela's)* • *That paper belongs to me; it is **mine**.* • *The future is **yours**.*
Reflexive Pronouns	When the subject and the object are the same by + reflexive pronoun = without others; without help	• *You should give **yourselves** a pat on the back.* • *They are playing **by themselves**.* • *I did it all **by myself**.*

Demonstrative Pronouns and Adjectives

Demonstrative pronouns and adjectives are used for a **person, place** or **thing** that **must be pointed to.** They are: *this, that, these* and *those.*

	When the object is <u>near</u> the speaker	When the object is <u>at</u> <u>a distance</u> from the speaker
Singular	**this**	**that**
Plural	**these**	**those**

IN CONTEXT

There Is/There Are

There is/There are is a common structure used to indicate that something is present.

Use **there** is with **singular** nouns and **there** are with **plural** nouns.

	There is	**There are**
Form	Singular noun	Plural noun
Affirmative	• *There is/'s a hotel on Main Street.*	• *There are posters on their walls.*
Negative	• *There is not/isn't a room available.* • *There is no room available.*	• *There are not any books there.* • *There aren't any books on the shelf.* • *There are no books there.*

> Watch out for the difference between **there** and **their** and **they're**.

Prepositions

A preposition is a word that is used to describe the relationship between other words in a sentence.

❶ Prepositions of Location (where)

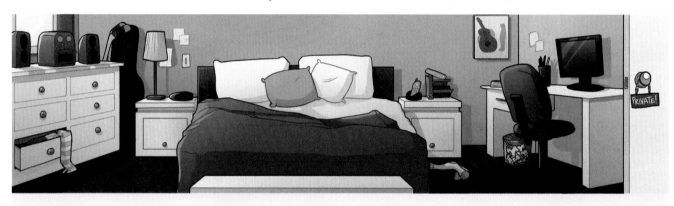

- The socks are **on** the floor.
- The papers are **in** the wastebasket.
- The basket is **under (underneath)** the desk.
- The light switch is **above (over)** the nightstand.
- The stereo is **between** the speakers.
- The dresser is **in front** of the window.
- The white pillows are **behind (in back of)** the blue pillow.

- The desk is **across from** the dresser.
- The guitar is **against** the wall.
- The alarm clock is **next to** the lamp.
- The hockey stick is **near (close to)** the guitar.
- The computer screen is **far from** the window.
- The pencils are **to the left of** the screen.
- The books are **to the right of** the telephone.

❷ Prepositions of Manner (how)

In English, we ride:

- **in** *a car and a taxi* (and we get **out** *of them*)
- **on** *a horse, bicycle, motorcycle*
- **on** *a bus, train, plane, boat, train*
- **on** *the subway* (and we get **off** *all of these*)

Prepositions of manner help you describe how actions are completed. The most common prepositions of manner are:

by: *Fabrice comes to school **by** bus.*

in: *Please do not write **in** red ink.*

like: *Stop crying **like** a baby.*

with: *I eat my peas **with** honey...*

❸ Prepositions to Show Direction (where)

across: over to the other side: *I swam **across** the lake.*

into: entering a place or building: *He went **into** the store.*

onto: up to the top of something: *She threw it **onto** the pile of clothes.*

through: in one side and out the opposite: *He drove **through** the tunnel.*

toward: in the direction of: *We walked **toward** the crowd.*

❹ Prepositions of Time (when)

Three Very Common Prepositions of Time

	Use	Example
on	– days of the week – dates	• *School begins **on Monday**.* • *I was born **on May 25**.*
in	– months/seasons – time of day – years – after a specific length of time	• *His birthday is **in September**.* • *The concert is **in the afternoon**.* • *She was born **in 1991**.* • *I will call you back **in twenty minutes**.*
at	– a certain time	• *I will call you **at 9 a.m.***

> Exception: **at** night
> • *The accident happened at night.*

Some Prepositions of Time in Context

before	*I will meet you **after** work. I finish at 5 p.m. so I should be there **between** 5:30 and 5:45, for sure **before** 6. We can have supper together, but I have to be home **by** 9, so I can stay **until** around 8:40.*
after	
by	
between	
until	

> For Telling Time...
> • *It's ten **to** seven. (6:50)*
> • *It's half **past** four. (4:30)*

Still More Prepositions to Show Time

Preposition	When to Use It	Examples
since	To show when the action began	• *She has been in Rimouski **since 1989**.* • *They have been married **since May 12, 2004**.*
for	To show how long	• *He lived in Boston **for five months**.* • *They have been married **for 12 years**.*
during	To show when (no specific time)	• *Carla slept **during the film**.* • *I had an accident **during the storm**.*
ago	To show when in the past	• *We saw that show **several years ago**.* • *That happened **two Saturdays ago**.*

Adjectives

Adjectives are words that are used to describe nouns.

In English, adjectives almost always go <u>before</u> the nouns they describe

> *(Examples: A **big** problem, a **messy** room, a **private** place, a **yellow** bird...)*

or <u>after</u> the verb **to be**.

> *(Example: He is intelligent.)*

More Than One Adjective

Sometimes, we want to describe a noun with more than one adjective. The general rule for deciding which adjective to place first is:

Opinion	BEFORE	Fact
(what you THINK)		(what is DEFINITELY TRUE)
Example: A ***pretty**,*		*pink purse*

You can also use the word **with** in your descriptions:

Examples:
- *A beautiful, new chair **with** large, red, vertical stripes*
- *A delicious chocolate sundae **with** whipped cream and a bright, red cherry*

For a **long string of adjectives**, here is the usual order:

Determiner	Opinion	Appearance	Age	Colour	Origin	Material	Purpose	Noun
		(size, shape, condition)						
Two	*beautiful,*	*big,*	*old,*	*red,*	*Chinese,*	*brass,*	*reading*	lamps.
An	*itsy-bitsy,*	*teeny-weeny,*		*yellow,*		*polka-dot*		bikini.
A	*fantastic,*	*shiny,*	*new,*	*black,*	*Canadian,*	*fibreglass,*	*hockey*	helmet.

(Note, however, that sometimes this order can be changed to show emphasis.)

Using Adjectives to Compare Things

Adjectives can be used to show comparisons:

	Equivalent	Comparative	Superlative
	Use to "equate" two things, or show their "sameness":	Use to compare two things:	Use to compare three or more things:
1. One-syllable adjectives	as... as as *fast* as	adjective + **er** + than *faster* than *bigger* than	the + adjective + **est** the *fastest* the *biggest*
2. Two-syllable adjectives ending in: -y, -le	as... as as *pretty* as as *simple* as	Change **y** to **i** adjective + **er** + than *prettier* than *simpler* than	Change **y** to **i** the + adjective + **est** the *prettiest* the *simplest*
3. Adjectives with two or more syllables	as ... as as *famous* as as *effective* as not as *interesting* as	more/less + adjective + than more *famous* than more *effective* than less *interesting* than	the most/least + adjective the most *famous* the most *effective* the least *interesting*
4. Irregular comparisons	as *near* as as *far* as as *many* as as *few* as as *little* as as *bad* as as *good* as	*nearer* than *farther* than *more* than *fewer* than *less* than *worse* than *better* than	the *nearest* the *farthest* the *most* the *fewest* the *least* the *worst* the *best*
		*Some adjectives use either form: *quieter, more quiet;* *simpler, more simple*...	*Some adjectives use either "-est" or "most": the *quietest, the most quiet*...

IN CONTEXT

*I'm definitely not **as superstitious as** my brother. He is **the most superstitious** child in our family. But I am **more superstitious than** my little sister.*
*Mom is **less superstitious than** my father and my grandmother is **the most superstitious** of us all.*

Be careful not to mix up
then and **than**:
then = next
than = comparison

Adverbs

- Adverbs are words that modify a **verb**, an **adjective** or another **adverb**.
- They add description and detail to your writing and speaking.
- Some adverbs are formed by adding **-ly** to adjectives:

Adjective Ending	Rule	Adjective	Adverb
Most adjectives	Add **ly**.	*quiet* *careful* *dangerous* *strange*	*quiet**ly*** *careful**ly*** *dangerous**ly*** *strange**ly***
-ble	When the adjective ends in **ble**, change it to **bly**.	*incredible* *responsible* *probable* *possible*	*incredi**bly*** *responsi**bly*** *proba**bly*** *possi**bly***
-y	When the adjective ends in **y**, change the **y** to **i** and add **ly**.	*easy* *happy* *lucky*	*eas**ily*** *happ**ily*** *luck**ily***
-ic	When the adjective ends with **ic**, add **ally**.	*ironic* *realistic* *scientific* *basic*	*iron**ically*** *realist**ically*** *scientif**ically*** *bas**ically***
Some adverbs are the same as the adjective.		*fast first* *hard early* *far*	*fast first* *hard early* *far*
Exceptions		*good bad*	*well worse*

- There are **four** basic categories of adverbs:
  1. Adverbs of frequency
  2. Adverbs of time
  3. Adverbs of manner
  4. Adverbs of intensity and degree

❶ Adverbs of Frequency

- Adverbs of frequency are used to indicate the **regularity** of actions.
- They are placed before the verb <u>unless the verb is *to be*</u>.

Examples:
- We **often** go to the beach in the summer.
- He **never** misses my birthday.
- You are **seldom** late for class.

❷ Adverbs of Time

- Adverbs of time are used to indicate **when actions take place.**
- They can refer to the past, the present or the future.

Past	*Examples:* • **Yesterday**, *I went shopping with my friends.* • *That CD came out* **last year**. • *We left* **on Sunday**.
Present	*Examples:* • *They are going to the mall* **this afternoon**. • *I am* **finally** *done practising!* • *He's* **still** *in the car sleeping.*
Future	*Examples:* • *He will arrive* **eventually**. • *She's babysitting* **tomorrow night**. • *She will be back* **soon**. • **Next week**, *I'm going to Florida.* • **On Saturday**, *we're having a party.*

❸ Adverbs of Manner

- Adverbs of manner are used to indicate **how actions are done.**
- Very often they end in –ly.

Examples: **carefully, completely, marvellously, frantically,** *etc.*

❹ Adverbs of Intensity and Degree

a) Adverbs of **intensity and degree** show extent.
   Adverbs of intensity modify adjectives
   or other adverbs.
   They go <u>before</u> the adjective or the adverb.

Examples: I'm **quite** *happy. You work* **very** *hard.*

b) Adverbs of degree modify verbs.
   They go <u>after</u> the verb.

Examples: He worked **a lot**. *We tried* **a little bit**.

c) When used as an adverb, the word **enough** is always placed after the word it modifies.

Examples: They didn't try hard **enough**.
   He practised **enough** *for one day.*

Asking Questions

There are three different types of questions in English:

1. Yes/No questions
2. Tag Questions (Yes/No questions with question tags)
3. Questions formed with question words.

❶ Yes/No Questions

Yes/No questions are questions that can be answered with either "Yes" or "No."

How to form Yes/No questions:

Auxiliary	Subject	Verb	Rest of the Question
Does	*Majid*	*train*	*every day after school?*

How to form Yes/No questions in various tenses:

Verb Tense	Auxiliary	Verb Form	Examples
Simple present	do/does	base form	***Does*** he live in the city?
Simple past	did	base form	***Did*** he go to the store?
Future	will	base form	***Will*** he study after school?
Present continuous	am/are/is	base form + ing	***Is*** he going to the party?
Past continuous	was/were	base form + ing	***Was*** he going home?
Future continuous	will	base form	***Will*** we be singing at the festival?
Present perfect	have/has	+ past participle	***Has*** he left yet?
Past perfect	had	+ past participle	***Had*** he received a gift?
Conditional	would	base form	***Would*** he come with us?

❷ Tag Questions

- Tag questions are **a form of Yes/No questions**. They are used in a conversation **to solicit a reaction** from the person you are talking to.
- Tag questions are usually used **in spoken conversation** and very rarely in texts.
- **Contractions are always used** with question tags.

How to form a tag question:

Affirmative statement → Negative tag
*This is exciting, **isn't it?***
*Vanessa's father's a lawyer, **isn't he?***
*She's coming to get us after class, **isn't she?***

Negative statement → Affirmative tag
*He's not from here, **is he?***
*You're not serious, **are you?***
*They didn't do their homework, **did they?***

Use the same auxiliary for the statement and the tag.

- *I can come, can't I?*
- *They have been through a lot, haven't they?*
- *We would travel all over the world, wouldn't we?*

You saw that film, **didn't you?**

Get out! Johnny Depp is incredible, **isn't he?**

Yes! The acting was great, **wasn't it?**

Yes! He's so cool!

❸ Questions Formed with Question Words

How to form a question with a question word:

Question Word	Auxiliary	Subject	Verb	Rest of the Question
Where	does	Rosie	go	skiing?
Who	will		become	the soccer coach?

Question Word	Use	Examples
Who?	About people	**Q** ***Who*** *is this man?* **A** *He is a **police officer**.*
Whose?	About possession	**Q** ***Whose*** *laptop is this?* **A** *It's **Jonathan's**.*
Which?	About choices	**Q** ***Which*** *film do you want to rent?* **A** ***The Day After Tomorrow**.*
What?	About things, objects, animals, actions, etc.	**Q** ***What*** *are you doing?* **A** *I'm **reading a novel**.*
When?	About time	**Q** ***When*** *are we leaving?* **A** *We're leaving **in two hours**.*
Where?	About places	**Q** ***Where*** *is your car parked?* **A** *It's in the **parking ramp**.*
Why?	About reasons	**Q** ***Why*** *are you laughing?* **A** ***Because** it's funny!*
How?	About ways or manner	**Q** ***How*** *did she figure it out?* **A** *She **paid attention to details**.*
How + adjective?		**Q** ***How far*** *is Sherbrooke from here?* **A** *About **150 km**.*
How + adverb?		**Q** ***How early*** *did he go jogging?* **A** *Very early... **at 5:30 a.m.***
How many	About things you can count	**Q** ***How many*** *cookies did you eat?* **A** *I ate **four**.*
How much	About things you cannot count	**Q** ***How much*** *do you like this movie?* **A** *I like it **a lot**.*

What's going on?

We just finished eating. Why?

I'm bored. Do you want to go out?

Where?

Sounds good!

How about catching a movie?

Toolkit • Grammar

Modal Auxiliaries

Like other auxiliary verbs, modal auxiliaries "assist" main verbs in expressing an action. They are used to show **capability** and **obligation**, make **requests**, give **advice** and grant **permission**.

Modal	Negative Form	When to Use It	Examples
can	cannot can't	• To express capability • To indicate permission • To make a request	• *She **can** play the flute. (She knows how.)* • *We **can** leave early. (It's okay.)* • ***Can** you help me, please?*
could	could not couldn't	• To make a polite request • In the negative, to express incapacity (past action)	• ***Could** you sing for us, please?* • *When I won the award last night, I **couldn't** speak. I was too surprised.*
should	should not shouldn't	• To give advice	• *You **should** study more.*
ought to	— (rarely used)	• To give advice • To express obligation • To express expectation	• *You **ought to** study more.* • *You **ought not** to drink so much.* • *Tim **ought to** get a promotion.*
may	may not	• To make a polite request • To indicate permission • To express possibility	• ***May** I go to the washroom please?* • *You **may** sit anywhere you like.* • *It **may** rain this weekend.*
might	might not	• To express possibility	• *We **might** watch the game tonight. (It all depends...)*
must	must not mustn't	• To express an obligation	• *He **must** help his father after school.* • *We **must not** smoke in public buildings. (It is illegal.)*
have to	not have to	• To express obligation	• *My marks are not good; I **have to** study more.*
will	will not won't	• To express intention	• *I **will** clean my room later, I promise.*
would	would not wouldn't	• To express something conditional • To offer a polite request	• *I **would** go with you if I had enough money. (But, I don't so I won't...)* • ***Would** you like more coffee?*

Conjunctions and Connectors

A conjunction is a word that <u>connects</u> words, phrases or clauses.

Some words are both prepositions and conjunctions:
- since
- for
- after
- before
- ...

First Part of the Sentence	Conjunction (connecting word)	Last Part of the Sentence
You	**and**	*Susan are so different.*
I'm running late	**but**	*I'll call you tonight.*
I can come and meet you	**or**	*you could come to my place first.*
We aren't going to the game	**because**	*my boyfriend has to work.*
I left early	**so**	*I could come and see you.*
Michael will come	**if**	*his brother can also.*
I was getting on the bus	**when**	*the storm really hit hard.*
Adam watches the news	**while**	*he eats supper.*
Serena went for her run	**although**	*it was cold and rainy.*

Transition Words

Try using some of the following words to help your conversation or writing flow from one idea to the next:

For a Shift in Time	To Summarize	To Conclude
• *At first, Initially* • *Before, Previously* • *After, Later, Subsequently* • *Then, Next*	• *Briefly* • *In brief, In short* • *Overall* • *To sum up*	• *Therefore* • *In conclusion* • *Thus* • *So*

To show order, you can use words like:

the next one: *I know the next answer.*
the one **after that**: *The answer after that is...*
the one **before that**: *The answer before that is...*
the next to the last one: *The next to the last answer is...*
the last one: *The last answer is...*

Active and Passive Voices

In the **active voice**, the subject of the sentence does the action.

In the **passive voice**, the subject of the sentence receives the action.

The preposition *by* is often used or implied. The passive voice consists of the verb *to be* followed by a **past participle**.

Verb Tenses	Active Voice	Passive Voice
Present	*John writes books.*	*Books are written by John.*
Present continuous	*John is writing books.*	*A book is being written by John.*
Present perfect	*John has written books.*	*Books have been written by John.*
Past	*John wrote books.*	*Books were written by John.*
Past progressive	*John was writing books.*	*Books were being written by John.*
Past perfect	*John had written books.*	*Books had been written by John.*
Future	*John will write books.*	*Books will be written by John.*
Future perfect	*John will have written books.*	*Books will have been written by John.*

Verb Tenses

Verbs are words that are used to express **actions, emotions** and **states of being**. Here is a table explaining the main verb tenses in English:

Tense	When to Use It	How to Form It	Examples
Simple past	• For an action that finished sometime in the past	Add **d, ed** or **ied** to the base form of regular verbs.	• *She played soccer <u>yesterday</u>.* • *I **lost** my cell phone <u>this morning</u>.*
Past continuous	• For an action that was going on in the past when something interrupted it • For two simultaneous actions	Past of **to be** (was/were) + base form + **ing**	• *We **were eating** supper <u>when</u> he got the news.* • *She **was talking** on the phone <u>while</u> she **was eating**.*
Past perfect	• For an action in the past that happened before another one	**had** + past participle	• *They **had** already **left** <u>when</u> Marina arrived.* • *I **had left** <u>before</u> you called.*
Present perfect	• For an action that is finished but that has a direct link with the present. There is more action to come.	**have (has)** + the past participle	• *The family **has visited** France <u>many times</u>.* • *Olga **has learned** to speak French very well.*

Tense	When to Use It	How to Form It	Examples
Simple present	• For habits or usual activities • For facts • For likes and dislikes	Base form	• *I **take** piano lessons <u>every week</u>.* • *Madrid **is** the capital of Spain.* • *He **likes** living in Toronto.*
Present continuous	• For an action that is happening right now • For an action that will happen in the near future • For irritations (with *always*)	Present of **to be** (**am, is, are**) + base form + **ing**	• *Mark **is planning** a surprise party.* • *We **are taking** a trip <u>in June</u>.* • *Julianna **isn't attending** the party.* • *Telemarketers **are always calling** us <u>at suppertime</u>.*

Tense	When to Use It	How to Form It	Examples
Future	• For an action in the future • To express a future intention • To make predictions	**will** + base form of the verb	• *I **will travel** to Australia in <u>two years</u>.* • *I **won't forget** to call your mother.* • *The Black Hawks **will win**.*
Future continuous	• For an action that will be taking place in the future	**will be** + base form + **ing**	• *Anita **will be playing** goalie <u>tomorrow</u>.*

Tense	When to Use It	How to Form It	Examples
Conditional	• For a hypothetical action • For an action that will happen only under certain circumstances	**would** + base form of the verb	• *I **would go**, too, but I am sick.* • *Jack **would love** to own a Porsche.*

Third person singular always ends in "s."

The Negative Form of Verbs

How to form the negative:

Verb Tense	Auxiliary	Verb Form	Examples
Simple present	do not/does not don't/doesn't	+ base form	*I **don't know**.* *He **doesn't care**.*
Simple past	did not/didn't	+ base form	*They **didn't come**.*
Future	will not/won't	+ base form	*We **won't go** there.*
Present continuous	am not/is not/are not isn't/aren't	+ base form + ing	*I**'m not reading**.*
Past continuous	was not/were not wasn't/weren't	+ base form + ing	*They **were not talking**.* *Linda **wasn't chewing** gum.*
Future continuous	will not be/won't be	+ base form	*She **will not** be visiting her cousin next summer.*
Present perfect	have not/has not haven't/hasn't	+ past participle	*She **has not seen** them.* *You **haven't been** there.*
Past perfect	had not/hadn't	+ past participle	*Barbara **hadn't seen** him.*
Conditional	would not/wouldn't	+ base form	*I **wouldn't go** there.*

Sequence of Verb Tenses

Verbs are divided into three distinct time frames: *past, present* and *future.*

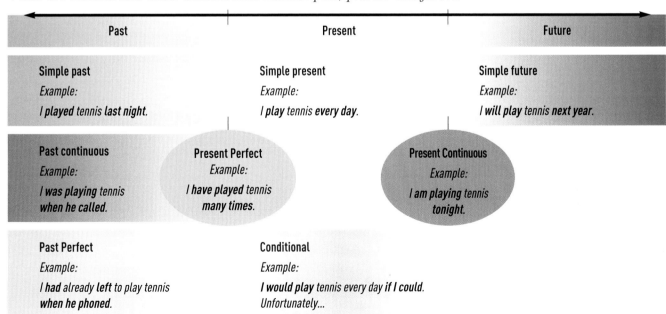

Capitalization

In English, capital letters are used for the following:

1. The first word in a sentence.
The cat is on the table.
2. The pronoun "I."
*I said that **I** would call him after school.*
3. The names of...

- **People:** *Terry Fox, Nelson Mandela, Meagan Winslow*
- **Relatives when used with the person's name:** *Uncle Tom, Aunt Agatha*
- **Titles when they are included with the person's name:** *Detective Brady, Major Lucie Madison, Ms. Jeannette Turner, **Dr.** Albert*
- **Places:** *Nova Scotia, Lake Louise, Harvard, New York City, the Eiffel Tower*
- **Planets, stars and constellations:** *Uranus, Earth, Venus, The Big Dipper*
- **Events:** *the Miss Universe Contest, the Quebec Winter Carnival, the Stanley Cup*
- **Days and months:** *Tuesday, Thursday, February*
- **Holidays and holy days:** *Christmas, Kwanzaa, Valentine's Day, Yom Kippur*
- **Languages, nationalities, races and religions:** *English, Chinese, Europeans, African-American, Jewish, Buddhism*
- **Organizations:** *the United Nations, the Salvation Army*
- **Organizations that use acronyms (all capitals):** *UN (United Nations), NHL (National Hockey League)*
- **Brands or trademarks:** *Jell-O, Kleenex*

4. Lists when the elements are on separate lines: like the above list
5. The first word in a direct quotation:
*He said, "**C**all me tomorrow."*
6. Only the first word in the closing of a letter:
Yours truly, Very sincerely, With love, Your friend
7. In titles, capitalize:

- The first word
- The last word
- All nouns, adjectives, verbs and adverbs
- All words with five letters or more
  - *A Tale of Two Cities*
  - *Life with the Man in Black*

Do NOT capitalize

- seasons:
  fall, winter, spring, summer
- directions (unless they are part of a name): *north, south, east, west, North Carolina, the West Island*

Punctuation Marks

Punctuation marks are signals to the reader. They help make the message clear. Sometimes, the meaning of a sentence can change completely depending on the punctuation.

Punctuation Mark	When to Use It	Examples
Period (.)	• To indicate the end of a complete sentence	• *My passion is singing.* • *He is an excellent artist.*
Comma (,)	• To separate items in a list • To separate two phrases • After introductory words	• *Please buy cheese, eggs, milk and bread.* • *Before you leave, please turn off the lights.* • *Dear John, tomorrow, I will do it.*
Question mark (?)	• To indicate a question	• *Where are you going?*
Exclamation mark (!)	• To indicate surprise or strong emotion	• *Wow! I can't believe you won!* • *That's fantastic!*
Apostrophe (')	• In contractions • To show possession	• *They don't want to take a taxi before seven o'clock.* • *Jane's phone number* • *the Smiths' address*
Colon (:)	• To introduce a list of items • In a business letter greeting • In time	• *This is what you need: a sleeping bag, a pillow, an extra blanket and warm clothes.* • *Dear Madam:* • *8:15 p.m.*
Semi-colon (;)	• To join related sentences into one sentence • For lists that already have commas in them	• *I told him not to go; it is too dangerous.* • *They toured: Toronto, ON; Montreal, QC; Halifax, NS and Moncton, NB.*
Hyphen (-)	• To make compound words • To write compound numbers • To join prefixes to words	• *Ghetto-blaster;* • *Seventy-seven;* • *Semi-colon; mini-mystery*
Parentheses ( )	• To give additional, non-essential information	• *She thinks that Gabriel (who sits in front of me in French) is really cute.*
Quotation Marks (" ")	• To indicate a person's words • For titles of poems, articles, stories and songs	• *"Make yourself at home," she said.* • *Who is the author of "The Last Dance"?* • *"What is the answer?" he asked.*

There is no **hyphen** in *New York,* *New Brunswick,* etc.

• **Commas and periods** always go **inside** the quotation marks.
• **Question marks** go inside if the question is part of the quotation and outside if it is not.

Spelling

Spelling in English can be quite complicated. There are lots of rules — and lots of exceptions! Sometimes, it's just as easy to use a dictionary as it is to try to learn them all by heart.

Here is a list of 100 words that are often misspelled:

1. a lot	21. changeable	41. height	61. omission	81. scissors
2. absence	22. committee	42. heroes	62. parallel	82. sincerely
3. accommodate	23. conscientious	43. humorous	63. parliament	83. soldier
4. accordion	24. criticize	44. independent	64. particularly	84. strength
5. achieve	25. defendant	45. insurance	65. pastime	85. studying
6. across	26. definite	46. interfere	66. permanent	86. success
7. address	27. develop	47. judgment	67. pigeon	87. surely
8. advertise	28. embarrass	48. language	68. possess	88. surprise
9. aggression	29. enough	49. length	69. precede	89. tariff
10. agree	30. equipment	50. lightning	70. privilege	90. through
11. apology	31. especially	51. literature	71. pronunciation	91. tomorrow
12. argument	32. exaggerate	52. lose	72. raspberry	92. traffic
13. athlete	33. exercise	53. marriage	73. receipt	93. transfer
14. basically	34. extraordinary	54. medieval	74. recommend	94. truly
15. believe	35. foreign	55. millennium	75. referred	95. twelfth
16. broccoli	36. forty	56. millionaire	76. relevant	96. until
17. business	37. friend	57. necessary	77. rhyme	97. vehicle
18. calendar	38. genius	58. ninth	78. rhythm	98. weird
19. carburetor	39. government	59. no one	79. ridiculous	99. wholly
20. cemetery	40. guarantee	60. occurred	80. rough	100. writing

Does the word "personal" take one N or two in English?

I'm not sure. You'd better look it up in the dictionary.

Phrasal Verbs

A phrasal verb is composed of a verb and a preposition. Adding the preposition gives the verb a new meaning. Here are some examples.

Phrasal Verb (verb + particle)	Meaning	Phrasal Verb (verb + particle)	Meaning
to **ask** *out*	to ask someone to go on a date	to **pick** *up*	to lift
to **ask** *over*	to invite someone for a visit	to **put** *away*	to put something in its usual place
to **break** *up*	to end a relationship	to **put** *back*	to return something to its original place
to **bring** *up*	to raise children; to mention a topic	to **put** *down*	to stop holding or carrying something
to **call** *back*	to return a telephone call	to **put** *off*	to postpone or to delay
to **call** *off*	to cancel	to **put** *on*	to put clothes on one's body
to **call** *up*	to make a telephone call	to **put** *out*	to extinguish a fire, a cigarette, etc.
*to **catch** *up*	to reach the same position or level	*to **put** *up with*	to tolerate
to **check** *out*	to borrow a book from the library	*to **run** *into*	to meet someone by chance
to **cross** *out*	to draw a line through	to **shut** *off*	to stop a machine or turn off a light
to **do** *over*	to do again	to **start** *over*	to start again from the beginning
*to **drop** *out*	to quit school or classes	*to **take** *after*	to resemble
to **figure** *out*	to find the solution to a problem	to **take** *off*	to remove something, especially clothes from one's body
to **fill** *in*	to complete a sentence by writing in a blank	to **take** *up*	to start a new activity
to **fill** *out*	to write information on a form	to **tear** *down*	to destroy a structure, like a building
to **fill** *up*	to fill completely with gas, water, etc.	to **tear** *off*	to detach something; to tear along a dotted or perforated line
to **find** *out*	to discover information	to **tear** *up*	to tear into small pieces
to **get** *along*	to have a good relationship	to **throw** *away/out*	to put in the trash
to **get** *in*	to enter a vehicle	to **try** *on*	to put on clothing to see if it fits
to **hand** *out*	to distribute something, usually to a group of people	to **turn** *down*	to decrease the volume; to decline an offer
to **hang** *up*	to end a telephone call	to **turn** *off*	to stop a machine or to shut off a light
to **keep** *up*	to continue	to **turn** *on*	to start a machine or to flick on a light
*to **look** *after*	to take care of something/someone	to **turn** *up*	to increase the volume; to appear somewhere
to **look** *up*	to search for information	to **write** *down*	to write a note on a piece of paper
to **make** *up*	to invent; to patch up an argument		
*to **pass** *away*	to die		

* These phrasal verbs are non-separable; the object of the verb must appear after the particle.
Example: *They are **looking** after their dogs.*
Incorrect: *They are **looking** ~~their dogs~~ after.*

List of Irregular Verbs

Colour Code	Examples:
A – A – A	bet – bet – bet
A – B – A	become – became – become
A – B – B	bend – bent – bent

Base Form	Simple Past	Past Participle
awake	awoken	awoken
be	was, were	been
beat	beat	beaten
become	became	become
begin	began	begun
bend	bent	bent
bet	bet	bet
bite	bit	bitten
bleed	bled	bled
blow	blew	blown
break	broke	broken
bring	brought	brought
build	built	built
burn	burnt/burned	burnt/burned
buy	bought	bought
catch	caught	caught
choose	chose	chosen
come	came	come
cost	cost	cost
creep	crept	crept
cut	cut	cut
deal	dealt	dealt

Base Form	Simple Past	Past Participle
dig	dug	dug
do	did	done
draw	drew	drawn
dream	dreamed/dreamt	dreamed/dreamt
drink	drank	drunk
drive	drove	driven
eat	ate	eaten
fall	fell	fallen
feed	fed	fed
feel	felt	felt
fight	fought	fought
find	found	found
fly	flew	flown
forbid	forbade	forbidden
forget	forgot	forgotten
forgive	forgave	forgiven
freeze	froze	frozen
get	got	gotten
give	gave	given
go	went	gone
grow	grew	grown
hang (suspend)	hung	hung

Base Form	Simple Past	Past Participle
hang (execute)	hanged	hanged
have	had	had
hear	heard	heard
hide	hid	hidden
hold	held	held
hurt	hurt	hurt
keep	kept	kept
know	knew	known
lead	led	led
leave	left	left
lend	lent	lent
let (allow)	let	let
light	lit	lit
lose	lost	lost
make	made	made
mean	meant	meant
meet	met	met
pay	paid	paid
put	put	put
quit	quit	quit
read	read	read
ride	rode	ridden
ring	rang	rung
rise (get up)	rose	risen
run	ran	run
say	said	said
see	saw	seen
sell	sold	sold
send	sent	sent
set	set	set
shake	shook	shaken
shine	shone	shone

Base Form	Simple Past	Past Participle
shoot	shot	shot
show	showed	shown
shrink	shrank	shrunk
shut	shut	shut
sing	sang	sung
sink	sank	sunk
sit	sat	sat
sleep	slept	slept
slide	slid	slid
speak	spoke	spoken
spend	spent	spent
stand	stood	stood
steal	stole	stolen
stick	stuck	stuck
sting	stung	stung
stink	stank	stunk
strike	struck	struck
swear	swore	sworn
sweep	swept	swept
swim	swam	swum
swing	swung	swung
take	took	taken
teach	taught	taught
tear	tore	torn
tell	told	told
think	thought	thought
throw	threw	thrown
understand	understood	understood
wake	woke	woken
wear	wore	worn
win	won	won
write	wrote	written

Iconographic References

LEGEND   r: right, l: left, t: top, b: bottom, c: center

Unit 1: page 4 a): © Reuters/Corbis • page 4 b): © Michael Brennan/Corbis • page 4 c): © Reuters/Corbis • page 4 d): © Bettmann/Corbis • page 4 e): © Franck Robichon/epa/Corbis • page 4 f): © Dimitri Iundt/TempSport/Corbis • page 5 g): © Bettmann/Corbis • page 5 h): © Reuters/Corbis • page 5 i): © George Tiedemann/GT Images/Corbis • page 5 j): © Reuters/Corbis • page 5 k): © Corbis • page 6: © Eric Marciano • page 8: CartoonStock [On line] • page 10 b: © moodboard/Corbis • page 12 r: © Max Rossi/Reuters/Corbis • page 15 l: © Bill Greenblatt/Corbis Sygma • page 15 r: © Matt Campbell /epa/Corbis. **Unit 2:** page 24 c: © Tony Baker/Brand X/Corbis • page 24 cr: © Thinkstock/Corbis • page 25 cr: © Robert Galbraith/Reuters/Corbis • page 25 b: © Bettmann/Corbis • page 27: CartoonStock [On line] • page 30: Paramount/The Kobal Collection • page 32 t: Photos12.com – Collection Cinéma • page 34 b: © Katy Winn/Corbis • page 35 c1(l): © John Atashian/Corbis • page 35 c2: © Reuters/Corbis • page 35 c3: © David Bergman/Corbis • page 35 c4(r): © Reuters/Corbis • page 37: © Joel Brodsky/Corbis • page 41 t: © Bettmann/Corbis • page 42 cl: © Michael Ochs Archives/Corbis • page 42 c: © Bettmann/Corbis • page 42 cr: © Underwood & Underwood/Corbis • page 42 b: © Underwood & Underwood/Corbis • page 43 cl: © Jacques Langevin/Corbis Sygma • page 45: © Bob Jacobson/Corbis • page 51 cl: © Richard Southall/Arcaid/Corbis • page 51 b: © John Richardson/Illustration Works/Corbis • page 52 t: © Andy Warhol Foundation/Corbis • page 52 c: © Bettmann/Corbis • page 52 b: © Neal Preston/Corbis • page 53 t: © Henry Diltz/Corbis • page 53 c: © Patrick Guis/Kipa/Corbis • page 53 b: © Contographer (r)/Corbis. **Unit 3:** page 58: © Ted Soqui/Corbis • page 65 r: © Maxx images • page 68 b: © Steve Allen/Brand X/Corbis • page 70 c1, c2, c3: Rideau Hall/© Bureau du secrétaire du gouverneur général du Canada 2008 • page 80: © Bob Krist/Corbis. **Unit 4:** page 82 c: © Tamara Staples • page 82 c: © Sinisha • page 82 b: © Igor Akimov/Itar-Tass/Corbis • page 83 tr: © Jutta Klee • page 83 l: © Hans Neleman • page 86: © Éric Gougeon • page 87 t: © Éric Gougeon • page 87 c: © Éric Gougeon • page 88 c: © Adrianna Williams/zefa/Corbis • page 88 b: © Jeremy Horner/Corbis • page 89 tr: © Corbis • page 89 c: © Michael Ochs Archives/Corbis • page 90 l: © Reuters/Corbis • page 90 r: © Michael Ochs Archives/Corbis • page 92: © Marie-Guylaine Dallaire • page 95: CartoonStock [On line] • page 96 a: © Plush Studios/Brand X/Corbis • page 96 c: The Art Archive/Bibliothèque des Arts Décoratifs Paris/Gianni Dagli Orti • page 96 d: The Art Archive/Bibliothèque des Arts Décoratifs Paris/Gianni Dagli Orti • page 96 f: © Josh Gosfield/Corbis • page 97 g: © Bettmann/Corbis • page 97 h: © image100/Corbis • page 97 i: © Bettmann/Corbis • page 97 j: © Bettmann/Corbis • page 97 k: © Underwood Photo Archives/SuperStock • page 98: © Gideon Mendel/Corbis • page 100 t: © Tamara Staples • page 104: © Igor Akimov/Itar-Tass/Corbis • page 105 cl: © Tamara Staples • page 105 b: Universal/The Kobal Collection • page 106 1: AP Photo/John Raoux • page 106 2: AP Photo/Herbert Knosowski • page 106 3: Courtesy Everett Collection • page 106 4: © Nina Berman/Redux Pictures • page 107: CartoonStock [On line]. **Unit 5:** page110: cr(2): © Corbis • page 110 cr (3): © Reuters/Corbis • page 110 br(4): AP Photo/Byron Rollins/CPArchive Photo public • page 111 cl: Photos12.com – Collection Cinéma • page 111 c: Columbia/The Kobal Collection • page 111 cr: AP Photo/Oded Balilty • page 113 c: © Bettmann/Corbis • page 115 l: © Construction Photography/Corbis • page 115 r: © Cultura/Cultura/Corbis • page 116: © Smart Creatives/Corbis • page 117 b: CartoonStock [On line] • page 118 b: © Image Werks/Corbis • page 119 b: Columbia/Tri-Star/The Kobal Collection/Sidney Baldwin • page 123 c: © Bettmann/Corbis • page 126: © Bettmann/Corbis • page 128: CartoonStock [On line] • page 130 b: © Carl & Ann Purcell/Corbis • page 130 d: © Alberto Pizzoli/Corbis Sygma • page 135 tl(1): Warner Bros/The Kobal Collection • page 135 cr (2): © Alastair Worden/Corbis Sygma • page 135 cl (3): Tetra Images/Corbis • page 135 b (4): Dr Jeremy Burgess/Science Photo Library • page 136 t: © Michael T. Sedam/Corbis • page 136 b: © Bettmann/Corbis • page 138 t: © Bettmann/Corbis • page 138 c: Photo by Alessia Paradisi /Abacausa.com • page 138 b: CartoonStock [On line] • page 139 t: AP Photo/Oded Balilty • page 139 b: CartoonStock [On line]. **Unit 6:** page 140 t: Daystar/United Artists/The Kobal Collection • page 140 c: Photos12.com – Collection Cinéma • page 140 r: © Colin Anderson/Brand X/Corbis • page 141 cl: Photos12.com – Collection Cinéma • page 143 c: © Bettmann/Corbis • page 144 tl: © Stefano Bianchetti/Corbis • page 144 cr: © Alex Gotfryd/Corbis • page 145 tl: © Corbis Sygma • page 145 cr: © Michael Nicholson/Corbis • page 145 cl: © Bettmann/Corbis • page 145 b: © Matthew Jordan Smith/Corbis • page 148 t: © Corbis • page 148 b: © Jane Sweeney/Robert Harding World Imagery/Corbis • page 149 t: © Virginia Cottinelli • page 151: Cartoonstock [en ligne] • page 153: © Michael Agliolo/Corbis • page 156: © Forrest J. Ackerman Collection/Corbis • page 157 tr: © Tim O'Hara/Corbis • page 157 bl: © Michael Agliolo/Corbis • page 158 c: © Corbis • page 159: © King Features Syndicate • page 160 tl (1): Photos12.com – Collection Cinéma • page 160 tc (2): © Louis Moses/zefa/Corbis • page 160 tr (3): © Bettmann/Corbis • page 160 bl (4): © Anne Marie Fox/Corbis Sygma • page 160 bc (5): © Bettmann/Corbis • page 160 br (6): © SW Productions/Brand X/Corbis • page 162 t: © Colin Anderson/Brand X/Corbis • page 164: Photos12.com – Collection Cinéma • page 165: bl (3): © Forrest J. Ackerman Collection/Corbis • page 165 br (4): Touchstone/The Kobal Collection/Phil Bray • page 168: Photos12.com – Collection Cinéma. **Unit 7:** page 170: © Stefano Bianchetti/Corbis • page 170 br: © SuperStock • page 172 tc (2): Knab, Ferdinand (1834-1902)/Private Collection, Archives Charmet/The Bridgeman Art Library International • page 172 bl (4): AKG images • page 175: © Bettmann/Corbis • page 176 b: AKG images • page 177 t: Knab, Ferdinand (1834-1902)/Private Collection, Archives Charmet/The Bridgeman Art Library International • page 177 b: © Archive for Art and History, Berlin, Germany/Superstock • page 178 cl: © Araldo de Luca/Corbis • page 178 cr: AKG images • page 179 bl (1): © Mimmo Jodice/Corbis • page 179 bc (2): © Dave Bartruff/Corbis • page 179 br (3): © Gian Berto Vanni/Corbis • page 179 l: AKG images • page 187 b: © Wolfgang Kaehler/Corbis • page 192: © Bettmann/Corbis • page 193 c: © Araldo de Luca/Corbis • page 193 b: © Michael T. Sedam/Corbis • page 197: Cartoonstock [en ligne]. **Project 1:** page 199 t: © Ted Spiegel/Corbis. **Project 2:** page 208 t: ©LWA-Dann Tardif/Corbis • page 209 t: © Marcel Hartmann/Sygma/Corbis • page 209 cl: © Kelly Redinger/Design Pics/Corbis • page 209 cr: © Kristy-Anne Glubish/Design Pics/Corbis • page 209 bl: © Don Hammond/Design Pics/Corbis • page 211: © Kristy-Anne Glubish/Design Pics/Corbis • page 212: © Colin Anderson/Blend Images/Corbis • page 213 bl: © Reuters/Corbis • page 213 br: © Reuters/Corbis.

ILLUSTRATIONS: Volta Creation
GRAPHIC DESIGN: Pige Communication